HOLLYWOOD DIRECTORS 1914-1940

HOLLYWOOD DIRECTORS 1914-1940

RICHARD KOSZARSKI

OXFORD UNIVERSITY PRESS

LONDON   OXFORD   NEW YORK

1976

OXFORD UNIVERSITY PRESS

London   Oxford   New York
Glasgow   Toronto   Melbourne   Wellington
Cape Town   Ibadan   Nairobi   Dar es Salaam   Lusaka   Addis Ababa
Delhi   Bombay   Calcutta   Madras   Karachi   Lahore   Dacca
Kuala Lumpur   Singapore   Hong Kong   Tokyo

This book is for my parents,
Casimir and Janina Koszarski

FOREWORD
BETWEEN
ACTION AND CUT
BY FRANCOIS TRUFFAUT

Years ago, when the cinema was invented, it was thought at first that its function was simply to reproduce life. Films were made of people strolling along the sidewalk, workmen leaving their factories and offices, babies eating, and horses vying with automobiles in the streets. In two famous shorts by the brothers Auguste and Louis Lumière, we see a train pulling into the station at La Ciotat and a fisherman in his dinghy.

Soon, however, both French and American film makers discovered that it would be much more interesting to intensify life rather than merely to *reproduce* it—the fisherman's dinghy could capsize in a squall, the locomotive could run off its rails—and thus, in a single blow, the novel lost its monoply on the art of narrative, and the fiction film was born.

Now, all narrative is based on dramatic situations, and there is not an unlimited number of these to choose from. In 1894 the theorist Georges Polti identified only thirty-six such situations: vengeance, deliverance, disaster, abduction, mystery, adultery, revolution, crime of passion, sacrifice, miscarriage of justice, and so on. Of course, several of these situations may be brought together within the framework of a single story.

While I was part of the Hollywood scene, I was struck by a significant difference in the way that Americans and Europeans go about making a film. An American, be he producer, director, or actor, begins by asking: "Who is the woman in this film? What sort of man, what sort of background are we dealing with?" A Frenchman, on the other hand, asks: "What is the plot?" This difference in initial perception illustrates very simply how naïve the Frenchman is, for he has not yet learned that all films, or almost all, tell essentially the same story (boy meets girl) and the background alone varies: a ranch, an airport, a circus, a campus, a cafe, etc.

The earliest films explored all the possible story lines in one, two, or three reels—that is to say, in ten, twenty, or thirty minutes. When it became apparent that the public could follow the same story for ninety minutes, the era of remakes began. Then the tales of vengeance, sacrifice, mystery, and so on—somewhat amplified and refined—were told once more.

It would be a very great mistake, however, to believe that silent films were too limited to tell subtle stories. *Lady Windermere's Fan*, for example, which Ernst Lubitsch adapted from Oscar Wilde's play in 1925, still enchants us today by the clarity, elegance, and wit with which it unfolds a tale of love and sacrifice that one could not have imagined being told without words. This is equally true of Hitchcock's *The Ring* (1927) and Murnau's *The Last Laugh* (1924), which had the distinction of not having a single caption.

The fact remains that the invention of the talkies gave rise to a new series of remakes, and the cinema began telling the same stories for the third time. In the process, characterization gained in truth, but the mise en scène lost through stylization. There is no doubt, even today, that a director who started his career in silent films has a far more decisive style than a man who came to Hollywood from Broadway in the thirties.

But to come back to those stories, those thirty-six dramatic situations, vengeance, disaster, mystery, sacrifice, adultery, etc., we can see that every fifteen years or so the cinema goes through a terrible experience which we call a "cinematic crisis." It always stems from the same cause: narrative has been, in a way, overworked. Whenever this crisis occurs, the press asks questions, and everyone gives his opinion. We are then told that the public is tired of seeing always the same stories, that the public has become *blasé*, that the public has become a script-writer and anticipates developments in the story. Some even brandish the terrible threat that the public is tired of fiction and wants true stories. Happily, that is not the case!

At this moment, however, the miracle occurs. A new technical invention saves the industry: after three reels, ten reels; after the silent film, the talkie; after the talkie, technicolor (one hundred percent natural, living color, of course); and after technicolor, cinemascope. These inventions—and their novelty soon wears off—thereby giving a little air of freshness to the oldest stories. Even eroticism, seen from this angle, can be considered a technical invention, because it allows remakes of Shakespeare, such as *Romeo and Romeo* or *Juliette and Juliette* . . .

The truth is that what gives any story a particular flavor—a style if you will—is the work of the director, the mise en scène.

We are often asked to define mise en scène. The only explanation, I believe, is that the mise en scène consists of all the decisions made in the process of telling the story. The more smoothly these decisions can be knit together, the more conclusive the execution of the film. For years it was thought that the quality of a mise en scène depended directly upon the means at the director's disposal. Nothing, however, could be farther from the truth. The man who shoots *Cleopatra,* for example, has every chance of creating a very bad mise en scène. His camera will never be well placed: first, he will come too close in order to shoot close-ups of the beautiful overpaid star (he will "focus on the money") and later he will move too far away so that he can show off the full extent of the over-lavish sets (there again, he will "focus on the money").

Orson Welles has said that nothing in the world is quite as foolish as a director talking about his own work. He was right, of course, but I would add: nothing as foolish, and nothing as wonderful. It is because reading it enthralled me so that I accepted with such pleasure the invitation to write a preface to *Hollywood Directors*.

What I like most in this book is this paragraph written by F. W. Murnau for *McCall's Magazine:* "One of my dreams is to make a motion picture of six reels, with a single room for setting and a table and chair for furniture. The wall at the back would be blank, there would be nothing to distract from the drama that was unfolding between a few human beings in that room. Someday I shall make that picture."

That dream which Murnau described in 1928 and which his death three years later in an automobile accident prevented him from fulfilling, was, I think, fulfilled by Ingmar Bergman in *Scenes from a Marriage* in 1974.

Before shooting a scene, the director calls: Action. When the scene is finished, he calls: Cut. All the secrets of the cinema lie there, in what happens in the mind of the director between action and cut.

Hollywood Directors gives us a glimpse of these secrets, and for that reason I hope that this book will have a sequel.

François Truffaut
March 1976

ACKNOWLEDGMENTS

For turning this ruckus manuscript into a real book I must congratulate, as well as thank, Sheldon Meyer, Leona Capeless, and the extremely supportive and professional staff of Oxford University Press.

For essential assistance on historical problems, Kevin Brownlow, Tag Gallagher, Anthony Slide, and especially William K. Everson.

For supplying many of the illustrations, the Museum of Modern Art Film Stills Archive, Academy of Motion Picture Arts and Sciences, Wisconsin Center for Theatre Research, and the William K. Everson collection.

For making it all possible without years of monastic drudgery on my part, the Xerox Corporation of America.

And for giving me the best possible reason to get this book published, my wife Diane, who is also extremely supportive and professional.

CONTENTS

xiii

CONTENTS

CONTENTS

III TRANSITION TO SOUND 1928-1933

IV THE DREAM FACTORY 1934-1940

CONTENTS

INTRODUCTION

The most creative and exciting period of Hollywood history spans the years from *The Birth of a Nation* to *Citizen Kane*, a quarter-century in which a new art rose up from sidestreet nickelodeons to dominate the imagination of the world. Before this period the movies had flickered noisily in darkened storefronts, an engineer's plaything tricked up for the amusement of the undiscriminating; by its close there would be museums of the cinema on both sides of the Atlantic.

By 1914, the year D. W. Griffith filmed *The Birth of a Nation*, the move to Hollywood had already begun. Production at studios along the Hudson (since Edison, the cradle of the American cinema) was already doomed, cramped by lack of space, scenery and sunlight. But the move west was symbolic as well as physical, a rite of passage for a young medium now leaving its infant days far behind.

During the period between the wars its grew in power and sophistication, transmuting the basic film grammar of the pioneers into the masterworks of a fabulous era. It created and met the technological challenges of sound and color, weathered the Great Depression, and seemed somehow destined to go on and on forever. Yet by the time Orson Welles flew out from Broadway cracks in the old foundation were visibly spreading. The American studio system was a felicitous union of tyrants and artisans busily engaged in the creation of screen entertainment for the masses. On occasion their work would rise above entertainment—though seldom beyond it—to produce something of special importance. Hollywood art was bought with the fruits of commerce, and so long as the whole system functioned profitably all was bright. But the unprecedented (and artificial) box office high of the war years was followed with an equally unprecedented down, a crash so calamitous that the whole comfortable system fell rapidly to pieces. Post-classic Hollywood which emerged from this disaster has a history of its own, less wonderful perhaps, less grotesque, less extravagant, and a lot less sure of itself. But that's another story.

This book traces the history of those days of self-assurance, when everything was right with the world and anything seemed possible, at least to the moviemakers. It is composed of articles, essays, and ephemera written by the great directors of Hollywood's golden age in the midst of their most creative years. Unlike today's misty memoirs, these essays are not seen through a dark glass, but are products of the period. The errors, omissions, arguments, and confusions are those of the day, not the legacy of long-forgotten grudges or inadequate reference books.

The filmmakers who contributed to Hollywood's classic period came from all backgrounds and displayed a wide range of aspirations. Some were studio journeymen content to breathe life into the impossible range of projects thrust upon them. Others were fired with the gospel of art and spent their energies battling over every frame. Most had a little of both these qualities, and the tensions generated between commerce and art power most of the great Hollywood films—indeed, are the hallmarks of the American cinema. Today the range of discussion that existed within the film industry as long as fifty or sixty years ago seems extraordinary, yet it must be remembered that a terrible enthusiasm drove these people. Conceptions of the nature of film, its relation to its audience and to the other arts, varied widely, and each director's opinion was as distinct as his or her films. Few attitudes had hardened, and a broad spectrum of opinion was voiced unashamedly. Here we have brought together everything from direct considerations of the film as an art to specialized discussions of color, acting, or design. And what these director/writers have to say not only draws a history of their times, but informs our understanding of their own work as well. Griffith, Stroheim, Murnau, Langdon—they address themselves to those problems about which their work raises our questions.

Of course, with all such writing there exists the problem of authorship. Major personalities in the arts, sports, and politics have often hidden behind ghost writers, too busy with affairs of their own to compose every word going out under their names. To whom do we owe the most eloquent of John Kennedy's orations, to which of his speechwriters? Surely it makes little difference since the words, ultimately, were his own. I think the same situation may exist here. These were serious people who considered themselves artists in the most modern of media, not starlets or studio heads being puffed by hired press agents. They have things to say, and like most creative types relish any chance to say them. Often the obsessions voiced under these bylines are so characteristic as to label their authors unmistakeably. But if at times a "written to order" piece has slipped in, the worst we can say is that it was issued as an authorized statement, and now exists as a puzzle for interested historians.

The essays are divided into four sections which break down the twenty-five-year span into smaller and more accessible units (the exact dates are somewhat arbitrary, and indeed could very well overlap). The Pioneers (1914-20) includes many whose work dates back to the origins of the story film and who had established the industry which was just now beginning to bloom. D. W. Griffith, Mack Sennett, and Thomas Ince are here, of course, but also some lesser-known figures, long neglected by established history. Alice Guy-Blaché, the woman who may have been the first to direct films with a plot, and Sidney Olcott, who made one of the first feature-length productions in 1912, only to find the theaters unwilling to play it. The Silent Age (1921-27) covers the heart of the silent film, and those who co-existed uneasily with the growing industry while producing the product needed to feed an ever increasing audience demand. Here are such workhorses of the silent screen as Allan Dwan, Rex Ingram, Marshall Neilan, and Herbert Brenon, and joining them the great clowns, Chaplin, Keaton, Langdon, and Lloyd. Transition to Sound (1928-33) is a mixed bag, a few short years in which many were coming to the end of their careers while others were arriving to take their places. Some chose to address themselves to the revolution, others to avoid it entirely. Borzage, Lubitsch, Murnau, and Ford are the major figures here, but, again, lesser-known directors like Edmund Goulding, Monta Bell, and William Cameron Menzies give us perhaps a greater insight into the triumphs and traumas of the day. The Dream Factory (1934-40) wraps up our first-person history with some of those who created the 30's classics that fueled the last years of Hollywood's golden age, men like Cukor, Mamoulian, Milestone, and King Vidor. Signs of coming times are already in the wind: Tay Garnett outlines the advantages of working for a percentage of the gross, and William K. Howard describes the joys and sorrows of shooting away from the studio—two of the most characteristic aspects of modern Hollywood.

These men and women will tell you a lot you never suspected about the good old days in Hollywood. That in addition to the worlds of "all work" or "all play" that some writers would have us believe in, there was another world, one of thought and investigation, of inquiry into the why and how of film-making. Some of this thinking was productive, some fruitless, some merely screwball. Taken together it gives us a context for all those wonderful films which still have a grip on our imaginations, long after the film world which created them has ceased to exist.

PIONEERS
(1914-1920)

EDWIN S. PORTER
(1869-1941)

Early film historians canonized Edwin S. Porter for his direction of *The Great Train Robbery* (1903), a work they hailed for a wide catalogue of film firsts (incorrectly as it turned out). It is noteworthy, then, that in this 1914 article Porter looks back not to *that* film, but to an earlier one as his chief contribution to the motion picture, the still neglected *Life of an American Fireman* (produced several months earlier). Only recently has this film become more widely available in satisfactory prints, and we can now see for ourselves why Porter felt it his most memorable early achievement. Although one of the first screen narratives, it is not at all "staged" in the generally accepted fashion of the early cinema. Instead Porter constructed much of his story from pre-existing scraps, what a later generation would call stock shots. Scenes of completely different fire companies are casually intercut with linking shots of the hero and his family in innovative and even revolutionary style. It is perhaps the first film "born" in the editing room, and as such the direct ancestor of the "Kuleshov Effect" in Soviet montage films some twenty years later. Unfortunately, Porter did not continue to develop the imaginative approach to editing, lighting, and camera position that we see in his earliest films. When he was given the chance to direct some of the first feature pictures in 1912 he completely repudiated his earlier experiments and adopted the worst excesses of a theatrical mannerism which even then was anachronistic. By 1915 he had gracefully retired.

EVOLUTION OF THE MOTION PICTURE

EDWIN S. PORTER

Looking back upon the past eighteen years in the motion picture business—back to the day when no one knew what a motion picture was—and realizing the wonderful strides the industry has taken since then, I am more than impressed. I am thrilled. Artistically and mechanically the motion picture has forged its way forward until today it is recognized as the greatest amusement factor in the world and the greatest educational force in the history of civilization.

Today the motion picture does even more than entertain and instruct; it has already gone beyond the present needs and desires of men, and will exert a tremendous influence upon posterity. It will record the histrionic achievements of the dramatic geniuses of the contemporary stage; it will chronicle and reproduce history as no other medium ever could or possibly will. As an illustration, the present Mexican conflict, through the motion picture, can be exhibited to future generations with such realism and exactitude as the spoken or written word could never convey.

In its artistic development alone, the motion picture has progressed within ten years to a stage reached by the oral drama only after thousands of years of development and evolution. In passing, however, we must record the assertion that the development of the stage greatly assisted the advancement of the film, because even at an early date in the history of the industry it was commonly recognized that the introduction of general dramatic principles in the production of motion pictures was desirable and necessary. The problem, however, remained as to the best means of utilizing the science of the drama so as to conform with the mechanical limitations of the film, and later, with the vast possibilities that these same mechanical factors presented.

From *The Moving Picture World*, July 11, 1914.

What does the development of the motion picture first suggest?

Natural evolution, an evolution assisted and enhanced by the demands of the millions who sought, and long sought in vain, clean entertainment at a minimum cost. Step by step, obstacles were overcome, difficulties surmounted, growth and development realized, not because there was money to be made through such development, but rather because the public demanded and made necessary the advancement that has been attained in the motion picture art. To the public, more even than to those who labored and struggled to give artistic presentations of the popular drama on the screen, is due the credit for the measure of improvement that has already rewarded the efforts of film producers.

My contention is this: if the public were content to receive and support the mediocre films that marked the inauguration of the business, this standard would still be acceptable. The public owes thanks only to itself for its ability today to see the beautiful, refined and artistic presentations of the screen. As for the producers, they should be content to know that public encouragement proved the inspiration that it did, and should be thankful that they were given the strength and the light to accomplish the great things which that public encouragement suggested.

I see as in a vision on the screen itself the days of 1899, the embryonic age of the motion picture. Today we hear that the picture is still in its infancy; if this general statement is true, at that time it was only a germ. There was no guide toward the right methods nor the pitfalls to avoid. The making of a picture depended most upon guesswork. Incidentally, the pictures at that time proved it.

At just about this time, when forty- or fifty-foot lengths was the vogue, I often wondered why it was not possible to produce a dramatic story in motion pictures. At this period I was chief producer of the Edison Company and it seemed peculiarly proper to me for the Edison Company to inaugurate this innovation. Accordingly, I conceived and prepared a story called "The Life of An American Fireman," a complete 800-

foot story based on a fairly good dramatic element and introducing the fireman's life in the engine house and in his home. The subject became instantly popular, and continued to run for a longer time consecutively than any film production previously. Encouraged by the success of this experiment, we devoted all our resources to the production of *stories*, instead of disconnected and unrelated scenes.

My mind jumps from this time to the early part of 1912, when the Famous Players Film Company was organized to present famous plays and celebrated stars in motion pictures. Between 1899 and this latter date the work of development and systematic formulation had been proceeding steadily, until at last it was possible not only to present short dramatic stories in motion pictures, but the great dramatic successes of the stage. These two dates must always represent decisive epochs in the history of the film. I am more proud than perhaps I should be to have been responsible for the first connected story in film and later to be associated with the first concern to undertake the presentation of celebrated dramas for the photoplay public.

What the future holds in store none can say. But its possibilities are as unlimited and incalculable as the difficulties and dilemmas that beset the producer in the early days of the art. That the men who have been largely responsible for this present excellence of motion pictures will reach out for better things seems certain.

ALICE GUY-BLACHÉ
(1873-1968)

When Léon Gaumont began mass-producing motion picture projectors in the last years of the nineteenth century he directed his secretary to take charge of the production of films to supply these machines. The secretary was Alice Guy, a woman of exceptional drive and ability. She established Gaumont's film-making arm, produced nearly all the films made by them through 1906 (specializing in the talking Chronophone films), and trained such future luminaries of the French cinema as Feuillade and Jasset. She married cameraman Herbert Blaché, who was soon after instructed to take charge of the company's American distribution office in Flushing. Alice Guy-Blaché gave up her position as Gaumont's artistic director, and the pair arrived in America in 1907. But she soon realized that what the American market needed were films specially designed for it by a domestic production unit, and to this end she organized the Solax Company in 1910 with herself as production head. Although no longer personally directing each film, she supervised every detail of production in a manner closely prefiguring the method of Thomas H. Ince. Solax prospered well enough to disappear into a merger a few years later. By the time this article was written she was nearing the end of a long and remarkable career. It was inevitable that her thoughts on sexual roles reflected the romanticized attitudes of the *fin de siècle*, but the biological determinism she speaks of is one modeled after her own successful professional life. Yes, she admits, women and men *are* physically and temperamentally suited to very different pursuits—and film-making, according to her, is very likely woman's work.

WOMAN'S PLACE IN PHOTOPLAY PRODUCTION

MADAME ALICE BLACHE

It has long been a source of wonder to me that many women have not seized upon the wonderful opportunities offered to them by the motion picture art to make their way to fame and fortune as producers of photodramas. Of all the arts there is probably none in which they can make such splendid use of the talents so much more natural to a woman than to a man and so necessary to its perfection.

There is no doubt in my mind that a woman's success in many lines of endeavor is still made very difficult by a strong prejudice against one of her sex doing work that has been done only by men for hundreds of years. Of course this prejudice is fast disappearing and there are many vocations in which it has not been present for a long time. In the arts of acting, painting, music and literature woman has long held her place among the most successful workers, and when it is considered how vitally all of these arts enter into the production of motion pictures one wonders why the names of scores of women are not found among the successful creators of photodrama offerings.

Not only is a woman as well fitted to stage a photodrama as a man, but in many ways she has a distinct advantage over him because of her very nature and because much of the knowledge called for in the telling of the story and the creation of the stage setting is absolutely within her province as a member of the gentler sex. She is an authority on the emotions. For centuries she has given them full play while man has carefully trained himself to control them. She has developed her finer feelings for generations, while being protected from the world by her male companions, and she is naturally religious. In matters of the heart her superiority is acknowledged, and her deep insight and sensitiveness in the affairs of cupid give her a wonderful advantage in developing the thread of love

From *The Moving Picture World*, July 11, 1914.

The ad taken by Herbert and Alice Guy Blaché in the 1918 *Studio Directory*. Note the importance given to Herbert through the composition and layout of the photographs.

which plays such an all important part in almost every story that is prepared for the screen. All of the distinctive qualities which she possesses come into direct play during the guiding of the actors in making their character drawings and interpreting the different emotions called for by the story. For to think and to feel the situation demanded by the play is the secret of successful acting, and sensitiveness to those thoughts and feelings is absolutely essential to the success of a stage director.

The qualities of patience and gentleness possessed to such a high degree by womankind are also of inestimable value in the staging of a photodrama. Artistic temperament is a thing to be reckoned with while directing an actor, in spite of the treatment of the subject in the comic papers, and a gentle, soft-voiced director is much more conducive to good work on the part of the performer than the over-stern, noisy tyrant of the studio.

Not a small part of the motion picture director's work, in addition to the preparation of the story for picture-telling and casting and directing of the actors, is the choice of suitable locations for the staging of the exterior scenes and the supervising of the studio settings, props, costumes, etc. In these matters it seems to me that a woman is especially well qualified to obtain the very best results, for she is dealing with subjects that are almost a second nature to her. She takes the measure of every person, every costume, every house and every piece of furniture that her eye comes into contact with, and the beauty of a stretch of landscape or a single flower impresses her immediately. All of these things are of the greatest value to the creator of a photodrama and the knowledge of them must be extensive and exact. A woman's magic touch is immediately recognized in a real home. Is it not just as recognizable in the home of the characters of a photoplay?

That women make the theatre possible from the box-office standpoint is an acknowledged fact. Theatre managers know that their appeal must be to the woman if they would succeed, and all of their efforts are naturally in that direction. This being the case, what a rare opportunity is offered to women to use that inborn knowledge of just what does appeal to them to produce photodramas that will contain that inexplicable something which is necessary to the success of every stage or screen production.

ALICE GUY-BLACHÉ

There is nothing connected with the staging of a motion picture that a woman cannot do as easily as a man, and there is no reason why she cannot completely master every technicality of the art. The technique of the drama has been mastered by so many women that it is considered as much her field as a man's and its adaptation to picture work in no way removes it from her sphere. The technique of motion picture photography like the technique of the drama is fitted to a woman's activities.

It is hard for me to imagine how I could have obtained my knowledge of photography, for instance, without the months of study spent in the laboratory of the Gaumont Company, in Paris, at a time when motion picture photography was in the experimental stage, and carefully continued since in my own laboratory in the Solax Studios in this country. It is also necessary to study stage direction by actual participation in the work in addition to burning the midnight oil in your library, but both are as suitable, as fascinating and as remunerative to a woman as to a man.

J. STUART BLACKTON
(1875-1941)

The most adventurous of the early American film companies was undoubtedly Vitagraph, and the man most responsible for its creative dominance, its co-founder and artistic director, J. Stuart Blackton. A badly neglected figure in film history, the centennial of his birth passed almost without notice in a year given over to lengthy tributes to D. W. Griffith. Yet Blackton's contributions to film were equally valuable, and of even more extraordinary variety. He was a pioneer in animated and trick films whom even the French acknowledge as their mentor; he was directing narrative films in 1897, and in 1898 was the first to use film as a propaganda tool. While heavily involved in early newsreel work he also demonstrated the possibility of fabricating news footage when he staged the Battle of Santiago Bay in a tub. He created a professional acting company at Vitagraph's Flatbush studio and used it to produce some of the first Shakespearean films. In 1909 he filmed *The Life of Moses* as a feature length picture and in 1922 produced and directed the first successful natural color feature, *The Glorious Adventure*, in Prizmacolor. One of the most interesting things about Blackton was the high regard he held for the film medium itself—this at a time when other filmmakers regarded it as little more than a fast-buck scheme. In the 20's he founded and edited the pre-*auteur* journal *Motion Picture Director*, put together one of the first film-on-film compilations, and lectured widely on the early history of film. The following piece is excerpted from one such lecture given to film students at the University of Southern California in 1929.

EARLY HISTORY
J. STUART BLACKTON

What is the future of the Kinetograph? Ask, rather from what conceivable phase of the future can it be debarred. . . . It is the crown and flower of nineteenth century magic, the crystallization of eons of groping enchantments. In its wholesome, sunny and accessible laws are possibilities undreamt of by the occult lore of the east; The conservative wisdom of Egypt, the jealous erudition of Babylon, the guarded mysteries of Delphic and Eleusinian Shrines. It is the earnest of the coming age when the great potentialities of life shall not longer be in the keeping of cloister and college, or money bag, but shall overflow to the nethermost portions of the earth at the command of the humblest heir of the Divine Intelligence.

Let the press agents of today laugh that off, if they can!

That was from the New York *Evening World* of April 21, 1896,[1] and I am proud to say that it was not written by myself, although I was, at that time, a cub reporter for the New York *Evening World*.

The day after the Vitascope was shown and these panegyrics appeared in the *World*, I was called into the City Editor's office and given the assignment to interview Thomas A. Edison about this wonderful new invention, the Vitascope. I went out to Orange, New Jersey, the following morning with my sketch book under my arm. I drew sketches and caricatures and cartoons and also wrote stories. On the *World* they called the stuff I did a "gold brick." The boys who wrote on space got paid for space exclusively—and those who sketched for the

---

1. This did not appear in the *Evening World*, at least not on April 21, 1896. It is actually the closing paragraph of the *History of the Kinetograph, Kinetoscope & Kinetophonograph*, published in 1895 by W.K.L. and Antonia Dickson.

Lecture given at the University of Southern California, February 20, 1929. Published in *Introduction to the Photoplay*, copyright 1929 by Academy of Motion Picture Arts and Sciences, Los Angeles. Reprinted by permission.

J. Stuart Blackton (right) discusses the workings of the Vitagraph camera with E. H. Sothern, the noted stage actor whom he persuaded to enter films in 1916.

sketch only, but as I both wrote and sketched, I got both, and so they called it the "gold brick."

This day I was sent out to interview Edison and to make drawings. I arrived at Orange, New Jersey, at ten o'clock in the morning. There I met Mr. W. E. Gilmore, the General Manager. He said "What do you want young man?" I told him that I was there to interview Mr. Edison from the New York *Evening World*. He said, "Why didn't they send a younger man?" I was then about nineteen years old. I passed that off the best I could and without further quarrel was later ushered into Mr. Edison's work room with the admonition that five minutes was all I could have and that if I took longer than that my life would not be mine. I went into this room, a room similar to this one and Mr. Edison was back there in the corner busily engaged. His back was to me. I said, "Good morning Mr. Edison," but he paid no attention to me. I said a little louder, "Good morning, Mr. Edison!" Still he took no notice. I said it several times and then I almost yelled, "Good Morning Mr. Edison!" I had been walking to and fro and then I walked right up to him and evidently he saw my feet there (that was the persistence of vision again), and he looked up and said, "Hello young man, what are you doing here." I told him that I had been sent out there by the New York *Evening World* to interview him. He said, "You will have to speak louder, I am stone deaf." He beckoned me around to his right ear and by means of a sort of bellowing I made him understand. He said, "All right, you have a good strong voice and I can hear you young man, sit down." And then he began to interview me.

Mr. Edison is probably the best informed man on the greatest number of subjects of anyone in the world, and he interviewed me about everything in the world connected with the newspaper business, the police court business, art, sketching, writing, everything. And then finally I got a few words in edgewise. And then he asked me "What is that you have got under your arm?" I told him it was my sketch book. He asked me if I could draw and said that was one thing he wished he could do. Then he asked me to draw something for him. I drew Levi P. Morton and several other men he knew and then he asked me if I could make a sketch of him. I said I would and he sat for me while I made a sketch of him. He was very pleased with it and said it was very good and he said he would give anything to be able to draw like that. Here was a boy of nineteen, seeing Edison, making sketches for him and of him, wasting hours that must have been valuable. He is the kindliest of men and the most colorful mind and man I have ever met, and yet to think of him, Edison, shut away from the world because of his deafness. In fact he really seems to have accomplished more because of that fact.

Then he asked me if I could draw that picture of him on a big paper, on a board. I told him that I could and he said, "You come on out to the Black Maria," and we did and he had them get boards and wide white paper and some charcoal, and right then and there he had the camera recording your humble servant drawing a picture of Thomas A. Edison. He said, "Put your name on that board," and "This will be a good ad for you, it will go all over the country in the show houses." I did and that was my entrance into the motion picture industry. I finished that picture with two others with the name of Blackton, Cartoonist of the New York *Evening World* written over the top of that board. Then I came out through the Edison work shop and shook hands with him. As I was leaving I asked if it was possible to buy one of those machines that make these pictures. He said he didn't know much about the business end of it, but he was sure they didn't sell them. Then he said, "I am getting a little machine together now and in about three, four or five months I am going to put it on the market. It will be called the Edison Projecting Kinetoscope, and will do everything the big machines would do. I told him that I would very much like to put in an order for one. He rang the bell for a boy and I gave the order for a machine.

I went out and there was Mr. Gilmore glaring at me. He said, "My God, what did you do to the old man, chloroform him?" I said, "Mr. Gilmore, we found we had many matters of interest in common between us." He said that I had been in there two hours and twenty minutes and asked me if I realized that. I said, "I made a couple of drawings out in the thing." And then I left him. I thought he was going to have apoplexy. That was the beginning of my close contact with the motion picture world.

A short time later we received a machine. I say we, because I rushed right down to my pal's room. He was Alfred E. Smith, who was working on John Street as a book binder and told him about the machine and said we must get one. He said all right and a few months later we received notice that machine No. 13 was waiting for us. I have always thought that thirteen was a lucky number for me since then. We bought it, we had to beg, borrow, and almost steal to raise the $800 and we bought the machine with ten films. There was *The Black Diamond Express, Shooting the Chutes, Fire Engines Responding to an Alarm, Blackton*, Evening World *Cartoonist*, and others making up the ten which was our stock of films, and which was the inception of The Vitagraph Company of America.

The Vitagraph Company of America for a period of 20 years, up to 1917 was the largest and most successful motion picture production company of America. In the beginning we rented an office at $10 a month, with a little skylight in the roof and it was about 10′ × 12′ in size. I mean that was the size of the room. And to follow through our trials, vicissitudes, and successes in one full sweep, we might say from that day of hiring an office in 1897 at $10 per month, by 1912-1913 our company was doing a gross business of between five and six million dollars a year. Not bad for a couple of kids just starting in.

I would like to tell you of some of the early endeavors. They are very interesting and I wish I had more time. Perhaps the Dean will let me come down again and tell you more about them. Now, we had no camera with which to take any pictures in the beginning and we could not buy one. So my partner took our projection machine and secured a different lens, made a contraption to take care of quantities of film and made a camera out of our projection machine. Then at night we gave shows and during the day time we took pictures with it. We gave exhibitions all over the country. The first real big audience we showed to was at a camp meeting in Massachusetts. There were six or seven thousand people in the audience. They had never seen a motion picture before. We had the train picture, *The Black Diamond Express*. Mr. Alfred E. Smith operated the machine and I was behind with a lot of pieces of sheet iron and wire things and poles to make a noise like a train. I tell you that it was very realistic. Here were six or seven thousand people who had never seen a motion picture before, and when that train came right at them on the screen they were amazed, with me behind making the "choo, choo, choo" and the bell and noises of a train and that thing coming right at them out of the screen, they went into a real panic and the first twenty rows of seats were emptied, and some went over backwards in the rush away from it, and one woman went out screaming and they never saw her afterwards. It is a fact, that was an absolute riot. The first showing of *The Black Diamond Express* sure amazed them.

After they recovered themselves we had to run it several times, in fact we could not help ourselves as it was a continuous thing, one end being fastened to the other end and it kept repeating. We must have run it twenty times for them. That was the first showing before a large audience. In New York they had shown to theatre audiences, but there were thousands of people at our showing. I tell you, at first they simply could not get enough of it. It was marvellous to them.

In Ohio there is one little thing that happened that I always like to tell because it is so true to human nature. We had been running our film through so much that it was getting worn and we had one that we cut into little pictures and put them in envelopes and gave them away to the audience. In this case we were at a county fair giving a showing there. It went over very big and then we went back to the hotel. Shortly after we got to the hotel a number of people came in and asked for Blackton and Smith. We came out and there stood the sheriff of the county. He said, "Are you the young men that have this moving picture thing?" I told him we were. He said, "What do you mean by this fake thing, giving away moving pictures?" I told him that we had been giving away pieces of film pictures, and he said, "I have been trying to make that move for half an hour, it don't move, it's a fake."

Now then, the machines were very crude and needed great improvement. One of the very greatest troubles with ours, and with all machines, was the flicker. In other words the shutter that went between the pictures and the light while the film was moved from one picture to the other was fifty percent of the exposure. Therefore, it was half on and half off the screen and made a flickering light. While riding back on the train one afternoon Alfred Smith, who was the mechanical partner, got an idea from watching telegraph poles going by and it reminded him of the motion picture machine, and the flicker on the screen. Then came along miles of picket fence and he said he noticed that although the pickets were closer together a whole lot more than the telegraph poles he could see through them and what was on the other side without the flicker caused by the telegraph poles. With that idea in mind and that simple beginning he worked out the "Flickerless Shutter." It was a shutter that instead of being in one piece, was split up into four pieces, and it ran four times as fast as the old shutter, and so with the four wings of the shutter it was possible to split up the diaphragm. That shutter was patented. Then there was another trouble we had to overcome. When the film was being run it would jump up and you would see the line that divided the pictures upon the screen, and there was no way to adjust that without throwing it out of line. (Illustrating with his hands.) Here is the light, here is the lens, here is the film. The light goes through the mechanism of the camera and through the little slot and through the picture, then through the lens onto the screen. If the light was lifted up the others were out of line. If the lens was adjusted the light was out of line. That was all you could do in those years. Well, Alfred Smith worked out a device for moving the whole mechanism up and down and leaving the light and lens stationary. He took what might be called the mechanism of the moving picture machine and mounted it on the board inside the camera frame and if the film jumped out of line all you had to do would be to raise or lower the whole mechanism as the case might be and the film came back to the line again. That was called the framing device. And the framing device and flickerless shutter were the first two great improvements in moving picture projecting machines. That was in 1897.

Now then, at that time the Edison Company was making films and selling them. The Selig, not a company, a man named William Selig, Lubin, Amet and Spoor (Lubin in Philadelphia and Amet in Chicago), were all making and selling films. These people were all struggling and poor like we were. The Edison Company was the only big company.

Then the Spanish American War broke out. It gave a very big impetus to the motion picture interests. The first war picture made by the firm of Blackton and Smith was *Tearing Down the Spanish Flag*. That was the first picture we made with our improved machine. It was made the day after the declaration of war with Spain. It was taken in our 10′ × 12′ studio room. Our background was the building next door. We had a flag pole and two 18″ flags, one of them an American one and the other a Spanish flag. Smith operated the machine and I, with this very hand, grabbed the Spanish flag and tore it down from the pole and pulled the Stars and Stripes to the top of the flag pole. That was our very first dramatic picture and it is surprising how much dramatic effect it created. The people went wild. Of course, it was war time and their emotions ran high and then while the flags were but 18″ in size the picture showed a big 36′ flag. That was the beginning of making the miniature look like the real large thing.

I cannot take the time to go through all this now, but we made several pictures—pictures of troops leaving, and showed them, making improvements as we went along. Just about then Dewey came back from his triumph in Manila. We took pictures of Dewey on his flagship the *Olympia*, of him driving through the streets, receiving the loving cup in front of the City Hall in New York City. Then at about the same time the Lipton Yacht Races were on. We went out and took pictures of the Lipton yacht *Shamrock* and of the races. On this occasion I became acquainted with good old Sir Thomas Lipton, and from that resulted a wonderful association of many years' standing.

We put on at Koster & Bial's Music Hall, which had been taken over by William A. Brady, the world's first news reel. We took the pictures of Dewey in the afternoon and at night of the same day we had them on in Koster & Bial's. The same way with the yacht races, the arrival of the regiments back from the war, etc. So there was established in 1897-1898 the first news reel.

In 1899 the great Windsor Hotel fire occurred, in which there was a great loss of life. We went with our camera and took a picture of it after the fire was all burned out. We took pictures of the ruins and then after in our little 10′ × 12′ office we constructed a little miniature model of the Windsor Hotel, made little street lamps and everything in miniature, making it as closely as we could like the pictures we had of the hotel and its surroundings. We had openings for windows and we put real fire into the building and then photographed it burning. I remember it very well. It created quite a sensation. It was shown as a re-creation of the great Windsor Hotel Fire all over the United States. The same theatres had shown our *Battle of Santiago Bay* which picture was also done in this little 10′ × 12′ room. We had a canvas tank, there was not much water. From here and there we had procured very good photographs of the well-known vessels of the day such as the *Iowa, Illinois,* and of the ill-fated Spanish fleet. We cut out the photographs of these vessels and fastened them onto blocks of wood and we floated them in the canvas tank.

At this time Amet had a lot of expensive models made of the vessels and photographed them. And when photographed they looked like models, but ours being photographs of photographs looked like the real thing, except when they jiggled on their wooden blocks. In those days the public received pictures like that with a lot of acclaim. There was a lot of smoke in that picture. It was mostly from among our friends who were on the side puffing smoke into the canvas tank and around the ships, and it was mostly cigarette smoke at that. That shows you the contrast with what is being done today. Those were early steps.

A man by the name of Rock joined us then, familiarly known as Pop Rock. He had a lot of these Mutoscopes he had hired from the Mutoscope Company and when he joined us we pooled our pictures together, what he had and what we had, and started out to do a large exhibition business, and also to make some films. Mr. Rock brought in one day a list of the takings of the various pictures for that day. They were as follows:

United States Battleship at Sea	1 day	$ .25
Joseph Jefferson (*Rip Van Winkle*)	1 day	.43
Ballet Dancer	1 day	1.05
Girl Climbing a Tree	1 day	3.65

We had been trying to decide just what kind of pictures to make and from this list we finally came to the conclusion that the people wanted to see more of the *Girl Climbing a Tree* type.

As to the early phases of the short films there was a little lull and the industry languished until 1902, and then from France came some very interesting films; for instance, there was *A Trip to the Moon, Cinderella, Blue Beard, Gulliver's Travels, Little Red Riding Hood*, and so forth. They gave new impetus and were Melies' ideas, painted the pictures and acted them himself. They were trick pictures and done by machinery. They were something entirely new. As I said that gave new impetus to the picture industry because the Spanish-American War had ceased.

Smith, Rock, and I conceived the idea of making dramas, making longer pictures. There had been some demonstrations made. Edison had *The Great Train Robbery*, and *The Life of an American Fireman*. Then we conceived the idea of doing a play and we erected our studio in Brooklyn. It was the first building actually to be built as a studio and was two stories in height with a flat roof. And in that building we made a great many films. The first picture to be photographed in this studio, which was built in 1900, was *The White Slave*, a melodrama. The second film to be made there was *Raffles, The Amateur Cracksman* which was playing in New York City with Col. Bellew, the stage actor, playing in it. I went to see George W. Lederer, the manager, and asked him if he did not think it would be a great advertisement for his theatre to have the play photographed. He thought it would and that is how much it cost us for the rights to make that picture. That was the first play, the first 1000' film that was made in the United States. And the lady who acted the part of the beautiful lady is sitting right up there now. It is Mrs. Blackton, but she was not Mrs. Blackton then. Mrs. Blackton is undoubtedly the first screen actress, although she does not speak of it now.

Having made *Raffles* and a few other long pictures we finally got to *Sherlock Holmes*, and all for nothing. The Kalem Company got more ambitious and decided to do *Ben Hur*. They did it, and it was in one reel and was directed by Sidney Olcott. They were sued by Klaw & Erlanger for $25,000 over this picture. The film cost them $3000 to make. The recent *Ben Hur* cost over $3,000,000.

Then came tribulations to the business in endless litigation. Without going through all the phases of the many legal battles, I will say that the Edison Company tried to enforce its patents, but finally we all got together and in 1908 the Patents Company was formed. Then, having pooled our patents we were sued as a trust, and later the trust was busted. And through all those hectic days it has been a tremendously interesting business—if you can call it a business. It is more than a business, it is more than an art.

SIDNEY OLCOTT
(1873-1949)

Sidney Olcott's name first appears in film history in 1907 when he directed a one-reel version of *Ben Hur* for the Kalem Company. Such adaptations were not uncommon for the period, and rights were never bothered with. But the copyright owners of *Ben Hur* sued, and won. The case established a precedent which in a sense legitimized the cinema's artistic ambitions. Movies were now to be thought of as the legal relations of theatre, literature and the other established narrative forms, a costly decision financially, but one which carried with it a long-sought air of legitimacy. The Kalem Company maintained no central studios and its production units were spread over a wide area—Florida was a favorite spot. Olcott soon became their chief director and led his own unit on a complex European tour, filming in Ireland, Germany, and Italy. Finally in 1912 he arrived in the Holy Land where he filmed a life of Christ entirely on actual locations. *From the Manger to the Cross* still displays an extraordinary visual grace, a real feat given the location's distance from any professional film labs or equipment houses. But at a length of six reels exhibitors were loathe to book it, since it completely upset conventional program standards based on one- and two-reel subjects. Two years later, in this rather disingenuous piece which refrains from mentioning his own connection with the film, Olcott was still gnashing his teeth about the treatment exhibitors had accorded his film. With the industry now inundated in a wave of feature length pictures, *From the Manger to the Cross* still remained largely unseen.

THE PRESENT AND THE FUTURE OF FILM

SIDNEY OLCOTT

The tendency and influence to-day in the cinematographic realm is undeniably for better things.

The truly lamentable late date of its arrival is also undeniably due to the shortsightedness of the very men (this without reflection upon those who have given their best efforts in the past) who to-day are scrambling pell-mell over each other, to embark in the very enterprise they so lustily berated in the not far distant past. Their glasses were steamed and their visions dimmed by breath wasted in condemning and belittling the new science of entertainment and instruction.

Men who knew nothing of theatricals, but who perhaps only recognized quick and ready money jumped in, and the stock phrase, "The worst season in years," came stalking in grim reality down the Rialto, up the stairs into the various agencies, and continued its march until it entered the portals of the Holy-of-Holies of showdom. And not until the big interests were handed—in the language of the vernacular—a nicely placed kick in the bank roll, did they wake up.

Then, with one hand on the seat of the pain, they announced, while wildly waving the other, that they were about to enter the "game." It looked easy: Acquire a camera; get some "people" together; adapt some of the threadbare success of the dim and distant past; and the other fellow would be wiped out.

But the "other fellow" had, during their long spell of sleeping sickness, been obliged to acquire something of a knowledge of showmanship; so that it was only after the expenditure of thousands upon thousands of dollars, and the discarding of old manners and means that finally the very men that should have been the first to recognize the new force were able to

From *The Theatre of Science*, edited by Robert Grau, New York, 1914.

25

Sidney Olcott in action on the set of *The Best People* (1925), one of his last films.

make for the commendable advance that is now so evident.

To a great extent, the splendid advancement shown by the various picture interests during the past year is largely due to the entrance of the gentlemen who were so late in arriving, but, having arrived, proceeded to make it known in their truly characteristic way. It is well they are here, for it means that each and all must bend their utmost energies to the production of subjects and spectacles that will, in a measure, overshadow the efforts of the past.

But of one thing all must be certain; great distinction must be made in the method of exhibiting the various subjects, for clap-trap and art will no more mix in moving pictures than upon the strictly legitimate stage. Striking examples of what is meant are to be found in those beautiful uplifting subjects, *From the Manger to the Cross*, and *The Miracle*. The exact methods that had tremendously enriched the coffers of the various manufacturers of the country, when applied to other productions, sounded the death-knell for these.

One firm, gentlemen of high ideals, are, I know, heartsick over the manner in which one of their subjects, they so generously financed, was released for exhibition. Not from a monetary standpoint, but from the fact that their admirable effort to give something of sterling merit, was so foully butchered in the hands of those apparently utterly devoid of discerning the difference of placing a biblical subject as against a "Give-me-the-papers" melodrama.

The subject in question involved the traveling of thousands of miles by a large company of artists, much laborious research, and a continuous movement through an arid inhospitable country, to the exact, or legendary spots in which the events in the life of the Savior, as we know them, were enacted.

Be it understood that in Great Britain, so well were the requirements for managing this masterpiece in a reverential and dignified way understood, that not only did the press and pulpit take it up and almost unanimously advise their hearers to see it, but it was, and is now, a common occurrence for a minister of the gospel to ask, or to be asked, to open the exhibition with prayer. And yet this work, a year or more after release date, has yet to be seen upon the screen in many of the larger cities of the United States.

If such elevating and worthy subjects as these, with their great adaptation for the betterment of all mankind, cannot be successfully put before the masses in this country, then the influence of the motion picture is woefully hampered by a stagnation of ideas relative to the handling of them.

But undoubtedly there are men, comparatively newcomers, upon whom we may depend to show the keen, and judicious foresight requisite in placing before the public in a masterly manner the various productions, in a way peculiar to their needs.

Those who have their ears to the ground know full well that the cry is for better things, and that the influence of the motion picture is a wonderful and absorbing thing, unlimited, and, as yet, unharnessed.

JAMES HORNE
(1880-1942)

The early serial film was a prestigious and financially important operation far removed from its pale Saturday matinee descendants of the 40's. In both France and America much of the top creative talent spent the years around World War I grinding out scores of "chapter plays" which contributed substantially to the evolution of later film structure. For the first time film-makers had to follow a narrative over extremely long stretches of screen time; a typical French serial might be as long as half a dozen contemporary features, while *The Hazards of Helen* ran 119 episodes. James Horne was one of the most important early American serial directors, although you wouldn't know that from studying the literature. He doesn't even appear in Sadoul's *Dictionnaire des Cinéastes,* and two recent books on the silent serial by an American film historian fail to mention his name either. The picture we get from this article of producing serials for the Kalem Company is one of speed and efficiency. While Horne flatly admits a desire to imitate D. W. Griffith, even more urgent is "the taking of 73 scenes with 100 people in six hours' time." Besides *The Mysteries of the Grand Hotel* his other serials included *Girl Detective, The Social Pirates,* and *Stingaree.* Later he became a comedy director of some success, receiving credit for Buster Keaton's *College,* and directing Laurel and Hardy in many films, including *Big Business* and *Way Out West,* arguably their best short and best feature.

JAMES HORNE'S OWN STORY
JAMES HORNE

When *Photoplay Magazine* asked me to write about myself and my work in staging *The Mysteries of the Grand Hotel,* and other pictures at the Kalem Glendale studios I wondered if they thought I might make up in literary talent what I lack in other ways. I'm afraid I have even less of literary ability than any other, so without attempting to write any "story," and without trying to write out a system for invariable success, I'll mention a few points that occur to me in my daily work.

I saw, in last month's *Photoplay Magazine,* this statement: art and efficiency are not only unrelated, but are not even speaking acquaintances. This was credited to a big dramatic producer. I believe in system—which is another word for efficiency—in active photography. I have my work laid out from day to day. I have found that everyone works better under a bit of speed pressure than when taking one's time.

I have a stock company which thoroughly understands what I want, and we seldom cover ground twice. Amazing as it may seem, my camera-man, Howard Oswald, has not had a retake in two years! And we "shoot" in all kinds of light, and have spent many working days when other companies have been at home waiting for the sunshine. I feel that the camera-man must be given equal credit with the director in any production. He can make or break the feature. While the director is watching the action, the camera-man has a hundred technical details to observe.

I aim to get the personalities of my players on the screen rather than my own. I give my people action and detail, but I want them to express these things in their own way. What is natural for me might be very unnatural and awkward for

From *Photoplay Magazine,* February 1916. Reprinted by permission of Macfadden Women's Group.

them. Too many directors make their actors imitate every movement and expression.

Dealing with extra people, in crowds or mobs, is one of my hardest problems. Usually the units in the mass are new to me, most of them are frightened before starting, and look to the director for permision to breathe. Two things, under these circumstances, I try to do: to make the new players utterly forgetful of the camera's little black eye; never to get angry myself.

During the taking of my last big production circumstances made me play a part myself—a thing I seldom do. The particular episode was a raid on a gambling house, which rehearsed in a wonderfully satisfactory way. When all was ready I gave instructions to the assistant who at the moment was wielding the camera, cried "go"—and away went the sensation, with burst-in doors, smashed furniture, over-turned tables, fainting women and even broken heads. When I had arranged my attire and recovered my breath I went to the camera to see how many feet this scene covered—and found but two yards of negative! The operator, languidly interested, had looked on calmly without turning the crank until the final moments of the play's big episode. I went outdoors and made some remarks appropriate to stupidity and the situation, and the vocal exhibition was what I believe the fans refer to as the "directorial temperament."

I think those directors who take animal pictures should at least wear the ribbon of the Legion of Honor. However docile the beasts are, they cannot understand what is said to them, and only infinite patience, kindness, and not a little of the element of chance must combine in results.

Children are easy to handle if you can make them forget the camera. But once "camera-broke" they are camera-broke for life, and if you are their friend, and have their good-will, they will do anything for you. Babies often refuse to show off when wanted, but even very little tots register purely assumed emotions which are surprising. I have had a little girl not yet three cry real tears for me at will, and, when the camera stopped, run to me dimpling with laughter as she stretched her hand out for the big silver dollar I had waiting for her.

In my pictures I aim only at life, and keep as far as possible from "acting." Life, I think, always has an under-vein of comedy—situation-comedy, the stage managers call it. This I strive to reproduce, and the finest of all humor-notes is that laugh which lies just above a tear. Mr. Griffith's great success has been in the simplicity, the reality, of his stories. Real human existence is in every one of his pictures. He is my master, and I am not ashamed to say that I would imitate him as much as possible.

When visitors come to our studio I always try to make them feel at home, but I am against the detailed exposition of all effects and artistic devices. There are directors who love to explain just how they did this, or how they did that, or how the scene was made up, or how the play was put together as a whole. I do not believe in this sort of thing because it spoils illusion—and illusion is only another name for charm.

GEORGE FITZMAURICE
(1885-1940)

That film deserves the same level of attention from its creators as do "painting, sculpture or any of the other arts"
was a foregone conclusion to George Fitzmaurice in 1916.
The motion picture was no longer a shoestring operation,
its makers no longer ambitious mechanics or sideshow
hucksters. The trend in serious film production was to the
"artistic," a phrase which conjured up an elegant visual
style modeled on the graphic work of the Beaux Arts tradition. Perhaps it was to be expected that Fitzmaurice
would share such views, and see painting and sculpture as
the first cousins of the motion picture. He himself was born
in Paris and trained there as an artist, although he apparently had no background in French film-making before
entering the movie industry here with Kleine and later
Pathé, where he began as a writer. Fitzmaurice approached
his films with considerable attention to detail and careful
analysis of his characters and their motivation (the "psychology" he talks of seems partly influenced by the writings of Hugo Munsterberg). As with later directors like
Hitchcock and Lubitsch, he knew beforehand everything
that he wanted to see on screen and expended the majority
of his attention on preparatory work far in advance of
shooting. Indeed, here he seems rather casual about his own
efforts on the set, claiming to "never bother" about things
like composition, even though his films were widely known
for their unaffected visual grace. But of course Murnau and
John Ford never looked through the camera, either.

THE ART OF DIRECTING

GEORGE FITZMAURICE

The right and proper direction of a photodrama is necessarily as much of an art as painting, sculpture or any of the other arts. It has its rules, its technique, its composition and, above all, its psychology, and it is this latter phase of the subject that is given too little attention by the average director which is largely responsible for the vast quantity of only mediocre pictures that are being produced today.

A comprehensive knowledge of psychology in all its branches is a necessary complement of good directorship, for motion pictures have progressed to such a stage that thought is the base upon which they are all built. The public of to-day demands something more than mere action; it demands a well-developed theme, and when you enter upon this you enter the realms of psychology. To incorporate human nature into a picture you must understand the science of mental phenomena, for it is this science that is guiding the guiding hand of realistic action.

To my mind the action of a director in producing a picture is largely subconscious. I can only speak of my own individual method. First there is the purely technical work of designing the sets. I work out every detail of this in advance, even selecting the design and color of the wallpaper. Then I pick out my furniture and work out detailed plans of just how it will be arranged in the completed sets. I even carry out this initial supervision so far as to accompany the women of the cast to the stores where they purchase their gowns in order to be perfectly sure before I start work that everything is in harmony. During all this time I am thinking deeply of the play as a whole, not in a conscious detailed manner, but absorbing the theme, the atmosphere, in a subconscious manner.

When it comes to the actual acting of the various scenes the

From *The New York Dramatic Mirror*, March 11, 1916.

During the silent period directors often formed close creative partnerships with their behind-the-camera collaborators. The production unit of George Fitzmaurice (left) included cameraman Arthur Miller and scenarist Ouida Bergere, here on the set of *To Have and to Hold* (1922).

whole idea is in my mind. I first send my people through a scene without instruction, for frequently they, in studying out the action of the picture, evolve ideas that are valuable. Then by combining the best of their initial work with my own previously conceived ideas, I arrive at the manner in which the scene should be played.

Composition is a subject that bothers many directors. Personally I never bother about it, except to notice when it is wrong. The ability to judge composition is something that is more or less born in one. One does not necessarily group his characters in certain definite positions, but should they group themselves in a manner that offends the rules of good composition the fault is at once noticeable to the good director.

D. W. GRIFFITH
(1875-1948)

D. W. Griffith was always, at heart, a man of the theater. Despite his complete failure on stage as an actor and playwright, despite the world-wide acclaim he had achieved following the release of *The Birth of a Nation*, it was always the theater to which his more serious thoughts drew him. In this article, reprinted here in its entirety for the first time, he compares the legitimate stage with its youthful offspring, and his conclusions are always in terms of theatrical effects. The film has already begun to replace the theater in the provinces, he writes, and will soon synthesize the remaining elements of spectacle theater—music and color—to create a new and irresistible medium of expression. He imagines a future audience watching "miniature pictures" by the comfort of their firesides, and speculates on how this will affect the more established forms of artistic expression. Griffith was always given to such crystal-gazing, and wrote widely on the future of the motion picture, though more typically in the late 20's when his own future in it seemed dim. But in 1916 he was at the height of his power and prestige as a film artist, with no seeming limits to his own future success. The scientific advantages of the cinema promised a hundred advances over the "sorry spectacle" of the theater, and Griffith easily categorizes the most notable. But somehow it is difficult to miss here a certain nostalgia for the "poor actor man" and his fellows, a romanticized troupe of backwater wanderers, now shunted completely off the main stage of life, rather like characters in a D. W. Griffith film.

PICTURES vs. ONE NIGHT STANDS
DAVID WARK GRIFFITH

No small part of my twelve years on the stage was spent with traveling companies. Some of these were "first companies" with celebrated actors or actresses, some were second and third and fourth. We actors sometimes had to take what we could get.

In these years I witnessed quite all over the country an interesting phenomenon. It was the devotion of thousands of Americans to a theater that was, taken generally, I think, as little deserving of such devotion as it ever has been in the long history of drama.

We played in communities large and small. The large communities were discriminating. They were exacting. They got the best. The small communities, which to me seem to make up America, got very little. We were accepted as a matter of course in the large communities; in the small our arrival was an event.

They were starved spiritually, these small communities all over the reaches of the land, else they would not have endured the theater that was given them. For weeks in vain the theater-goers in the little centers watched for announcements. At last into town we limped, as it were, usually very tired after long stretches of one-night stands. We acted and we were away again. Sometimes we carried scenery, more or less; generally we did not. As I look back now it seems a crude, almost humorous spectacle—this spectacle of the theater using the same scenery, yes, and the same music, often, for nearly every play, whether comedy or tragedy, a dirge or a delight.

It was all crude and inadequate, this business of our traveling to the small community that needed enlightenment most, of the storekeeper or real estate man who owned the theater opening its cold and cheerless desertion to receive us, and the

From *The Independent*, December 11, 1916.

Wearing his characteristic broad-brimmed hat, D. W. Griffith directs a scene from *Intolerance* (1916) as Billy Bitzer crouches behind the camera. This is the photo which illustrated this article on its first appearance.

faithful who came to see us perform. They paid down their dollars and dimes to enter the theater. The manager stoked the furnace; the town orchestra tuned its rusty strings. The orchestra struggled, the building was warmed, the old and familiar interiors and garden scenes retouched with paint now and then were presented to view, and we actors acted in true "high-falutin" style with what enthusiasm we could muster for this one of many audiences we knew we should very unlikely ever see again. They loved the stage, these faithful, surely. I know of no better illustration of the hunger in us all for the traditional form of entertainment. And they paid, because they had to pay, very greatly for what they enjoyed, crude though it was. For the business man of the theater made clear to them that he had a hundred expenses to meet, interest on a building expensive to build, to maintain, to heat, light and advertise; that he had to charge from twenty-five cents up to two dollars or more for each seat because the theater was used only once a fortnight or so.

Doubtless this sorry spectacle would have continued thru many decades had not Science come to the rescue of these typical Americans in the small places.

Science looked askance on the poor actor man and told him his one-night stands were over. Science made an end of a chilly theater and a backward play. It made an end of inadequate scenery, magically, as it were, snatching the faithful from the old, old interiors off to beautiful hours in the glorious spots of the earth. Already the motion picture is the world's chief form of entertainment, the greatest spiritual force the world has ever known. Here in America it has worked in the course of seven years or so a phenomenal change and it is expanding by leaps and bounds. Already it is the fifth industry in point of riches in America and by all odds the most powerful in point of influence.

Here in America actors, managers, playwrights and producers soon discovered the workings of a tremendous change in the traditional form of entertainment. They watched the end of traveling companies. There are practically none now; those that try the road, save to reach the largest centers, die miserably. Here before me are figures, in fact, that show that last year in twelve months one of many copies of a single film in Illinois and the South played to more people and to more money than all the traveling companies that put out from New York played to in fourteen months. Disregarding the few exceptions, from which I hope something unexpectedly good may come, the old stage is gone, and the new stage is here. It is here, I think, primarily because of the working of economic law, because the man in the small center, and in the large—the typical American, in a word—has discovered that Science offers him something vastly more satisfying, more interesting and more influential for ten cents, or even for five, than the old stage gave at two dollars, or could give at any price at all.

After years of experience on the stage as playwright and actor, I am quite sure not only that the new stage will continue to improve, but that it has vastly greater potentialities than the old, not only in point of reaching vastly more millions of people but in actual and intrinsic artistic power. For it is clear to me that not only can a producer express any old-stage idea on the new stage at least as effectively as could be done on the old stage, but more effectively. And there are many ideas that I can express, and have exprest, with the pictures that could not be exprest on the old stage at all. Within the limitations of the old stage, to illustrate only one phase of the situation, it was impossible to employ more than two plots and difficult enough to have even two. In my "Intolerance," which I take because it comes first to mind, there are four plots, each in a different century, each in a different part of the world, all drawn together at the end. And I can conceive a play set in one spot, in one stretch of time, with six or seven plots all woven together.

Within the limitations of the old stage it was impossible to employ many technical means that are used with fine effect in the motion pictures. I can accelerate action in a great many ways—by letting two or three stories or plots race along side by side; I can open a play with so simple a thing as a glimpse of a rose, or a glimpse of a beautiful picture; and in a flash I can take the audience from the banks of the Euphrates in Biblical times down to Medieval France, or down to the story of a little girl of today.

Acting itself has been improved with this development of the technical means of the play. Many actors have told me that they thought that acting on the old stage was difficult, but that it is nothing compared with acting in the new. Not often, in fact, do we find an actor or actress trained in the old school who is successful in the new. Those who succeed are those whose art is simplest and finest. Mrs. Fiske was very successful in her "Tess." Leo Dietrichstein would be successful, I am sure. Irving or Mansfield would be wonderful. Two years ago there was hardly any real actor depending upon the motion pictures. We paid very little attention to the old-stage actors. And when at last we took them and tried them we found they were far beneath in real acting power the ones we had trained. The problem of the old stage and of the new is the same—to permit a playwright to express himself to his audience. The technique is different. The results, I believe, in the new are vastly more effective than in the old, and surely the motion pictures are satisfying millions whom the old stage never satisfied at all.

I use the word "satisfying" deliberately as descriptive of the needs of our civilization. We have little time for art. We make no pilgrimages to its shrines. Art, in short, satisfies a passion that we Americans are prone, the great mass of us, to satisfy in the form that is nearest to hand because we have so little time between the swift stretches of our increasingly busy life. I have observed often that hunger for beauty in the forms of any particular art is usually appeased by gratification in another. I have observed this particularly in Americans. Few indeed of us go from a motion picture play to a theater, or from a theater to an opera, or from an opera to a circus. Surely most of us would not feel after seeing whole reels of beautiful color pictures the passion for paintings that we felt before seeing them.

I think that this observation has point. It makes clear, I believe, that from reasons of time no less than of money most of us are likely to select the art that satisfies us most and is most convenient and least costly. I should be little surprised, to illustrate, if many devotees of the Metropolitan Museum of Art in New York City have discovered that they can get at a neighboring theater for ten cents, with little expenditure of energy, of time and with as little loss of money as they would spend in carfare to reach the museum, something that satisfies their hunger for beauty and for entertainment.

And still the motion picture as it is, is not at all comparable to what I expect it soon will be. Let us imagine a Massenet writing great music to great films or producing great films to be shown with great music. Would not opera and orchestra as they now are suffer as a result? Let us imagine miniature pictures designed for home entertainment, by the fireside, and for library reference. Let us suppose that color pictures are perfected. May I ask if, after seeing a play set in the Grand Canyon of the Colorado, say, with all its marvelous scenery seen even more accurately than the eye without aid of camera lens can see, we should care to visit any art museum? And who, having heard while seeing this composite the music of a Massenet, would have spiritual energy left for opera?

These developments of the motion picture doubtless seem to many most farfetched. And yet I need but point out that science is busied with its share of these improvements and has already, by dint of several years of intensive work by six or seven scientists, got the motion picture camera perfected so that, without tinting, without limitation or liability to error such as prevailed in the only color pictures ever employed, pictures may be taken without considerable additional cost and with all the colors of the universe.

I do not know what will be the future of the motion picture because the achievements of science are nearly always impossibilities until they appear. But I do believe that the arts and the passion for them must always endure quite in the forms that we have them. Surely there will be music as long as people live. And books and poems and short stories. Surely we shall always love beautiful objects of art such as we find in the museums. These old arts will not be lost. Yet I think they will in their forms be altered. Perhaps, for us busy Americans, science with wonderful hands will shape them into a single medium that the most sanguine of us never have dreamed of.

Certainly those who love acting and the play meanwhile need suffer no apprehension. I am sure that acting and playwriting are not gone; rather they are to enjoy a lusty growth, with rewards in terms of money greatly increased, and rewards in terms of influence such as we writers long have dreamed of. See what promise there is offered by such a film as *The Birth of a Nation*. With the old stage the playwright and the actor each evening could reach a thousand persons or so. One evening not long ago while twenty-four copies of *The Birth of a Nation* were being played to full houses in the United States at prices up to two dollars and in South America at opera prices, the same film was being shown in Canada and in Australia, and at the Drury Lane Theatre, in London.

I know, finally, that because I am a producer of motion pictures, that because I left the old stage for the new, I am likely to be criticized to my own hurt for the conclusions that I have drawn. Yet I have merely tried to make clear that the arts in form are susceptible to a kind of economic and artistic determinism that works ruthlessly to the survival of the fittest.

WILLIAM S. HART
(1870-1946)

By 1917 William S. Hart had given up the main directing chores on his films, but as this article indicates he still had quite a say in the proceedings. Demanding realism in the settings, making up lines for the *other* actors to mouth during shooting, or dictating the proper and improper use of close-ups, he made sure that his own personality intruded into his films as much as possible. Although modestly demanding to be on screen only 40 per cent of the time, Hart knew that it was not merely his physical presence, but the entire design of his films that audiences recognized. They knew a Bill Hart film from a Broncho Billy through the integration of landscape and action, the characteristic psychological dilemmas of the protagonists, and the gritty realism of even the studio interiors. Hart was obsessed with all of these details, and made sure *they* dominated the screen 100 per cent of the time. Audiences saw and appreciated. But as Hart eclipsed Broncho Billy Anderson in the late 'teens, so he himself was succeeded in popularity by Tom Mix in the early 20's. Mix did not surpass Hart in realism, but offered something else entirely, a dream-cowboy who catered to the broadest-brimmed fantasies of jazz-age Western aficionados. The new audience gradually tired of Hart's dour realism and increasingly moralistic scenarios, and Hart would not stoop to "tricks" to recapture them. When public tastes changed, he and Tony retired in style, and from the expanses of the Hart ranch cast a wary eye on the drugstore cowboys who rode the Hollywood range well into the 40's.

LIVING YOUR CHARACTER
WILLIAM S. HART

"Putting over" a lead character on the screen requires thought and common sense. This sounds like a truism—I mean common-sense in forgetting one's studied technique and carriage and simply dressing and *feeling* the part.

"Live the character, if it is a true one," is my motto, and forget everything else. Think as he would think, and you'll do as he would do. If a story demands that I assume the role of a minister, then, thruout six or seven weeks that are filled with producing the story, I try to forget that William S. Hart is just a plain actor, and try to think, study and live as a Right Reverend would. Then I am governed by what my inner judgment tells me the character would do under the conditions prescribed by the author's scenario.

If the role is that of a bad man, all my feelings are those of a desperate character thruout the play. And so it goes in all my parts, which, for the most part, are of a Western nature. When the picture is complete I relax and become myself again. This state of pleasant, personal freedom generally lasts about four or five days, until the study of a new story begins by Doctor Jekylling myself into a new character.

It is strange, when you take up the character of another, how you can enter into the emotions and feelings of the rôle, As an illustration, in taking a scene in *The Patriot*, some time ago, I was called upon to weep hysterically over the grave of my dead son. His death had occurred while I was away from home, and, as a result, I was turning traitor to my country. Subconsciously I knew that I was kneeling by a mound of earth and that no one was buried there, least of all any child of mine; but the emotional qualities of the character so worked

From *Motion Picture Magazine*, May 1917. Reprinted by permission of Macfadden Women's Group.

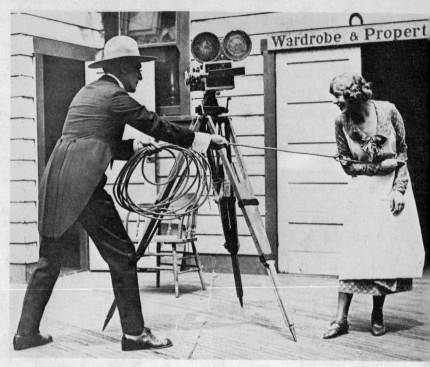

William S. Hart and Seena Owen off-camera during the shooting of *Branding Broadway* (1918).

on my imagination that it was easy to play the scene. I was tortured with hate, and grief, and self-pity, and with the thought that I was turning my back on my country. I just naturally turned loose and cried.

When an actor feels the character that he is playing, the "close-up" is an invaluable asset. If it is a tense scene, where the character is under great mental stress and his facial mobility is such that he can put over that emotion to his audience, then, despite all rules of technique to the contrary, I claim that the scene demands a "close-up" of the actor's face cut quickly into the main scene. The "close-up" is often used, unfortunately, when unnecessary, when it only serves to distract the attention of the audience from the principal scene, but it is really the only medium by which an actor can accurately register a particular emotion.

I want all my "sets" just as accurately made as possible, as this gives the atmosphere and is a material assistance in feeling the part. I make up extemporaneous lines for myself and for the rest of those in the cast, always striving to maintain the author's original intent and atmosphere. It is remarkable how a few lines help; they drown out the whir of the camera, and one can speak as the character would speak under the same circumstances, thereby joining the last dividing link between himself and the part. I do not believe in useless dialog, which is unintelligible on the screen and likewise distracting, but a few snappy lines here and there, particularly in moments of crisis and climax, are certainly very much in order.

Tricks are not my forte. I spoke of using common-sense, and this is one of the places that applies. The public always spots any little theatrical and stagey tricks a lead character "pulls" for the purpose of riveting attention on himself. True characterizations do not need tricks to push them thru. Perhaps I had better explain what I mean by tricks little, cute things, not necessarily funny, but done at a moment when another player is rightfully entitled to the attention of the audience and "pulled" for the purpose of turning that attention on himself.

Some actors hold to the belief that if they are contracted to play leads they must appear in nine-tenths of the scenes. I believe that the lead character is not necessarily the one to receive the most footage. The leading character naturally enjoys the center of interest, but let the footage take care of itself. I prefer about forty per cent. of the total footage, provided the part gives me an acting rôle. By "acting rôle" I mean the part that I can feel and play in such a manner that it is vital.

I think the most disagreeable part that I ever had was in *The Aryan*. It was hard for me to really feel it, being that of a white man who, forswearing his race, makes outlaw Mexicans his comrades and allows white women to be attacked by them. It is difficult to put all one's decent instincts aside and live and think as such a despicable character must have done. But by allowing myself to think only of the terrible wrong that the white race had done me—pure imagery—I settled into it, and I am sure Bessie Love at the time believed I was the typical brute.

I suppose every actor has his own ideas on how certain rôles should be played. I try for true understanding and naturalness and leave the rest to the cameraman. And I find that I am seldom called upon to re-enact a scene for want of color. I am not a person who permits enthusiasm to run away with my better judgment, and I do not think I overfeel a part. The public, of course, must judge my efforts.

LOIS WEBER
(1882-1939)

Lois Weber had good reason to be proud of her new Sunset Boulevard studio, which was nearing completion as she wrote this article. For the preceding few years she had worked with her own unit at Universal City, and had rapidly achieved prominence as the top director on that enormous lot. Her films tackled such controversial issues as birth control, divorce, and abortion, and while raising storms of controversy and censorship pulled millions of dollars into Universal's coffers. By 1917 she had the power to demand that the company sponsor a private studio for her, carefully designed to her own specific requirements. This was the highest goal of any of Hollywood's early producer-directors, allowing freedom from executive pressures while providing a sustaining distribution relationship. Universal would pay for and distribute her films, and she would make them in her own way at her own pace, in "an inspiring and delightful environment" free from the factory-like atmosphere of Universal City. Weber's films were nothing if not personal, for she controlled every aspect of production herself, even acting in them when the time allowed. Each was designed to help promote various moral and spiritual values in an entertaining as well as inspiring fashion, and no director in the early cinema worked from more high-minded ideals. But eventually the fundamentalist zeal of her productions began to work against her. As the 20's approached her audiences dwindled, uninterested in the conservative moral universe of her films. By 1921 she was forced to close the doors of the Sunset Boulevard studio for the last time, and in the future found employment only on the fringes of a much changed industry.

A DREAM IN REALIZATION

Interview with LOIS WEBER by
ARTHUR DENISON

Miss Weber, the editor of the *Moving Picture World* wants a story from you. He would like you to talk about the thing nearest your heart if you can do it in a thousand words."

"That's an outlandish thing to ask any woman to do," Miss Weber replied, "to say an even thousand words and then stop. But say I may talk about anything I choose. That's an inducement. And I think I should like to talk about courage at this moment. It would be rather timely, anyway, wouldn't it? And if you have ever tried taking a cheque book and a good deal of real enthusiasm and in two weeks converting them into a motion picture studio, you'll understand the kind of courage I mean. I'm certain that it doesn't take more to face a regiment. That is what I have been doing; but when my studio is finished, it will be worth all the time and effort that have gone into it. For it will be unlike any other I know of.

"For a long time it has been a dream of mine, as I suppose it has been of many another director, to have a company and studio of my own. Now that dream is about realized, for I have the grounds; the stage is fast nearing completion and we are already in some of the buildings. And not only is it a complete and efficient studio, but it will be the pleasantest to work in of any of the large number I have seen. We have taken a charming old estate here in Hollywood and converted it into our workshop. We have acres of ground, and shade trees and hedges and gardens, to say nothing of a tennis court. That may sound sentimental and feminine to many; but I am sure that we will make better pictures all the way round from having an inspiring and delightful environment in which to work.

"Of course, the thing nearest my heart at the present time is the picture which I am making, and those which I am to do in the future. And my using the word 'sentimental' brings to mind

From *The Moving Picture World*, July 21, 1917.

50

Lois Weber (center) appearing as an actress in one of her own productions, title unknown, a short time before the construction of her own studio.

a point about those pictures which I intend to produce. It lies in the difference between sentimentality and true sentiment. You know, I think, that I can count on the fingers of one hand all the pictures which I have seen that were founded on true sentiment. And the number that have sprung from purely sentimental ideas is appalling. Believe me, this is something more than a mere juggling with words. The fault isn't limited to the making of motion pictures. There's not a doubt in my mind but that ninety per cent of the trouble in the world is caused by the general inability to distinguish between sentimentality and the matter of true sentiment; between the sham and the real. And the motion picture industry, or the motion picture art, if you prefer, is not going to attain the position of honor which it should occupy until it learns to make that distinction. I know what the common answer to all this is. That the public as a whole is sentimental and that unless you give them what they want you're not going to make any money. And let those who set themselves up as idealists chatter as much as they please about their art, the commercial side cannot be neglected. We're all in business to make money. But there are at least two ways of going about it. You can pander to the whim of the moment; or you can build with an eye to the future. Personally, I prefer the latter. Results may not come so fast; but they are surer and more stable when they do come.

"I've produced many pictures that I think contained a liberal dose of ideas, and they've made money. And I don't think the ideas were sentimental. To be quite frank with you, I used to be a good deal of a sentimentalist myself. But many years of hard work has taken that out of me. And after nine years of making motion pictures if I see anything clearly, it is that the frothy, unreal picture is doomed. I know that for a long time the picture public has liked to think that the hero can do no wrong. But that's an illusion which can't last forever. I think it's riding to a fall now.

"The time can't be far off when the man or woman who comes to a picture is going to look about and realize that no such perfect creature as the time-honored hero exists either on this earth below or the heaven above. And they are going to even more willingly pay their nickels and their dimes to see a flesh and blood person whom they can recognize out of their own experience than they ever were to see a dummy concocted of all the impossible virtues a scenario writer could imagine.

"I've told you I have a pleasant studio in which to work. Naturally that pleases me. But the public isn't going to know that I stood in the shade of a California pepper tree when I directed such and such a scene. It is the quality of picture which comes out of that studio by which I shall stand or fall. And consequently I shall labor hard and long to make them constructive pictures of real ideas which shall have some intimate bearing on the lives of the people who will see them. If I can swing that big a contract successfully, I shall be happy.

"One thing which I have never been able to do before and which I shall do now that I have my own studio is to have every set needed in a picture ready before I begin to take a scene. In that way I shall be able to take my whole picture practically in sequence. I think the inability to do that has been one of the greatest difficulties under which both actors and director have labored. Always before, it has gone something like this: Mrs. Smith is in her kitchen for Scene 8. Mrs. Smith comes back to her kitchen for Scene 200 and the director tells her, 'Now, Mrs. Smith, your husband has left you, your baby fallen out of the third story window and your bank has failed since you were here last. Please convey those things.' If the picture is taken in its proper sequence Mrs. Smith will have experienced those things before she is called upon to display their effect, and the characterization can be built accordingly. If I am able to carry out that one thing, it should go a long way toward knitting a picture into a more plausible and connected whole. And I have several kindred experiments which I shall give a fair trial.

"But in the end, I pin my faith to my story, for all the sumptuous settings in the world and a cast of two dozen stars will not and cannot carry a bad story to a legitimate and pronounced success. And I pin my faith to that story which is a slice out of real life."

MACK SENNETT
(1880-1960)

The king of Hollywood's "fun factory" has often been credited with developing most of the great comic talent of the silent film, but while Mack Sennett has a secure and valued place in the history of screen comedy it is surely not as a developer of individual talents. Although Arbuckle and Chaplin, Langdon and Lloyd were all on the lot at one point or another, they developed their styles only in spite of Sennett, and grew to their artistic peaks only away from his influence. This was not because of any extraordinary short-sightedness on Sennett's part, but because of the basic operation of the "fun factory" itself. Comedy routines were interchangeable among the Keystone regulars, and scenarios were produced on an assembly line basis with little or no thought given to the peculiar personalities of various comics. Having a funny moustache, or crossed eyes, or an extra two hundred pounds, was as much individualization as was required. When screen comedy followed Chaplin's lead and began to focus more on personality than situation, Sennett and his troupe of grotesques were left behind. But in their pre-1920 heyday they created a vigorous new style of motion picture comedy founded on speed, insolence, and destruction, which won them the undying affection of the French dadaists, and which (as can be seen here) was more consciously crafted than many had thought.

THE PSYCHOLOGY OF
FILM COMEDY

MACK SENNETT

There was no doubt about it; the comedy looked like a flop.

In the scenario, it read like a yell. In rehearsal, it was still better. When they were taking the picture it seemed as tho there would be a laugh in every foot of film. Even the camera-man laughed, beyond which there is no possible tribute.

But when I saw it in the projecting-room, the thing went bla-a-a—— Especially the big scene with the china closet.

It was a very funny idea. Paddy McGuire and Chester Conklin were papering a room. One end of their scaffolding rested on the top of a cabinet of fancy china. Suddenly the end of the plank slipped and crashed into the Limoges; it took another bump and smashed all the Haviland on the next shelf. And so it went, bump, bump, bump, thru all the grades of fancy crockery to the floor.

In front of the camera it had been uproariously funny—frightfully comic, as our overseas Allies say. In the projecting-room it fell flat.

Comedies are not like murderers, however. They get more than one trial.

When one of our comedies is finished, it is usually about five times as long as it is when the public finally sees it. During the period of cutting it, we give many little performances in the projecting-room. Sometimes the projecting-theater is crowded. Sometimes there is an audience of only half-a-dozen scene-shifters and mechanics—a very discriminating audience, I may remark by the way.

We tried this gag on all of them. It didn't get over. Yet I knew that it was funny.

At last the reason dawned upon me. I cut the film and tried it again on a mixed audience made up of actors, scene-shifters,

From *Motion Picture Classic*, November 1918. Reprinted by permission of Macfadden Women's Group.

A moustachioed Mack Sennett visits the set of his *Small Town Idol* (1921).

directors, mechanics and counting-room clerks. This time they yelled their heads off.

The reason the gag was not funny in its original form was due to the way it was placed in the film. Just before the scaffold broke thru the china there was a very exciting chase. Two or three men were pursuing a scared little fellow around a swimming tank, shooting at him with guns. It was funny, but it was too long. In order to really "get" that scene with the china you had to be paying very close attention. You had to see and appreciate the fact that it was expensive china before the scaffolding began bumping into it. Chester Conklin was trying to surprise his wife by papering a room of their house. You can imagine the lady's surprise when she came home and found what had happened to her china. To thoroly "get" this gag you had to very clearly appreciate the fact that it was her treasure and pride. The shooting scene left you a little tired, mentally, and in no mood to give the close concentration necessary.

It is a curious thing to say that a noise spoiled the gag; but it really did. You failed to hear the imaginary crash of china on account of the greater imaginary noise of the shooting.

I took out most of the chase and transposed the position of what remained. Then the gag got over. I didn't make it any funnier. It had been funny all the time. All I did was to give it a chance to make itself heard.

Gozzi, the famous Italian dramatist, demonstrated conclusively, as the result of examining thousands of plays, that there are only thirty-six possible dramatic situations. There are only a handful of possible jokes.

The chief members of this joke band may be said to be:

The fall of dignity.

Mistaken identity.

Almost every joke on the screen belongs, roughly, to one or the other of these clans.

For instance, here are some of the old, reliable veterans:

Two detectives masquerade as burglars to catch another burglar and catch each other. Mistaken identity.

Rich old uncle comes to visit his nephew to whom he is to give a hundred thousand dollars on condition that nephew marries and produces an heir. Uncle, on arrival, is mistaken for a servant and put to work in the kitchen. Mistaken identity again.

Young hubby plans to scare his wife by masquerading as a burglar. She finds out the scheme and entertains a real burglar under the impression it is her husband. Mistaken identity.

Hotel clerk gets room numbers mixed. Young hubby comes home unexpectedly and finds a man in the room where he expected to find his wife. Mistaken identity.

Pie-throwing in comedy is based directly or indirectly upon the fall of dignity. There is nothing funny about hitting a man with a pie. The joke is in throwing a pie at one man and hitting another; in aiming at a tramp and hitting your rich, old aunt.

Parenthetically, it may be remarked that comedy directors

often fail with a gag thru lack of discrimination. There are certain characters whom the public wants to see roughly handled; there are others who are immune from rough stuff. It is not always clear why.

For instance, you can always be safe in hitting a policeman—a comedy policeman, that is to say. There is no American who, as a boy, has not dreamed of caving in the helmet of a cop with a mighty swat that will send it down around his ears. Most of us have never gotten over the feeling. Nearly every one of us lives in the secret hope that some day before he dies he will be able to swat a policeman's hat down around his ears. Lacking the courage and the opportunity, we like to see it done in the movies.

The copper is fair game for pies, likewise any fat man. Fat faces and pies seem to have a peculiar affinity. If the victim is fat enough the movie public will tolerate any kind of rough stuff.

On the other hand, movie fans do not like to see pretty girls smeared up with pastry. Shetland ponies and pretty girls are immune.

It is an axiom of screen comedy that a Shetland pony must never be put in an undignified position. People don't like it. You can take any kind of liberties with a donkey. They even like to see the noble lion rough-housed, but not a pony. You might as well show Santa Claus being mistreated.

The immunity of pretty girls doesn't go quite as far as the immunity of the Shetland pony, however. You can put a pretty girl in a comedy shower bath. You can have her fall into mud puddles. They will laugh at that. But the spectacle of a girl dripping with pie is displeasing.

Preachers in comedy have to be handled with tact and sagacity. If the preacher has side-whiskers and goggles they like to see things happen to him. If he is young and smooth-shaven he is as immune as a blond young lady.

I will not attempt to analyze the reason, but American comedy fans are rather ruthless with old age. The worst mishaps often happen to old people in screen comedies. Especially if they are well-dressed old men. An elegantly dressed elderly man with whiskers is headed straight for misfortune in the movies. He hasn't a chance.

No doubt this is an evidence of the reluctant awe that young America feels for wealthy old age; it is very much like the secret resentment against the policeman. The attitude of a comedy audience toward a judge is very peculiar. For some reason I have never been able to fathom, they like to see them get into domestic scandals. The spectacle of a solemn, old judge being led away by the ear by his irate wife makes a movie audience hug itself with delight.

That pie targets so frequently wear side-whiskers and top hats is rather to be regarded as a convenience of stage mechanics rather than as a settled prejudice against people with zits.

Explanations must be Hooverized to as great an extent as possible in the movies. By custom side-whiskers and stove-pipe hats have come to be recognized as the badge of the official goat of the comedy. Just as a white lawn dress and curls are the sign of the heroine in drama.

These conventions are more marked in comedy than in other forms of movie drama. In comedy the events are piled on too rapidly to admit of much character drawing. You can't go into the personality of a preacher to show the audience that he is not a proper candidate for sympathy. When you put side-whiskers on him and top him with a stove-pipe hat the movie fans understand the trade-mark. They know that he is due for disasters.

So much for the material out of which comedies are built. Most of the materials are old. All jokes are old, and there are only a few of them. One of the earliest inscriptions found in Egypt was a joke about a mother-in-law told in hieroglyphics.

Skillful comedy direction consists of arrangement of these comedy elements. And the arrangement involves a knowledge—either instinctive or studied—of the psychology of the man sitting out there in the dark in front of the screen. You must know how he thinks and how fast he thinks. The extent to which you get in tune with him is the measure of your screen success.

Like a diamond, a joke depends very largely upon the setting. Nine times out of ten if a gag fails it is because of the poor paving of the way up to it.

This is true of any joke. How many times have you seen a good story ruined because the teller chose a time when his audience was not in the mood to pay attention!

THOMAS H. INCE
(1882-1924)

This lengthy narrative of Thomas Ince's first years in Hollywood is interesting not just for his recollections of names and events in those days, but for the attitude he takes toward them. Ince arrived on the coast in 1911, joined Triangle in 1915, moved over to Paramount, and established his Culver City studios in 1918. This article was written in 1919, hardly a great many years after the first of these events, but his assessment of "the early days of the cinema" is already antiquarian. Things had moved so fast, not only for Ince but for everyone else in the film business, that he could take no other attitude. But by the dawn of the 20's this rampaging progress had slowed, and Hollywood wore largely the same face it wears today: the Culver City studios built by Ince were later the home of Selznick and Desilu. While Ince had already halted his personal direction of pictures by this time, he maintained tight control over his entire studio output by close supervision of each detail of production, from scripting onward. He devised the system of studio production which made assembly line filming possible, but (at least until 1919) he somehow avoided mass-produced look. His best films were all recognizably Ince pictures, yet each was carefully individualized and could stand on its own merits. By the time of his death in 1924 the writers and directors he had trained could not function without him, and his entire studio disbanded.

THE EARLY DAYS AT KAY BEE
THOMAS H. INCE

When I was first assigned to write the story of Kay Bee, I didn't realize how difficult the task would be—nor that the chief difficulty would be to keep it within the prescribed bounds. Harking back to the early days of the film industry in Southern California is much like trying to recall one's childhood days, although scarcely more than a half-decade has elapsed since the pioneers on the West Coast were objects of mingled pity and contempt.

Yet, as someone has said, five years in filmdom has been a century for achievement.

In the library of my home in Hollywood I have a collection of books containing the still photographs of every motion picture I directed, supervised, or had any connection with since I came to California seven years ago. This collection, to me, is priceless. It was to these leather-bound photo-albums I resorted to freshen my memory of the early days and from them I could write and write and write—but perhaps I attach too much importance to my own participation in the development of the old "movies" to a great international industry. Still, in turning over the pages of these interesting volumes, two things occur to me that somehow or other had not entered my mind before. One, that a list of the faces pictured therein would read like a directory of "Who's Who" on the stage and screen to-day. The other, that not a few of the photo-dramas we made in those days could run the gantlet of the critical screen experts of to-day and would be graded with the best of the current product. However, that's a subject that can easily be made controversial, so we will shun it. The editor said he wanted me to write about persons, the players who came to our modest early studios from stage—or stable, as the case might have been.

From *Photoplay Magazine*, March 1919. Reprinted by permission of Macfadden Women's Group.

Thomas Ince studies the script of *Human Wreckage* (1923) with Mrs. Wallace Reid. This anti-narcotics drama was one of the last films produced by Ince before his untimely death.

As the early crop of fans will recall, I had made a number of pictures in the East, notably those with Mary Pickford, before coming West to join the New York Motion Picture Company, which I believe was the second or third in the field in California at the time. I had been offered the munificent salary of $150 a week, and the journey was quite a financial undertaking, so much so in fact, that Mrs. Ince gave me a diamond ring to pawn in order to get the first month's rent for the house she had discovered in Hollywood.

The New York Motion Picture Company was then making the "Bison" brand of films at the studio in Edendale which is now a part of Mack Sennett's studio. Fred J. Balshofer, now an independent producer, was both director and manager as well as a partner in the concern. The office was in the remains of a former grocery store which also provided the stage. The scenery, props, wardrobe and art department filled another room.

Of the members of that little company nearly every one has come up with the business. Our leading woman was Anna Little, now a Paramount star. Miss Little's activity was confined largely to Indian roles. Nearly every story had a young Indian squaw and Anna worked regularly. Each story likewise had a colonel or a sheriff, and J. Barney Sherry, whose work is known to film followers in every part of the world, was the colonel or the sheriff as the case might be. Prior to my arrival he was the Indian chieftain in the Western thrillers so that he had already attained more or less advancement. It was in the following Kay Bee days that he was again advanced to the role of the ingenue's father, usually a ruined banker, a role in which he excels. Mr. Sherry, I believe, was the first recruit to the screen from the legitimate stage. Like others who made the jump early in the game, he was a little ashamed of it. At any rate he did not use his right and also his stage name, which is J. Barney Sherry Reeves. Unlike others, Barney didn't return to the speaking stage.

Another member of the company was E. H. Allen, for many succeeding years my business manager. Mr. Allen at that time played cowboy roles and made himself generally useful. The important Indian parts were taken by George Gebhardt.

I had brought with me from New York as leading lady, Ethel Grandin, at the time one of the most popular of film heroines. My cameraman was Ray Smallwood who afterwards became Miss Grandin's husband. Had she remained in the business I believe that Ethel to-day would be among the highest paid stars, but apparently she preferred the quietude of simple married life.

At that time a single reel production—the standard length then—contained twenty or twenty-one scenes. My first picture contained fifty-three scenes, and it was freely predicted that I would be fired for wasting so much time and film. Around the studio I was generally designated as "one of those New York guys that know all about the picture business." My salutatory was a comedy which greeted the public as *The New Cook*. I believe it was three days in the making. We were supposed to turn out two single reel dramas each week. Many of those early pictures have been done over and over since as five reel features.

Our removal to Santa Ynez Canyon on the ocean front, afterwards named Inceville, forms one of the most interesting chapters of the early days of the industry. George Gebhardt had discovered the place as a dandy Western location and we acquired the right to work in the Canyon. It was about that time that Lo, the poor Indian, became an integral part of motion pictures. I must not be considered unduly immodest if I claim most of the credit.

At about that time a circus came to the Coast to winter. It was a wild west show known as Miller Bros. 101 Ranch Circus. Up to then we had made up Mexicans to play the part of Indians. After some negotiating, I was authorized by the firm, with a great deal of trepidation, I fear, to engage the entire circus at a cost of $2,000 a week. There were a half hundred Indians, 300 horses, buffaloes, etc. Every morning they left Venice, their winter quarters, and proceeded to the Canyon; worked all day, or whenever they were wanted, and then hiked back.

With the big expense of the wild west troupe, it became necessary to get more money for the pictures, so I conceived the idea of discarding the single reelers and making 2,000 foot dramas. We never went back to the single reels and were the first to establish the double reel standard.

The first picture made with real Indians was *Across the Plains*. Ethel Grandin was the girl and the boy was a young chap named Ray Myers. Afterwards he went to Kalem and since has quit the pictures.

Harold Lockwood, whose sad death recently was such a shock to the film folks as well as the public, was engaged to play the leads then. The lead usually was a young lieutenant. Harold was a fine young fellow who had attracted some attention while at Selig's. He had no peer in that day as a juvenile. Later I loaned Harold to Famous Players to play opposite Mary Pickford in *Tess of the Storm Country*. That advanced him farther in his profession. New prospects opened up for him and he did not come back to us.

The heavy dramatic parts of those early productions were inevitably entrusted to Francis Ford, without doubt one of the most finished of all the pioneer film performers. It was nothing for him to play an Indian hero in the morning and make up as Abraham Lincoln for the afternoon's work.

Our first plant at Inceville consisted of two dressing tents, one for the ladies and one for the gentlemen. Then we built a small platform upon which we staged our few interiors. My particular pride then was a real stone fireplace, the first ever shown on the screen. Throughout all the changes which came with the development of the studio into one of the chief factors of the film industry, I always saw to it that that old fireplace remained undisturbed. I regarded it as a sort of monument to pioneer realism.

Between Santa Monica and Inceville there lies on either side of the coast road, a Japanese fishing village, the inhabitants of which are Japanese and Russian fishermen and their families. This also was utilized for scenes. I remember one instance of the use of one of the houses as an old Southern home. Although the camera was so placed as to ignore the presence of various exotic impedimenta, one of the still pictures accompanying this article, prominently displays a Japanese sign surmounting an adjoining building. Another time we used this location for a Western street.

The early days in Santa Ynez Canyon were not momentous by any manner of means. One of the most exciting incidents of our early picture making there was a grass fire that nearly wiped out everything we had. The fire was caused by a smoke pot igniting the grass and everyone, actresses as well, turned to with water buckets, blankets and other apparatus to fight the flames. I can visualize Ethel Grandin made up as a bride attired in the once-fashionable crinoline, dashing madly about with her bridal veil wrapped about her neck, taking frequent swipes at the fire with a wet blanket.

Another exciting period was the near-battle which followed the legal fight over possession of our plant between the then organizing Universal Company and the New York Motion Picture Company. At one stage of the proceedings bloodshed was only averted by the belligerent attitude of our troop of cowboys and Indians, all of whom were ready to do real fighting at a drop of the hat. However, this recital has to do with persons rather than business fights.

But this legal mixup brought about the birth of Kay Bee as a picture play brand. The courts awarded Universal the right to the title of "Bison 101," so there was born Kay Bee, taken from the initials of Messrs. Kessel and Bauman, principal owners of the New York Motion Picture Company. Early fans will also remember our Broncho and Domino pictures.

Another of my early standbys was Charles K. French, who came to us from the Pathé studio, and there was also Raymond West, now one of the industry's best directors, who was assistant cameraman of the original company when I came West.

When we had been in the Canyon about a year Miss Little left us and Louise Glaum was selected to play the Indian squaws. Like Miss Little, Miss Glaum soon won to stardom by her splendid acting ability and unique personality.

Another early acquisition was Charles Ray. He was just about twenty then and had had some experience in musical comedy. Like others he was driven to the pictures by a bad season on the stage. Fortunately for him, and also for me, Harold Lockwood had just left and I needed a juvenile to take his place. So Charlie got his name on the payroll opposite the figures $25. (Salaries were not computed by the day, needless to state.) That was about six years ago, and Mr. Ray has literally worked his way to the top. He has played heavies, character parts and practically everything around the studio that came within the purview of the male player. But it was not until *The Coward* that he approached the dimensions of stardom. His work in that picture stamped him as a splendid performer.

Others who came to me in those days were Rhea Mitchell and William D. Taylor, both of whom had been playing in stock companies in San Francisco. Taylor later became a highly regarded director and is now with the British forces in France. Another of the early leads was Elizabeth Burbridge, nicknamed "Tommy," who has dropped out of sight in recent years. The list also includes Clara Williams, who came to us from Lubin; Winnie Baldwin, now a prominent figure in vaudeville; Jack O'Brien, also destined to become a prominent director, and Grace Cunard. The child parts were generally entrusted to Mildred Harris (now Mrs. Charlie Chaplin). Mildred was then about twelve years old, and she is perhaps the first of the child screen players to develop into a dramatic star.

The first person of stage prominence to join us in the Canyon, I believe, was Bessie Barriscale, who had made her debut in *The Rose of the Rancho* for the then new Lasky company after a highly successful career on the stage. At that time no players were featured or starred. It was considered bad policy even to publish the cast. The producers feared even in that early period what eventually occurred, practical possession of the business by the stars, so far as the big end of the money was concerned. But the public was attracted to the picture shows in those days by personalities, so the development of the star system was really due to the public's insistence upon seeing the players it liked.

As I recall it Miss Barriscale and Sessue Hayakawa were among the first players we featured, although at that time Sessue's brilliant little wife Tsuru, whom he married shortly after they joined us, was the more prominent partner of the two. Miss Aoki had been brought to me by a Los Angeles newspaperwoman and I conceived the idea of making some Japanese photoplays. Before we began, Miss Aoki one day brought Hayakawa into my office and introduced us with the remark that he was a very good Japanese actor who would also be a good picture actor. Tsuru was an excellent prophet.

My first picture with them was *The Wrath of the Gods* and it created a sensation. But Sessue wasn't particularly impressed with the cinema in that first vehicle because he had to wear a crepe beard. He certainly objected to that facial adornment but he had to submit. He never wore another, however.

William S. Hart I suppose may be classed as my greatest find. Bill and I had been old stage friends and we renewed acquaintance when he came to Los Angeles, playing a character part in *The Trail of the Lonesome Pine*. At the close of the season he returned to the Coast and we did a few two-reelers with him. It wasn't long before we reached the conclusion that Screen was Hart's middle name. His first big hit was made in his first vehicle that went over two reels, *The Bargain*. It established a new era in western film dramas. This was followed by *On the Night Stage*, in which Robert Edeson was the ostensible star. These were of that interesting pre-Triangle era when our big productions were Mutual Master Pictures.

One of our chief woman players of that day was Enid Markey, who has, I understand, deserted the screen for the stage, her first love.

Of the actors who played with us in the old Inceville days who have since attained prominence as directors there are included also the names of Reginald Barker, Chester Withey, Richard Stanton, Howard Hickman, Frank Borzage, Charles Miller, Jerome Storm, Charles Giblyn, David Hartford, Walter Edwards, and others whose names do not occur to me at this time.

Another of the early recruits from the stage was the late Henry Woodruff, of *Brown of Harvard* fame. He was a finished player on the screen just as he was on the stage and our association was a very pleasant one. Willard Mack, another stage celebrity, came later, starring in *The Conqueror* as his first screen vehicle. Billie Burke, H. B. Warner, William Desmond, Julia Dean, Jane Grey, the late Franklin Ritchie, Orrin Johnson, who came west to do *The Three Musketeers*, Bruce McRae, Frank Keenan, George Fawcett, George Beban, House Peters, Lew Cody, Arthur Maude, Lew Stone, Mary Boland, Gladys Brockwell and Truly Shattuck were others recruited from the speaking stage, all of whom, I believe, made their film debut under my auspices.

Two of these drew record breaking salaries for that day. When Mr. Keenan was engaged to play the father in *The Coward* he was paid what I am told was the highest salary ever paid a male star up to that time. There was no question as to Miss Burke's salary being a record breaker, as she was given $40,000 for the picture, which consumed about five weeks in the making.

Peggy, in which Miss Burke starred—her first film play by the way—was one of the greatest photoplays ever made to my manner of thinking, both as to the star, the cast, which included William H. Thompson, William Desmond, Charles Ray and others, and the photography. All of the beautiful light effects were obtained without the use of an artificial light. (As a matter of fact I never used imitation sunlight until we moved to Culver City.) The direct rays of the sun and the use of mirrors were the only mediums used in the filming of *Peggy*.

Although Dustin Farnum was a stage celebrity when he came to us to do *The Iron Strain,* which by the way was my first release to Triangle, he had already acquired some fame on the screen as he had done *The Squaw Man* and *The Virginian* in the early Lasky days. But I have always considered his work in *The Iron Strain* as his greatest contribution to screen literature.

Mr. Warner also did splendid work in the two pictures in which he was starred, *The Raiders* and *The Beggar of Cawnpore*. George Fawcett, one of the best character men on stage or screen, did his best work for me in *The Corner*. Miss Dean made her film debut in *Matrimony* and Katherine Kaelred, the original stage "vampire," did *The Winged Idol* with House Peters supporting her. Dorothy Dalton was a recruit from the stage, who did her first screen work at Inceville but she did not attract attention until her performance opposite Hart in *The Disciple*. Stardom came soon after.

The list would not be complete without the names of Dorothy Davenport, now Mrs. Wallace Reid; Webster Campbell, the late George Osborne, Robert McKim, one of our ablest villains, who has pursued Dorothy Dalton and other stars through countless feet of celluloid; Tom Chatterton, who is not playing now, but whose serial activities are well remembered; Shorty Hamilton, well known for his western portrayals, and Leo Maloney, all of whom had their first camera experience under my direction or supervision in the early days of the cinema.

IDA MAY PARK
(D. 1954)

Like Lois Weber, Ida May Park was one of several women directors employed by Universal in the late 'teens, but here the resemblance ends. Weber was totally committed to the cinema as a tool for moral betterment and strained all her energies to this end, one of the cinema's few true idealists. Park, on the other hand, was a hack with no pretensions to art or education whatsoever. A slave-driver known generally around the studio as "Mrs. Simon Legree," she subordinated all else to getting the product out on time and under budget, the very model of a modern studio functionary. While she was a prolific screenwriter and director, her films (*Vanity Pool, The Model's Confession*, etc.) are completely unknown today, so little can be said of her directorial abilities. But she *was* chosen to write the entry on film directing for the 1920 anthology *Careers for Women*, a book that sought to indicate newly opening career possibilities for its readers. With her no-nonsense attitude toward the business, she was probably a better choice than Lois Weber, although hardly as well known. While her thoughts on the general background for a director are fairly standard, it is interesting that she shares the view of Alice Guy-Blaché that women directors have an advantage in the "natural . . . superiority of their emotional and imaginative faculties." But if they had an advantage, Hollywood took no use of it. When *Careers for Women* was reissued in an updated and expanded edition in 1934 the entire entry on motion picture directing was dropped. There was only one woman director working in Hollywood.

THE MOTION-PICTURE DIRECTOR
IDA MAY PARK

The vocation of the motion-picture director is one that commands so comprehensive a knowledge of the arts and sciences, economics and human nature, that it is particularly difficult to describe. To the almost unlimited mental demands on the director is added the necessity of an invulnerable physique. Perhaps that is why the number of consistently successful directors, both male and female, is relatively so small. But having these things there is no one, man or woman, who might not take up the profession with a certain degree of confidence in his or her ultimate success.

Because it is so obvious, I have not mentioned the necessity for a well-developed dramatic instinct. Perhaps more than anything else that instinct is the deciding factor of the success or the failure of the motion-picture director. Like acting, this ability to direct is an inborn talent, but it can be cultivated to a certain degree through the mediums of training, proper reading, and environment. But again, as it is with acting, the cultivated art can never equal the natural; it will always lack the fire of genius. From the beginning of the production, when the story is being moulded to scenario requirements, the director is the supervisor, the dominant note of the production, and (I am now writing to women alone) it is her sense of dramatic value that imparts to, or withholds from, the picture that indefinable something which can raise it to the ultimate peak of picture perfection or relegate it to the vast scrap-heap of "rubber-stamp" productions.

Second to this in importance is the artistic eye, for at all times the picture must be perfect in its angles, composition, and grouping. Our chief aim is to please, first and foremost, through the vision.

Preparation, since the demands on knowledge of all kinds is boundless, must necessarily be very general. A college education is a great help if it has not been concentrated on any particular subject to the detriment of others. The whole motion-picture industry is so young and the recognition of the value of good direction so recent that, so far as I know, there is yet no school established which teaches the strictly technical side. Knowledge of camera operation, of lighting effects, and of all the hundred and one less important mechanical details must be gained through work in the studio itself. The difficulty of obtaining a position as apprentice or assistant is unfortunately very great.

Once in the game the aspirant to a directorship will find the opportunities limitless. Such a statement is not half so extreme as it sounds. The perfect picture is still a thing of dreams. An industry can develop only as the intelligence which directs it develops. The interest of big minds is a thing that until recently has been glaringly absent from the motion picture. But now converts, intelligent converts, are flocking to the banner and results are bound to come in the form of better pictures.

The financial return is likewise unlimited. A thousand dollars a week is a small income for a successful director. It might well be called a minimum. There is no maximum.

While production is on there is no rest. No eight-hour day is known to the director. Often work extends far into the night, many times through it, and the next day brings no respite. Given a certain number of weeks, a certain number of dollars, and a troupe of actors, you are under a terrific nervous and physical strain that does not let up until you have completed the work. The obstacles which arise are frequently enough to try the greatest patience. The director must never lose her poise, must never betray the slightest annoyance unless she wishes to jeopardize the success of her picture. In all the world there is no more difficult lot of people to handle than a company of actors. When vacation finally does come, it is never more than two or three days. For the first time in six years I am taking a ten-day vacation, and even now the tentacles of the great cinema octopus reach out at intervals and threaten to drag me back, my vacation half over, into the maelstrom of the studio.

As for the natural equipment of women for the rôle of director, the superiority of their emotional and imaginative faculties gives them a great advantage. Then, too, the fact that there are only two women directors of note in the field to-day leaves an absolutely open field. But unless you are hardy and determined, the director's rôle is not for you. Wait until the profession has emerged from its embryonic state and a system has been evolved by which the terrific weight of responsibility can be lifted from one pair of shoulders. When that time comes I believe that women will find no finer calling.

MAURICE TOURNEUR
(1876-1961)

Of all the film-makers who flourished in the Griffith period, the one with the most prepossessing artistic credentials was undoubtedly Maurice Tourneur. Born in Paris in 1876, he began as an illustrator and designer, and he worked as assistant to Auguste Rodin and Puvis de Chavannes. Soon he turned his attention to the theater, where he fell under the influence of André Antoine, whose *théâtre libre* movement had brought the naturalist revolution to the Paris stage. By the time he entered films in 1912, Tourneur had already acquired a fondness for experimentation and for innovative approaches to staging and decor. In 1914 the Eclair Company sent him to their large new studios at Fort Lee, New Jersey, where he began producing films at a terrific rate—three dozen in the next six years alone. Tourneur set high standards for himself and was universally praised for the "artistic" qualities of his work, but even he could not produce so much art to order. Here he complains about some of the pressures he faces as a motion picture director, and one cannot help sensing a tone of despair. His screen work after this point grew less personal, less ambitious, and less successful. In 1926 he quarreled with M-G-M and returned to France, where he continued directing with some success until 1948.

MEETING THE PUBLIC DEMANDS
MAURICE TOURNEUR

Oliver Goldsmith once said, "The little mind which loves itself will write and think with the vulgar; but the great mind will be bravely eccentric, and scorn the beaten road." Had Goldsmith been a present-day producer of motion pictures he would probably never have spoken that line, for the mind that tries to be eccentric and scorn the beaten road in pictures usually leads the head in which it is contained to disaster.

Making pictures is a commercial business, the same as making soap and, to be successful, one must make a commodity that will sell. We have the choice between making bad, silly, childish and useless pictures, which make a lot of money, and make everybody rich, or nice stories, which are practically lost. Nobody wants to see them. The State right buyers wouldn't buy them; if they did, the exhibitors wouldn't show them.

I remember how delighted I was when I read what the reviewers had to say about my *The Blue Bird*. Do you know, amongst the hundreds of exhibitors in New York, how many showed it? To my knowledge Mr. Rothapfel and a few fellows uptown.

Those of us who are familiar with the productions of the articulate stage know very well that every time we go to see a show we sit before the curtain in a thrill of anticipation, waiting for the magic moment to come, feeling certain that we shall get an excitement of some sort or other. The orchestra plays, the footlights go on and the curtains part.

But what do we see if it is the screen? A sneering, hip-wriggling, cigaret-smoking vampire. She exercises a wonderful fascination upon every man that is brought anywhere near her, and so far as I have been able to judge, the only reason for this strange fascination is the combination of the three attri-

From *Shadowland*, May 1920.

Maurice Tourneur uses his *Beaux Arts* training to good advantage as he touches up Wallace Beery's warpaint during location shooting on *The Last of the Mohicans* (1920).

butes I have already mentioned. They are good enough to apparently kill any man at fifty yards.

If it is not a vampire, it's a cute, curly-headed, sun-bonneted, smiling and pouting ingenue. She also is full of wonderful fascination. She runs thru beautiful gardens, (always with the same nice back-lighting effects), or the poor little thing is working under dreadful factory conditions that have not been known for at least forty years. Torn between the sheer idiocy of the hero and the inexplicable hate of the heavy, is it any wonder that her sole communion is with the dear dumb animals, pigs, cows, ducks, goats—anything so long as it can't talk.

If it is not either a vampire or an ingenue, it is a band of cowboys, generous-hearted, impulsive souls. They never do a stroke of work; they couldn't—they have not got time. They must be hanging around the saloon, ready to spring into the saddle and rescue the heroine, whether she is a telegraph operator or a lumberman's daughter, or a school-teacher up in the mountains. I saw all that many times, but I have yet to see a cowboy looking after a cow.

Next comes our old friend the convict. He is always innocent, but unjustly imprisoned. Altho the picture is one of today and the clothes of everybody were bought last week, our unhappy convict's sole consolation is the fact that he is able to wear striped clothing, abolished years ago. He insists on wearing it; it is the one thing that reconciles him to the rigors of the prison existence, from which he escapes so easily whenever he has a mind to do so.

Another old friend is the screen doctor. Carrying always his little black bag, he enters the room where the patient lies unconscious; he feels the pulse, listens to the fluttering motions of the heart, and then one of two things occurs. If the patient is a man, the doctor steps back from the bed, takes off his hat and looks sadly at the floor. This indicates the patient is dead. If the patient is a girl, more particularly if she is the leading lady, he gives her a glass of water, and whether she fell from a thirty foot cliff, was poisoned by the villain, shot in the back by a Japanese spy or run over by the Lumberlands Express, she is instantly cured. You would imagine that the doctor would express some sort of delight at such a miracle, but he doesn't; he remains comparatively unmoved. It is only when a patient dies that he develops an intensity of sympathetic grief such as he would exhibit if the patient were his own twin brother. One thing is certain; if many of his patients die, his own life will be seriously endangered, a merely human constitution being unable to withstand many such shocks. I could keep on describing types like those from now till the middle of next week. Up to the present time the public has not seemed to realize how bad the average picture is, because they have been rather fooled by the fact that directors have introduced new lighting effects, by the personality of the star and by tricks generally.

I would rather starve and make good pictures, if I knew they were going to be shown, but to starve and make pictures which are thrown in the ash-can is above anybody's strength. As long as the public taste will oblige us to make what is very justly called machine-made stories, we can only bow and give them what they want.

Prunella was one of my productions that the reviewers spoke of as an artistic achievement. The first time I saw it shown to the public was in one of the side-shows in Atlantic City. An automatic piano furnished the musical score, which consisted of popular dance music. A week or so later it was shown in one of the leading New York theatres with success, but the managers of the smaller houses thruout the country considered it "too high brow" for their patrons. *Broken Blossoms* was a very good picture, but suppose it had been shown without the two Russian orchestras, the two prologs, and about fifty thousand dollars' worth of publicity, who would have gone to see it? Suppose Mr. Cecil De Mille made *The Admirable Crichton* as Barrie wrote it, instead of putting on *Male and Female* as Mr. De Mille saw it, what would have been the result? The picture wouldn't have made any money, which is not so important, but it would not have been shown, and this is the main thing to a producer, and to my mind it is going to be the greatest event of next year.

The American producers will have to change entirely their machine-made stories and come to a closer and truer view of humanity, or the foreign market is going to sweep us out with their pictures, made in an inferior way, but carried over by human, possible, different stories. I am not going to elaborate on the mental anguish of the director who has been talked into accepting a bad script that he knows is bad, because this has happened to me four times out of five and I would rather not think about it, as it is too painful and I remember only too vividly the feelings of gloom and depression with which I have walked away with a script of this sort under my arm, wondering how in the name of heaven I was going to live the next few weeks without committing suicide, or what sort of new stunt I could invent to make it get by.

Good stories are not only a necessity, but some day they will actually come. The industry is founded on the firm basis of providing healthy entertainment, and I look forward to the future with confidence. If anyone wants to awake the sleeping beauty, I certainly do, but the poor lady has been sleeping for so many years that at times it seems like an impossible job.

SILENT AGE
(1921-1927)

REX INGRAM
(1892-1950)

For men like Griffith the theater was the obvious bench-
mark by which motion picture progress was to be measured, but others in Hollywood were drawn just as strongly
to the non-narrative arts. Rex Ingram was one of these, and
here presents a set of rules for film direction modeled completely after the workings of an artist's studio. Born a
Dubliner, Ingram shared with many of the French ex-
patriates a background in the graphic arts that would
translate itself into some of the silent film's most breathtak-
ing imagery. *The Four Horsemen of the Apocalypse, Mare
Nostrum,* and *The Magician* are filled with images that
seem designed to hang on the walls of Edwardian art gal-
leries. Indeed, that is their curse as well as their glory.
Ingram's films seem today distressingly static, and if seen in
prints of substandard quality nearly all traces of their once
widely heralded beauty will have vanished. When Louis B.
Mayer began exerting studio pressures on Ingram in the
mid-20's, the director packed up his entire unit and established studios for himself in the south of France. His wife,
Alice Terry, starred in these films and John Seitz was cine-
matographer. Making heavy use of Mediterranean locales,
with side trips to Paris for their cityscapes, the group prospered until the coming of sound, when increased difficulties of production, and Ingram's by now fragile health,
forced them to disband. With the supervision of Irving
Thalberg awaiting back in Hollywood, Ingram decided to
remain in Europe. He tried his hand at one independently
produced talkie, but it was unsuccessful. He never directed
again.

DIRECTING THE PICTURE
REX INGRAM

Yesterday it was an industry; today it is an art. There, in a nut-shell, you have the history of the progress of the making of pictures. As an industry the film might have continued indefi-nitely to create dividends for investors; as an art, it has become the medium for conveying to the world the message that the great masters of all time have attempted to give us.

Fifteen years have seen the cinema develop from the state where its choicest temples contained but a dozen seats. The public was charged the sum of five cents to enter a nickelodeon, which was disguised as the observation platform of a railroad train, from which they watch a flickering representation of landscape slip away behind them into the distance. It was an illusion obtained by the projection of a motion picture film which had been photographed from the back of an observation car.[1]

Today great theatres, seating thousands of people and con-taining lobbies which are in themselves as large as an entire legitimate theatre, are devoted exclusively to the presentation of the motion picture. If this remarkable change has come about in the theatres, it is not probable that the development of the cinema, as an art, has remained at a standstill.

It assuredly has not. The motion picture was destined from the beginning to become more important than the legitimate drama because of its tremendous scope. We realize there is no limit to its range when we consider that where one theatre presents a stage play, it is possible for hundreds of motion pic-ture theatres to present identically the same screen production at the same time in all parts of the world.

1. The reference is not to any simple nickelodeon store-show, but to a related, though somewhat more complex entertainment which flour-ished at the same time, Hale's Tours and Scenes of the World.

From *Opportunities in the Motion Picture Industry*, Photoplay Re-search Society, Los Angeles, 1922.

Rex Ingram with Rheba, an Arabian dancer he discovered and featured in his 1924 production, *The Arab*.

Hundreds of thousands of people in the civilized world know nothing of the work of Rembrant, Michalangelo, El Greco, Corot and Doré, and would in all probability be little interested in them. Yet, to these people the same message will be brought through the medium of the cinema—the message that the masters of art have given to those of their students who are today engaged in film production.

For the inevitable is coming to pass. Slowly but surely, the cinema is coming into its own, taking its place, if not beside sculpture and painting as an art, most certainly ahead of the spoken drama. The motion picture's unlimited possibilities where sweeping, smashing dramatic effects are desired; the many opportunities it affords to accomplish results not to be dreamt of behind the footlights; the intimacy that can be made to exist between the audience and the characters in the film play—all go to prove that this great new art—until recently termed "industry"—potentially combines that which fine sculpture, fine painting, and the best that the theatre has to offer can give us.

Art is as important as the scope and power of its message. We believe that a fine piece of sculpture which stands in a public square, or part of a city, exerts an ennobling influence upon the citizens. A fine painting that hangs in a public building undoubtedly leaves an aesthetic impression upon those who see it.

We know that our daily lives are greatly influenced by the masters of the spoken drama. Yet, when we stop to consider that for every one person who sees the work of a sculptor, or a painter, for every hundred persons who are present when a spoken drama is enacted—a million or more carry away impressions from the cinema theatres. Just what these impressions are, depends upon the play.

Where sculpture, painting and the legitimate drama belong to the art-loving minority of the nation, the motion picture belongs to the whole people. Therefore, being the most universal, the most easily understood of all the arts, it is bound to take its place in time as the most necessary of them all to a better civilization—going upon the premise that the chief object of art is to exert an aesthetic influence upon those who come in contact with it and are reached by its message.

In 1913, when I was studying drawing and sculpture at the Yale School of Fine Arts, a motion picture play, founded upon Charles Dickens' famous story, "A Tale of Two Cities," came to New Haven. It followed in the wake of many cut and dried one-reel subjects, and while this picture was necessarily full of imperfections, common to all pioneer films, it marked a tremendous step ahead in the making of them.

I left the theatre greatly impressed; absolutely convinced that it would be through the medium of the film play to the production of which the laws that govern the fine arts had been applied, that a universal understanding and appreciation of art finally would be reached. I brought several friends of mine, most of them either students of the art school, or members of the Yale Dramatic Association, the following day to see this picture, which had been made by the Vitagraph Company of America, and each and every one of them was as much impressed as I. All of us thereupon decided to enter the motion picture field. After leaving New Haven, I lost track entirely of the other members of that party.

But some months later I was fortunate enough to take part in a film play, directed by William Humphrey, the man who had produced this version of the Dickens' story.

As time went on, I began to realize how valuable my training at the art school was going to prove. In spite of inattention, I had gained an understanding of the laws that govern perspective, composition, balance, construction, form and the distribution of light and shade, thanks to the repeated lectures on these subjects. And it is through producers who have acquired knowledge and training of this kind that the cinema can advance further than all the other arts in influencing an entirely modern civilization, as only an art which belongs peculiarly to this day and age can.

Allowing for the difference in medium, practically the same laws apply to the production of a film play which has artistic merit, as to the making of a fine piece of sculpture or a masterly painting.

The rough preliminary sketch made in a plastic medium or on paper by the sculptor for his proposed job has its parallel in the synopsis made before the motion picture scenario is blocked out.

Before a scene is taken in a film play, provided ideal conditions exist in the studio, the scenario is completed. For without a well-constructed script, the efforts of the director will fail to convince.

He may have the human note, humor, pathos, fine characterization and photography, well composed pictures and good lighting, but unless he convinces in the telling of his story, all these things stand on a foundation that wabbles.

The sculptured figure or group of figures first takes form in an armature, or firmly constructed frame built according to the proportions of the job. This frame is composed of steel braces, wood and lead piping, all wired together. Upon this structure, the clay is then roughly massed.

Just as the moving picture director must have a thorough knowledge of the scenario construction, the sculptor must be familiar with this part of his work, whether he does it himself or whether it is done for him, for if the armature is unskillfully put together, it will not stand when the great weight of the clay is put upon it, and his efforts will be to no purpose. For even if portions are unhurt when the figure collapses, the mass will not hang together again.

The armature is the sculptor's scenario.

As the sculptor has to compose his grouping, to fit a certain space, on a pediment or a monument, so the director must place his people within given lines, according to the distance they are from the cameras, in order that the massing of figures, the distance, and the arrangement of light and shade will go to make up something that has pictorial value.

However, in this the film often presents a more complicated problem than either paint or clay. The compositions of painter and sculptor are studied out, and when finished remain as their creator left them, but the moving picture composition changes every moment.

Often a fine bit of grouping that has taken the director a long time to compose will be changed to an unbalanced, disconnected mob scene through some alteration in dramatic action. This change sometimes may necessitate an entirely different arrangement of lights, and a different dressing of the set, although in most cases, a different camera set-up or a change of foreground will be sufficient.

There is a tendency in film production when one is striving to make something of beauty, to sacrifice, or lose sight of, the story theme. In moving pictures, this is particularly dangerous. For in sculpture and painting, although the finest examples of both arts have a theme—certainly a meaning—neither are linked so closely to literature as is the screen.

Something rarely sought for on the moving picture screen is form. As with clay and paint, form is one of the most vital adjuncts to the film. Take the close-up for instance. Without knowledge of the construction and forms of the human head it is only by chance that the director can light it in such a way that the modeling is brought out. Lack of modeling will make a head thrown upon the screen appear to be flat and without character, and in doing so weaken the characterization of the player.

It is modeling obtained by judicious arrangement of light and shade, that enables us to give something of a stereoscopic quality to the soft, mellow-toned close-up, which takes the place of the human voice on the screen and helps to make the audience as intimate with the characters as if they had known and seen them constantly in everyday life. Form and modeling help a characterization one hundred per cent.

The most noticeable racial characteristic of the Chinese head is the high, bony structure of the cheeks, a peculiarity that will be accentuated by the source of light coming from above at all times when photographing this particular character. The top light throws a shadow under the prominent cheek bones and gives them a more pronounced effect than could be obtained by any high lighting that a clever make-up artist might use in his efforts to gain this effect.

Sculpture teaches us that color is deceptive. The fact that from a live mask or fine portrait bust of a friend we invariably learn more about the character of the original than we knew before, proves that the theory has something of truth in it. Thus, except in the rare cases when both sculpture and film are colored, the sculptor and director are working in a mono-tone medium and both are striving for the same result—the one in the round, the other on a flat surface, and the director sim-ulates the form which is not there by an arrangement of light and shade calculated to create an optical illusion.

In saying that all arts are kindred we are uttering a platitude. The making of poor pictures is not art just as surely as the modeling of an inferior statue or writing of bad music is not art. The big things in all art, we know, are the simple things—those which are stripped of all the pretenses and affectations of the artist.

John Sargent's "Frieze of the Prophets" in the Boston Mu-seum, and the saints in the reredos of the Church of St. Thomas on Fifth Avenue, New York City, by the sculptor, Lee Lawrie, are among the finest examples in America of the splendidly simple thing in art.[1]

In them we see not the surface, but that which lies beneath. When the screen shows us what lies behind the actions in the hearts of those whose reflections are thrown upon it, then it also is accomplishing something toward this end.

What do you think the producers look for in a man when they engage him to take charge of one of their producing units? What qualifications are considered necessary in a successful director? May I tell you?

First, I should say, the ability to create. A broad acquaintance with the world at large; an intimate knowledge of the races; an understanding of how people live in the countries throughout the earth; and the power to visualize the written word in picture form.

You sigh, and say to yourself, "This is indeed a hard profession to break into!" But, I ask you, is it? Would it not be equally as hard for one to break into your own profession, whatever it may be, unless one had the training for it? Of course it would. If it were an easy thing to become a motion picture director, the studios would be full of them. It is because it is not an easy thing to become a director, that the work is so attractive. To those unfitted for it, there is no use allowing this work to make an appeal.

The potential director had better be certain that he is a close student of human nature. To make his work stand out and achieve success, it is necessary that the characters he portrays on the screen appear as actual living, breathing persons. One of the surest ways to study human nature at first hand is to mix with all classes of people in all walks of life. Once you are able to do this, you will come to know life, and be able to depict it humanly on the screen.

The director should also be a lover of books. And natural tendency to analyze different dramatic situations will help immeasurably when you are finally qualified to handle the megaphone.

1. Ingram was at one time a student, and later an assistant to Lee Lawrie, or so he later claimed.

There really is no sure road to the position of director for a motion picture producing company. Some of the rank and file of men and women now directing stars of the screen drifted quite naturally from the legitimate into studio work. Others have served long apprenticeships as actors, writers and cameramen before they were qualified to direct a motion picture.

To know the camera is to know what is possible of it. Therefore a good many of our present day directors have graduated from the ranks of cameramen. First of all they have the knowledge of the limitations or possibilities of the camera. Then they have gained a vast store of information by observing the methods of the various directors when they have served as cameramen.

Since the players are as clay in the hands of the sculptor, as paint at the tip of an artist's brush, it is desirable that, like the artist, the director should have a true sense of art values. He moulds them into the forms desired and called for by the author's script, in one instance, or he places and blends them on his canvas to conform with the story told by the author in another.

MARSHALL NEILAN
(1891-1958)

Neilan's career was one of the truly meteoric Hollywood nightmares: an early, almost instantaneous acting and directing success, followed by long years of decline, neglect, and oblivion. His matinee-idol good looks had won him a certain following in leading man roles for such companies as Kalem and Flying A, and by 1914 he had promoted himself into a director's chair as well. At Kalem these responsibilities were wide ranging and swung from melodramas featuring himself to the bizarre slapstick antics of Ham and Bud, one of the screen's first comedy teams. Major success came the following year when he directed Griffith heroine Blanche Sweet (whom he married in 1922) in a successful series for Goldwyn. Soon Mary Pickford hired him for her own films, where he displayed extraordinary talent in such films as *Stella Maris*, *Amarilly of Clothesline Alley*, and *Daddy Long Legs*. Pickford never before or since had a director with greater dramatic skills, or one who could better handle the more interesting elements of her own personality. His reputation for handling actresses no doubt elicited this piece on the essential elements of screen acting, all of which are slanted toward women, and none of which include talent. Neilan at his best was able to synthesize performances at the editing bench out of the raw material provided by a pretty face—something Sternberg took credit for years later regarding the work of various actresses in his own films. But by the time he wrote this article Neilan's career had already peaked. A great, if undisciplined talent, his later years traced a sorry decline, broken unexpectedly at the very end by a striking cameo role in Kazan's *A Face in the Crowd*.

ACTING FOR THE SCREEN:
THE SIX GREAT ESSENTIALS
MARSHALL NEILAN

When an actor has gained distinction as a great comedian, he invariably expresses a desire to play Hamlet. When an actress has become famous for her ability to wring tears out of a stony-hearted skeptic, she is usually quoted as saying that she longs to play comedy. Some comedians have transferred their efforts to tragedy and with startling success. Some sob-sisters have gratified their ambition to play comedy, and have played it well. But these were the exceptions, and except in one or two cases, they have gone back to their original types.

There are, of course, some actors and actresses so versatile that they can enact any type of role, but most of them specialize in some particular sort of characterization. And why not? All other art forms are expressed in a variety of ways; one artist specializes in etchings, another uses pastels and a third will devote his time to portraits in oils. Each has, of course, mastered the technique and he could work with other media, but he is at his best when using that one with which he has specialized.

So it is with acting, and particularly acting for the screen. It is needless to mention the fact that the screen demands a great deal more from its recruits than does the stage. But this buga-boo has been greatly exaggerated, and has discouraged many persons who possess real talent.

The amateur, and particularly the woman, does not often realize the extent of her ability. The urge for expression is there, and the desire to act. Often her greatest asset lies in some little peculiarity that she has constantly bewailed. In fact most of the "ifs" and "buts" that keep the average amateur from making her first try for fame in moving pictures result from

From *Opportunities in the Motion Picture Industry*, Photoplay Research Society, Los Angeles, 1922.

Director Marshall Neilan with his wife and onetime star, Blanche
Sweet. Photo taken in the mid-20's.

the work of those pestiferous little devils, Super-Modesty and
Self-Criticism.

For instance, says one pretty girl as she holds up the mirror
to nature, "Oh, dear! Why did God get tired out when he
started making my nose? Who can tell? I might have been a
motion picture star but for that."

Says another dainty maid, taking a disappointed inventory
of her personal charms, "I'm so thin, I'm afraid the camera
would miss me, if I ever did get a chance to try for the movies."

Wails a third, "What good does it do me if my features are
perfect as long as I haven't any personality?"

But you're all wrong, girls. You forget that the precious
spark of fame and fortune comes many a time from just such
a little personal eccentricity as yours. While you are not the

type, perhaps, that you admire, so you fail to sell whatever marketable attributes you have *just* because you haven't Mary Pickford's eyes, or a smile like Constance Talmadge's or the dash of Nazimova.

You must stop to think of one very important fact. *No one*, not even the starriest of these famous ones *has everything!* Some have more personal advantages than others. Oh, yes! We'll all agree on that. But just glance over the foremost constellation and see what you'll see. Everyone in the group has, perhaps, several points of attractiveness but you will note that in each case, one of the *six great essentials* to success has been featured to a more striking degree than any of the others.

Sometimes this is true to such an extent that in your intense admiration, you are conscious of nothing less than perfection. *Yet*, with all due credit to these splendid artists who give us something to think about and dream about in our pleasure-seeking moments, perhaps if you could have a confidential boudoir chat with each one, she would tell you, with a bit of suppressed longing, of some little thing she wishes nature would do, or some little thing she wishes nature hadn't done for her. And you will be surprised to think you had never noticed the triviality of which she speaks, just because no one is, really, so mercilessly critical of us as we, ourselves, are.

But you are getting impatient to learn what are the *six great essentials*. And you shall have them. First of all, you know I'm going to say *beauty*. That, of course, needs no explanatory remarks. Another one is *personality*. Another, *charm* (there's a difference between these two that you'll understand later). Next there is *temperament*, then *style*, and sixth, *the ability to wear clothes*.

The most striking, and perhaps the most interesting way to force this truth upon your minds, is to point to six great favorites who have not only made a sensational hit but who have by subsequent achievements proved that their popularity is not a thing of the moment, but is based upon qualities and characteristics that are sure to attract today or a hundred years from today. There are many that we could choose as graceful embodiments of one or more of the *six essentials*, but after conscientious, impartial consideration of the screen's great galaxy of artists, we have selected what are perhaps the most striking examples.

For sheer *beauty*, perfection of features and a portrait-like magnificence, who can call forth more admiration than Katherine MacDonald? If you are attracted to her, you will instantly recognize that it is primarily her rare physical loveliness which appeals. The role makes very little difference with Katherine MacDonald. So long as she stays young and beautiful, we will continue to be awed worshipers at her shrine.

Hardly have we written the next essential, *personality*, when the magnetic name and presence of Mary Pickford flashes before you. You just need to recall one of her radiant smiles, one of her delightful impersonations, or one of her raggedy roles in which her natural personal charm was almost obscured in the intensity of her characterization, to realize that you love Mary Pickford, first, last and always, because she is Mary Pickford. She has something that irrespective of looks or age or anything else, will live on. She has *personality*.

Charm is a more quiet, a more subtle expression than is personality. It is none-the-less attractive, however, to many fans, as witness one of the most popular of its possessors, Elsie Ferguson. Something more spiritual, more elusive than personality, something that is enhanced by beauty but not necessarily dependent upon it, clings to this lady who has fittingly been called the aristocrat of the screen.

You are probably thinking that Norma Talmadge should have been included long before now, but an analysis of this attractive star's success places her in the forefront of those who hold their admirers through *temperament*. Often it is attributed to actresses but seldom possessed to such an extent as Norma Talmadge possesses it. It is her extreme sensitiveness to every possible emotion, her poignant response to a hundred different moods, which, expressed in vivid play of features and gestures, mark her as a truly superior personality.

Style, a semi-mental, semi-physical quality, is more superficial than the above characteristics. It depends not merely upon clothes, but upon an innate knowledge of how to walk, how to stand, how to conduct oneself generally. A number of comediennes can boast of it, but none more rightfully than Bebe Daniels. A poise that never flags, self-assurance, an accurate understanding of her best features, and the knowledge of how to "put herself over," are evident in every one of this clever young woman's efforts.

The ability to wear clothes is no small asset. Is there anyone who can flaunt a superb wardrobe with more dash than Gloria Swanson? To the smallest detail of ornament such as a buckle on a headdress or a wrist trinket, this young woman has a knack of lending to her apparel a certain significance of modernity that makes you unconsciously think that whatever she happens to put on is, of course, *the very latest thing*.

The important question, is, which one of the *essentials* is yours? Most everyone of you has at least one of these. *First* of all, you must realize which is yours (that is not such a small task either, as self-knowledge comes with development, not nature). *Then*, you must cultivate this, emphasize it and perfect it until everyone about you is forced to recognize that you are beautiful, charming or chic, or that you have personality, temperament or style. The chances, ten to one, are that you have not merely one, but, as each of our six fair examples, several of these *essentials*. But there is *one* in which you excel. Which one is it? Study your mirror with a candid eye, and be sure, be very sure, that you are not too modest.

That is different advice, is it not, from what our grandmothers and Sunday School teachers give us? But the movie profession *is* different. It has brought forth new standards of self-appraisal. It requires a supreme confidence in all the gifts that the good Lord has bestowed upon us—mind you—not an exaggerated idea of our own beauty or cleverness—but a strictly fair opinion, unhampered by super-modesty.

Your own personal experience reminds you that there are hundreds of beautiful girls, charming girls—hundreds of the other four kinds of girls—who will never get any closer to the screen than the front row of their favorite theatre. Perhaps the hosiery clerk in the biggest department store in your town has a face and figure more beautiful than has ever been photographed. That girl, if she only knew it, might be making $5,000.00 per week instead of eighteen.

You may not be quite as beautiful as she, *but*—you may have ten times her personality and brains.

Did you ever think of that? If not, think of it now and keep thinking of it. Don't listen to discouragement from "friends." Don't believe that there is some mysterious key to success in this particular profession. Don't believe that the gates are closed except to a few fortunate ones who know somebody who is assistant to some Great Person who holds jurisdiction over this profession.

Speaking as a director, I can give you a bit of interesting information. There is no such thing, among men of our profession, as being satiated with beauty or talent. We are none of us at the stage, professionally speaking, where we do not get a thrill from the first sight of anyone who has something new or distinctly pleasing to offer. There is no one of us who does not instinctively feel the urge to create something artistic when he sees a promising subject. Instantly there is the double-sided curiosity within us—first, "What am I capable of doing with this personality?" And second, "What can she do with herself?" From then on the work is co-operative—and fascinating.

Another very important consideration—

It may be that you are unusual enough, either in appearance or personality, to play, not a conventional leading role, but a strong character part. You may not have the qualifications of a screen idol, but you may be a type so true to life that you are indispensable to the screen. I have in mind a woman who, without youth or what is commonly known as beauty, and with no reputation whatever, startled the whole country with her marvelous characterization of a mother role. You will all remember Vera Gordon in "Humoresque." You will never forget her, will you? Because she fitted the conception of what a mother should be, and for no other reason whatever, she was assigned that role. As a result she has identified herself with this type of role, so that today, you can't think of Vera Gordon without thinking of a plump, wholesome, kind woman, who loves her children.

Less and less, as time goes on, does success in the movies depend upon mere prettiness. What you do with whatever ability you have counts far more. As in a sales office, so in a motion picture studio. Can you take orders? Are you receptive to honest suggestions from someone who has had the advantage of a wider experience than yours? If so, you have a great fundamental quality without which nothing can be accomplished.

Stars, as you may know, are never made overnight. Most of them "arrive" after months, maybe years, of hard labor—not work, but *labor*, spent in playing obscure parts. But if you have real dramatic talent, obscurity and competition cannot hold you down. You will in time force the director, your rivals, and the public, to admit that you are no longer an extra, or a secondary, or somebody's leading woman, but a star.

The field is a wide one. Never before has so alluring a profession held out a greater variety of opportunities to a greater variety of aspirants. The fruit crop is bounteous this year. Success is on every bough. Reach for it.

Let the pretty girl whom we referred to in the second paragraph take another, more tolerant view of her looks. She doesn't like her nose, she says, "It's too stubby." Now right there is where we differ with her. It may be stubby, but it isn't too stubby. Let her ask her boy friends who have been her admirers since the days of aprons and pigtails, or her new, grown-up beaus, what it is that they love about her. As sure as she wants to be a movie star, they'll say, "I don't know, sweetheart, unless it's because you have such an adorable little nose!"

And the girl who never can grow fat, no matter how much buttermilk she drinks—let her stop and think a minute next time she sighs before a full-length mirror. Let her forget the plump beauty of her chum who patronizes her because she weighs only 98 pounds. Consider some of our slender screen fairies, who, far from disguising their slightness, deliberately accentuate it. You know them—Anita Stewart, Constance Talmadge, Lillian Gish, Nazimova. For that matter, any fashion magazine has pages and pages of encouragement for the girl who is not only slender but (oh! direful word) skinny. She can wear a style of clothes that is forbidden to any one with any inclination whatever toward stoutness.

The third little girl who bewailed her lack of personality has a snap, because as we said, she has the face of an angel. She can cultivate personality by cultivating an interest in persons and things outside her own immediate circle. She can test out her own conversational ability because people will always listen to her. She is so beautiful. The trouble with marvelously pretty girls is often that they are lazy, too lazy to be interesting. But with a little initiative and an incentive, they can develop that absurd, charming, magical something that we call *personality*.

In repetition, as the rhetoricians say, lies emphasis. In repetition also, we might add, lies monotony. We don't want to bore you but we do want to impress you with the great and mighty rule for success in the world of shadow-shapes. Don't underestimate your own distinctive charm, and don't, don't, don't indulge in a friendly folly of imitating when you can CREATE.

CHARLES CHAPLIN
(1889-   )

It was highly appropriate that Chaplin in 1924 wrote an article called "Can Art be Popular?" After his First National features and *A Woman of Paris*, Chaplin had achieved the wildest critical acclaim ever bestowed on a director of Hollywood movies. Although he relished the accolades of his highbrow admirers more than he would admit—and the praise of crowned heads higher still—he is here obviously (and I think sincerely) made quite uneasy by it all. "I have not much patience with a thing of beauty that must be explained to be understood," he writes, suspicious of those who would analyze his work to death. If Chaplin has kept up with these explainers he must today have an entire library full of critical commentary on the films of Charlie Chaplin, over a half-century of (often less than profound) exegesis on the how and why of Chaplin's art. His suspicions have long since been borne out. In the 20's and 30's sociological critics made his tramp an icon for the oppressed masses, in the 40's and 50's political critics were blinded by the glare of his private life, and today cinematic formalists analyze his articulation of space and scrutinize his sketchy narratives for long-neglected semiotic codes. For fifty years Chaplin has been grist for everyone's mill, and will no doubt continue to be so as long as critics can avoid coming to terms with his own thoughts on "film art."

CAN ART BE POPULAR?
CHARLES CHAPLIN

Usually the term "art" is applied to dull academic things which scare most people away. Great art is a feeling which cannot readily be defined. But the greatest subject in the world can be so simplified that anyone may appreciate and understand it, and that is—or should be—the highest form of art. If there is any subject so profound that it cannot be expressed so as to be generally understood, then there is weakness in the artist's method of expression, or else his great subject was not so worth while after all. All of us who are healthy are born with the same emotions, and we will react to the appeal of beauty in much the same way.

Children have definite conceptions of love, hate, fear and revenge. These, expressed fully in terms and things that come into the circle of their lives, are bound to be liked. Some people tell a story badly to a child; others do so well; in either case only the subject matter is understood. *Alice in Wonderland* and certain fairy tales—which are unquestionably admitted to be classics and works of art—were not explained into that proud position by grown-ups who liked them, but rather became classics because of their real appeal to children, who love beauty and a good story well told without knowing why.

It is in its subject matter that art—or that which is acclaimed as art—must find acceptance and accord, if it is to be popular. To the materialist art is something which stands for truth as he knows it, whether it is pleasant or unpleasant. He will not be interested in the feeling of a thing that is too optimistic. He will condemn such a work because it is perhaps false in logic or sloppy in sentiment, sometimes both. But this is just as one-sided

From *The Ladies' Home Journal*, October 1924. Copyright 1924 by Curtis Publishing Company. Reprinted by permission of *Ladies' Home Journal*.

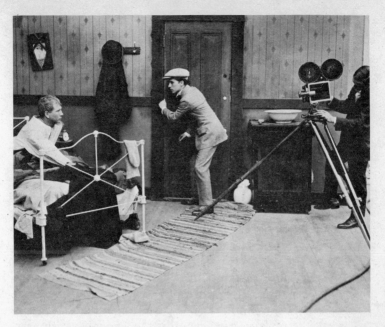

Out of costume, Chaplin directs Tom Wilson in a scene from *Sunnyside*, a First National release of 1919.

and intolerant as the person who insists that good art is all sentiment and optimism.

Art to academicians—and to some critics—is a matter of rules and can be defined, at least to their own understanding; and thus they make of it a preachment, which it is not. I have not much patience with a thing of beauty that must be explained to be understood. If it does need added interpretation by someone other than the creator, then I question whether it has fulfilled its purpose. Rules to the creative artist are sometimes a help to playing safe. I do not trust rules any more than I trust figures; but by avoiding all things which are generally thought to be wrong, one can turn out something which a good many people will say is right, but it will not be very original, nor will it have any great effect on the emotions. Art is not a study. It is beauty which gives joy and entertainment; it is a matter of feeling.

But because art is largely feeling, the creative artist has not the right to have what we see in his finished work called art just because it may have been sincerely felt. The fine spirit and feeling that we find in any great work of art must have some wider appeal than to a few persons who fool themselves. Because I do not like certain types of modern art, I do not mean that in painting and sculpture I like only things that have been seasoned by time. In my judgment there is altogether too much reverence for the things that have come down through the years. A thing is not art because it is old any more than it is because it is said to be sincere.

For the purpose of a play it is consistent enough with life that an unprincipled character, through roguery and deceit, eventually gains worldly goods. But this will annoy many people, even though the sheer irony of the success of weakness may be the subject matter of the play. They will be aroused to such a state of antagonism that they will forget that their emotions have been played upon and that the whole has been very real to them. All this turmoil has been created within the spectators, and yet they will swear that it has not been entertainment at all. But, after all, what is entertainment but to lose one's identity and live in another world?

Tragedy is likewise not ordinarily popular. The public is apt to dislike the subject matter for personal reasons and not to appreciate it as good work well done. If a tragedy is drear and drab, as it is wont to be, it creates fear that reflects on the spectator. If he could only get away from his personal view, he would see the beauty in the unhappiness. He, however, is apt to take it as preachment, cautioning him what not to do.

I am frequently told by people who have seen my films that they like the pathetic touches. An intelligent woman that I met in New York, when I was last there, told me that she did not like film comedies, but that she liked the pathetic parts that cropped up unexpectedly in some of mine. While I cannot agree with her, for I do love the good, honest slapstick—I mean the slapstick honestly arrived at—her view of the tragedy that is often behind comedy is one that is shared by a great many persons. Such tragedy is of course never misunderstood, for of all people in the world of make-believe the clown is the loneliest. No one is like him. It does not matter what he does so long as he does not approach too close to outright vulgarity.

We, as audiences, like the tragic in the comic and not tragedy in itself. We carry our inconsistency beyond this, and though we do not like tragedy, it impresses many of us and we would agree that it is art perhaps and that low comedy is not. But a slapstick comedy can be just as great a work of art as a Greek tragedy. Both play on the emotions, both apply the same technic in their construction, and each has its own system of logic by which it arrives at a conclusion or climax to create an emotion, whether it be a shudder or a guffaw. Both have the same mysterious, logical forces weaving through the construction. The building up and the establishing of a condition that makes a climax—even if in a comedy that point is no more than the mere slapping a man over the head with a stick—must be worked out just as inexorably and logically as anything in tragedy, if the laughter over the head hitting is to be genuine. The outward aspect of things in comedy does not seem so important but the climax must be reached—as in tragedy—through the channels of character, surprise and suspense.

Slapstick is cheap as it is generally understood, but—looked at impersonally—there is something cheap in the conduct of every man. If we could only bring to the viewing of tragedy the same impersonal spirit that we bring to slapstick, tragedy would be more popular. As I have said, the clown is so removed from us—at least we think so—that no one thinks to rant about his philosophy or conduct, and yet if both the clown and the tragedian give us emotions then the clown's conduct is as important and should be taken just as seriously as that of the tragedian with his code of morals.

A great many persons, when they come to a discussion of the films, will be quite positive that there is no art in them, for the very nature of the business with its thousands of theaters to supply necessitates that the films must be liked by a great many people. In other words, a film must have popular appeal, and in order that the greatest numbers may like it, it must be obvious. This may be true, but it does not follow that, because the thing is liked by a great many people, it is either viciously obvious or inartistic. There may be little art in the films, but it is due to reasons other than their popularity or their attempt to be popular. There have been bad stories that have been artistically done, and there have been stories in which the subject matter has been good and the rendition mediocre. On rare occasions we have had good stories combined with good treatment, and these pictures have been enormous successes. The highbrows will look condescendingly at such a film, as the exception that proves the rule or as one of those accidents that will happen when they, the self-appointed guardians of what is artistic, are not looking.

The film creates emotion through the eye. It arouses emotions in a direct way. Of all mediums of art it seems to me the most direct. It translates, denotes and suggests emotions which convey beauty. Why isn't this art? In an earlier article in this magazine I pointed out that the unhappy ending in films has often been inartistically arrived at.

In the business of making pictures and around the studios, the unhappy ending is often mistaken for art, and the exhibitors look askance at the picture. Most of the films with unhappy endings have been poor films, and they have not been successful. That they have not been does not mean that the great public which is attracted to the picture theaters throughout the world does not appreciate art. The unhappy ending should not purposely be sought. The material and the subject matter dictate what the ending shall be. It is not a matter of plot. Anybody can invent plot which is only crossing and crisscrossing. I think I hate plots.

When I was working on *A Woman of Paris,* which was a great deal of an experiment for me—an experiment because it was the first picture directed by me in which I did not act myself—I tried to state vividly a certain phase of life, to show the absolute cosmic scheme of things from the view of a sentimentalist—in this case a woman. My underlying idea was, of course, that she was not strong enough for life with its relentlessness. This picture has been extravagantly praised—too extravagantly, I fear—and it has caused resentment which seems to me out of all proportion to what is a slight thing after all—just one more movie.

Most of the resentment has been occasioned by the subject matter rather than the rendition. The treatment was one of repression—that is, understating things rather than overstating them, a conscious attempt to show by suggestion everything that could be so handled. I have talked to a number of people about this method, and without exception they pick out two things. First, the showing of the arrival and departure of a train at a railroad station without showing the train, and second, the lapse of a year in the woman's life without any attempt to explain or account for the lapse. We see her alone, destitute on the railroad platform, deserted by her lover, and we next see her gay and splendid in a restaurant in Paris and with another man. Of the people I have talked to personally, there is no question about the first attempt to economize in expression—that is, the train. But apparently most of those I have talked to would have liked to see the meeting of the man and the woman, though it has nothing whatever to do with the story. This objection may be well founded, because it brings in the personal element. They want to see when and where the leading characters meet.

It often seems to me in our discussions of pictures and the theater, and the acting in either or both of them, that we take ourselves pretty seriously. There is a reason for this, of course, because it is all so fleeting.

Fashions in plays have constantly changed, and of all literature I suppose the play is the most ephemeral. The modern theater is more; it is topical; it often seizes for its theme something that is talked of in the newspapers. This may supply an interest for the time; but anything which is to live should have truth as to fundamental things, and often these everyday themes are seized upon before there has been time to ascertain whether the basic conditions are really sound.

Only the true in art can survive, and the trash is thrown away; but the play that seems old-fashioned today might be acclaimed after a lapse of five hundred years.

The films can be preserved longer than plays on the stage,

but it is a good deal of a question whether people one hundred years from now will care to look at the pictures of the present day. We laugh at the films that were done fifteen years ago, but add fifty years to their life and how can we tell that someone, looking at them, might fail to recognize any difference between those that we now think are foolish and those that we are working on seriously this month to release two or three months hence.

In the world of amusement I think there has assuredly been progress toward art, both in the creation and in the reception by the public. Certainly in subject matter there has been progress. The plays are no longer so stilted.

They deal with life as we know it.

I see no reason to believe that the public will not today accept sincere art in any form. Of course it is never wise to speak with too much authority in a discussion of art. It is likely to lead one to the uttering of mere platitudes. In my own work my object has been to express certain phases of life and emotion in as artistic a manner as my talent and equipment have allowed me.

ROBERT FLAHERTY
(1884-1951)

Robert Flaherty is considered the father of the documentary, not because he was the first to take his cameras out into nature but because he pioneered in bringing the dramatic narrative form to the already flourishing actuality film. The vehicle of his success was *Nanook of the North*, a record of his explorations among the Eskimo. Not content with presenting scene after scene of northern life in the accepted newsreel fashion, Flaherty turned the film into a drama of man's struggle for existence against nature's overwhelming power. *Nanook* was a tremendous world-wide success, and the erstwhile explorer had become a film-maker. He signed with Paramount and his first assignment was the unnamed project he discusses here, *Moana*, which appeared in 1926. But while the studio had expected another *Nanook*, what they got instead was a South Seas idyll, the story of an island paradise whose people knew nothing of the daily struggle for existence that dogged the Eskimo's every waking moment. Fish filled the water and fruit dropped from the trees. In order to give some dramatic impetus to his film Flaherty had the natives re-create a long discarded *rite de passage*, but even this harrowing procedure failed to offset the image of indolence created in the minds of pragmatic 20's audiences. The film failed at the box office, and with it Flaherty's hopes for future studio funding. The rest of his thirty-year career was largely spent scraping up financing for a variety of unhappy projects, and a handful of classic titles are all that exist today of his efforts.

PICTURE MAKING IN THE SOUTH SEAS

ROBERT J. FLAHERTY

During my first few weeks in Samoa I was disgusted. The drenching heat did not help my feeling for the charm and spirit of the country; the natives I could only see as mobs and rabbles. The fortunes of the film seemed low indeed. These reactions, however, were simply those of any superficial traveller hovering around Pago Pago or Apia, the two ports of call. Only when I left the white man's settlements and settled down here in this incredible spot, became acclimated and began to personally know the Samoans, to live amongst them, to have them in my house, to journey with them, did my interest and enthusiasm revive. We are living in one of the finest native villages in all Samoa. Our house is one that is leased from the sole white inhabitant, trader David, here twenty-seven years. It stands within the shelter of the tall rocking cocoanuts. Beyond the screen of trees and the outline of the chocolate-topped thatched fale (house of the village chiefs) is the strip of sea, blue as blue, save for the single thin line of white which is the booming, grumbling reef (without which no South Sea island is complete).

We have put verandas around the house to screen it from the flies. Here we have our long talks with the village chiefs—speculations and discussions on the material and incidents for the film, gossip about the village—and drink our bowls of kava. Adjoining the veranda looking into a clear space among the cocoanuts stands the diminutive cabin which shelters the electric plant and projector. Farthest from it is the skeleton frame upon which is hung the motion picture screen. Our film nights are epochs in the lives of the Samoans. From villages for miles around they come—venerable gray-haired chiefs striding with the dignity of kings; the oldest of old men and women, with scampering youngsters as thick as flies around them; and the

From *The Film Daily Yearbook of Motion Pictures*, 1924.

MGM·9275

Robert Flaherty on Samoa during the shooting of *Moana*.

singing throngs of young men and girls, wearing flowers in their hair—until the matted ground overflows with humans crouched eager, tense and expectant for the projector's magic eye to open. But we keep them waiting, for a pageantry of village chiefs are waiting on the veranda, where at centre Taioa, our Samoan girl, the Mary Pickford of our film to be, in the strictest, most punctilious ceremony, is making our bowl of kava. While this is going on, the high chief's talking man, solemnly and with tremendous dignity arises, and resting his hand on his cane begins to speak. Unintelligible words—a pause —then trader David translates:

"We come here tonight overjoyed to find that you are well; that your family are well; and that all that belong to you are well. We are overjoyed to know that you have been well; that your family and all that you have have been well." And as the chiefs gravely nod their heads the speaker goes on. Again David translates: "And we hope that the good God will keep you and all that you have and your family well," and the chiefs' heads nod again. Then come more and more unintelligible words. The heads around us seem to have become more thoughtful, more solemn. The speaker warms to his subject. We turn to David, but his face, rapt, is turned toward the speaker. We are impatient. We shuffle in our chairs. Our gaze wanders. We almost give up, when, with a low sweeping bow, the speaker at last sits down. Eagerly we turn to David—they are overjoyed that I am well; that my family are well; that all that I have are well; that the good God may keep me and my family well, and all that I have well.

"The finest speaker on this side of the island," says David in an aside, "more words than any of 'em."

Suddenly Samuelo, our house-boy, shouts out a rapid fire of words. In slow measured time we clap hands, and Taioa, stooping low, holds out the dripping bowl of kava. "Manuia!" each drinker calls, and gulps it down. With the same punctilious ceremony (wars have been fought over the etiquette of kava drinking) from chief to chief the cup goes round. With the last drop done we all file out to join the patient throng within the deep gloom of the cocoanuts.

Karl, son of David, my right-hand man, shoots the projector light out upon the screen. The babble of voices suddenly stops. There is no sound save that of the plumes of cocoanuts rocking in the night "trade." The film comes on. In Samoan Karl calls out as best he may each title as it flashes by—which, with their Samoan slant, vivify the picture, a thousand fold. The inevitable triangle develops—the lover, the girl and the crafty villain. Comments begin to fly. This is from Karl: "Did we ever see such a handsome man? See how he hungers for the girl! What a dog the villain is! By lies he keeps the girl and man apart." For a long, long hour the audience hovers between ecstasy and deep despair, but finally a crash, a thunderclap of exultation rings out upon the night. The villain is "getting his." This from Karl as the film nears its inevitably happy end: "Watch the man get near the girl. Ah, she smiles at him! He smiles at her. Now watch—ah, yes! see, he takes her in his arms —and look, she likes him! Look at her face—how she loves him." And then, amid guffaws from the men, hoots and catcalls from the youngsters and giggling from the girls: "Oh, my! If our girls were only half so kind."

Half a minute's walk through forests of mangoes and cocoanuts brings me to the laboratory which we built deep-set among the trees. The branches of one breadfruit almost overspread it. Here is where we do most of our film work, the drying and the printing—invariably to the accompaniment of the staring eyes of children peeping through the doors and windows at every little thing I do, and on the alert to pick up any scrap of paper or waste bit of film I throw away. Facing the laboratory are the great mouths of two caves which wind underground to blind unknown ends. Into the gloomy depths of one mouth the villagers come now and then to bathe. The mouth of the other we have boarded up and fitted with a door and laid steps within which lead in a half-curve to where we have placed a large platform over the cave's deep, cold, clear water. Here the film developing tanks are set, their tops just poking through the platform, so that the cave's cold water forms a jacket around them. I spend hours developing in the blackness of this cavern, and whilst in the feeble light of the red lamp I watch the clock tick the minutes away, the choruses of my two Samoan helpers re-echo through the gloom. Natives squat waiting outside the cavern's door for us to file out with our dripping racks of film. They peer over our shoulders as we hold the frame up for inspection against the light.

It has been no easy task to get the right characters for the film. Like the Eskimo the photographable types are few. Taioa, the taupo (village virgin) of Sasina, was my first find. Here should follow the inevitable picture—raven hair, lips of coral, orbs (meaning eyes), etc. etc. But to you, not knowing the fine type of Polynesian, such a passage at words would mean nothing. I can only say that when, after a feast of pigs, taro, breadfruit, wild pigeons, mangoes and yams, to the accompaniment of siva sivas and ta'alolos hours and hours long, I bargained for and bought her from the proud and haughty, albeit canny, chiefs of Sasina, and she and her handmaid came up the palm-lined trail to Safune, the old women here told her between their teeth that they would see that she was killed by dawn.

Competition as to who shall be in the white man's film is never-ending. Countless little imps of children in shapes and sizes and faces as various as a bag of mixed candy come hovering around our veranda and with utter artlessness assume poses or dance siva sivas or bring us a lizard or a bird or some strange flower, all for the purpose of attracting our attention—we might use them in the film.

One night Malai ("Flying Fox"), highest of all the chiefs, brought along, with his talking man, his counsellors and his two old women (always the most deadly of the tribe), his taupo, and before the glinting eyes of Taioa assured me how much more beautiful his taupo was. Whereupon, imperiously he waved his hand, his men struck up a song and his taupo bounded up and danced—not before, but at me—and the old cats of women who danced accompanying her at either side did not hesitate to put their bids on their taupo's behalf into words: "Is she not most wonderful? When does one ever see such dancing?" and all the most alluring phrases they could muster. Taioa, quiescent up to now, bounded up as soon as their siva was done and danced as she had never danced before. But Malai, his talking man, his counsellors and the old women, angry, turned their gaze away. Only a supper and good cigars which my wise house-boy thrust forward and my promise to make a separate film in which appeared no women save the taupo of the great Malai prevented a breach there and then.

All of this was not for gain, but for nothing more than to

advance the glory of Malai's beloved town. How much that prestige means to the Samoans you might gather from the following. There were, as is the custom, ceremonies without end when first we came—sivas by the young men, the women, the old women and the children, ta'alolos by the chiefs themselves and a great feast of wild fowl, huge wild pigs, roasted on bananas, taros, yams, mangoes and from the reef baked fishes in all the vivid colors of the rainbow—all of this to the accompaniment of speeches without end—the freedom of their town was ours; we were under their protection. They adopted us as their children, and all that they had, could say or do, was ours.

Now Annie, nurse, all the way with us from New York, has red hair—glorious red hair. The Samoans spend years bleaching their head with coral lime in order to turn it the dull color of rust—the nearest they can approach to such a crown as Annie wears. So Annie—"Mumu" they call her—has become famous the island round. One day as she and Haioa and the children strolled off to swim she was brought up with a start by someone tugging her hair, and before she could turn a Samoan stepped before her. By signs and gestures he indicated his regard, tapped her shoulder, then tapped his—he was the right man for her. But Annie (Irish) gave him such a lashing with her tongue that, abashed, he slunk away. When we heard the story naturally we were indignant. To Malai a complaint was made. We had almost forgotten the incident, however, when at dusk a messenger flew up with a note from Mr. David: "Do not come out on the veranda. Stay indoors until I come." He relieved the tension, however, by coming himself in a moment more, saying the chiefs were coming, all of them to beg our pardon. We glimpsed a procession walking funereally through the gloom toward us, heads bowed low, half shielded with branches of palm. "Let them come, let them come," said David, "Do not show yourselves. Keep them waiting—it is fa'a Samoa (the custom)." The procession crouched in the open space before the veranda, their heads bowed toward the ground, the palm branches still held over them. Before them all a solitary figure, shielded by the folds of a priceless mat, knelt on the ground. Without sound or movement they awaited the interval of our displeasure. Then Tugaga, David's spokesman, spoke up. Three times he asked them why they came, expressing his great surprise at the manner of their coming, urging them to speak, because it grieved us to see them so. Thereupon said Maumea Levu, Flying Fox's talking man: "Oh, Tugaga, let us live! Let us live!" Such was the beginning of the ceremony, whereupon the chiefs took it upon themselves to atone for the fault of one of their number who had brought disgrace upon them all and upon the good name of their beloved town. Their spokesman told of how we had to come from America, the far, far country—we had come to Safune because Safune had been well spoken of to us—how they, the chiefs, had given us the highest chief names and had taken us under their protection—and now what a wretched mess it all was, the good name of Safune wrecked forever! Could we forget? Could we forgive them? There were tears in the eyes of David's spokesman when he replied in our behalf, and as he concluded, the kneeling form before us suddenly came to life, and bowing low presented us with the priceless mat, an heirloom of the offender's family, generations old.

It was quiet in Safune the following day. Not a chief or talking man could we see. Said I to David: "Good heavens, are they in mourning still?" "Hell, no," replied he, "They are all in the offender's fale, feasting, cramming, stuffing themselves on all the precious fowls and pigs and bananas and taros and yams the poor devil owns."

Malai, the "Flying Fox," it is who has been chosen for my principal film character. He, the great chief of Safune, is the head of one of the oldest chief families of all Savaii. He is one of the big figures in Samoa and one of the few great hunters of the sea. We live side by side. My house is his house; his house is mine. There are no journeys save the ones he leads; and through him the services of every one of his townsmen are always at my call.

ROBERT FLOREY
(1900-   )

Robert Florey, part of the second generation of French film-makers in Hollywood, arrived after the war and quickly carved out a career as technical adviser or assistant director to such Hollywood luminaries as Chaplin, Sternberg, and Vidor. As a director on his own he showed great promise with a series of independently made experimental films in 1927-28 (including *The Life and Death of a Hollywood Extra*, made with Vorkapich), but most of his later years were devoted to low budget melodramas which even *his* considerable wit could brighten only sporadically. Still, *Murders in the Rue Morgue*, *The Florentine Dagger*, and *Face Behind the Mask* all demonstrate a considerable talent that was never properly utilized either by Hollywood or by Florey himself. Why this happened is uncertain. Florey was a free spirit who valued his personal liberty within the studio system, but, unlike Chaplin, Sternberg or Vidor, he never had the commercial clout to make that system work for him. So he amused himself with second-string projects and B-picture budgets, relatively minor efforts on which he could work undisturbed, casually inserting a personal touch here and there. His success at this mode of directing made him extremely suitable for television work, and he enlivened over 300 episodes of series like "Wagon Train," "The Twilight Zone," and "Alfred Hitchcock Presents" with his characteristic stylistic flourishes. Indeed, for Florey (as well as a whole raft of lesser talents) the B-picture never really disappeared, but changed, practically overnight, into television.

FOREIGN ATMOSPHERE FOR
THE AMERICAN SCREEN

ROBERT FLOREY

The evolution of the motion picture technical director might be traced beyond the early days of the screen to one early period of the stage, when his prototype used for the tools of his trade, only a flow of language and the imagination of his audience.

"Ladies and gentlemen," he would say, "picture, as our drama unfolds, a forest on all sides of our scene, a great feudal castle on a wooded hill in the background, and winding down toward us, a road—"

Yet the early motion picture setting was not so many cycles ahead of the Shakespearian wagon show. Heroic days, those, when the settings of a scene were painted on framed canvas, windows could not be opened, and doors had to be shut carefully, to avoid shaking the whole painted structure. Painted clocks eternally registered the same hour, and to knock a flower pot off a tenement window sill, the knocker would have to erase it with a damp cloth.

Heroic, too, were the men who, regardless of obstacles and financial limitations, pioneered the development of present-day technical art—beauty, realism, accurate detail. Their innovations stimulated a demand by the patrons of the novelty of that day, the art of this, for a more realistic and beautiful reproduction of the surroundings of screen drama.

So while the directors were evolving more realistic screen stories, and the actors were learning proper screen make-up, the directors began to build realistic sets—walls more solid, windows that would open, real flowerpots that would fall from real window sills.

Naturally, it proved far easier, faithfully to reproduce local conditions than foreign conditions, contemporary conditions than those of remote periods of the past. Yet the demand for

From *The Motion Picture Director*, January 1926.

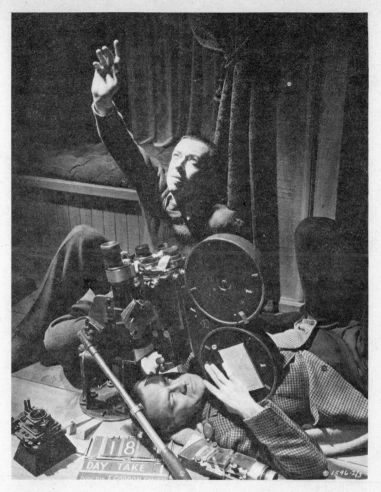

Robert Florey (above) directing *The Preview Murder Mystery* (1936), which was set against a Hollywood studio background. The "director" lining up the shot is Ian Keith.

colorful pictures has ever been on the increase, and ultimately this demand created the modern, highly developed type of technical expert.

It became the hobby of many producers to engage as technical directors or at least as consulting experts, natives of the countries in which pictures of foreign locale were laid. Results were not always satisfactory. Naturally, in filming pictures of past ages, it proved impractical to engage men who had lived in those times. Communication with departed spirits even now has not reached that stage of perfection that would enable them to procure, for instance, the services of an expert who had lived in colorful Venice of the fourteenth century!

The idea of having a Russian supervise the technical details of a picture laid in modern Russia, just because he is a Russian, gradually came to be looked upon as the same sort of fallacy as getting one of Nero's lieutenants to oversee the technical details of *The Burning of Rome*. It proved that only an expert of long and varied experience in research, with in addition other background and equipment, could help a director build the proper atmosphere around his plot—regardless of nationality.

Just as an example of some of the things that go into the making of a technical director of today, let us consider my friend Jean Bertin, who is now assisting Clarence Brown to put the Parisian atmosphere into *Kiki*, Norma Talmadge's present vehicle. He studied to become a naval officer, then became a painter, then a fashion designer in Paris. Then he went on the stage, both acting and directing. Only after going through these and other experiences of a broadening and cultural nature, did he consider himself able to co-operate in the making of a picture!

I myself have been a motion picture director in France and in Switzerland; I have travelled extensively all my life; I have learned a lot in many ways. Yet I find that I need every bit of my experience, everything that I have learned, not to make mistakes. Only long experience, and a deep and almost universal knowledge can adequately fit a man for the position of technical director with a large picture company.

Given sufficient natural and acquired equipment, and armed with unlimited facilities for research, one man may attend to pictures of domestic and foreign locales, past and present periods, far better than the less broadly experienced man who is a specialist in any one type of picture. The man who is inexperienced is certain to give too little detail, unimportant detail, inaccurate detail and sometimes totally wrong detail. It is not only a question of knowing what style of furniture was in use during the reign of Louis XVIII. Any dictionary can tell you. But, for instance, what is the difference between Louis XVI and Rococo, two styles almost alike, but used in different centuries? Or what kind of a wig did Louis XV wear, and who during his reign was still wearing the dark, long-haired Louis XIV wigs?

These are the sorts of puzzles I have had to solve:

"Describe a religious procession in French Brittany, and design a costume for a Swiss-Italian bride."

Because I was familiar with French Brittany, was I able to solve the first riddle without research? Not at all. My knowledge of the country, people and customs simply enabled me to make short cuts.

"How does the average passer-by in Paris look to the tourist?" Ah, that's an easier question. It is something one has noted many times, and there is a certain latitude that takes it out of the exacting class of problem. But suppose the problem is,

"Furnish and dress the room of a demi mondaine in a provincial town of Southern France in 1830. Or,

"Of what material should one make the *litham* (veil) of the Touregs, those African bandits who sweep the desert."

Research! And that in itself is a formidable problem; the largest library one can collect cannot cover all the reference needed, as the demands are infinite. "Describe a third-class funeral procession in Paris!" Sounds simple—but just where would the man who is not an expert in research start to find out about it? If he chanced, within a few hours, to find a man who had been pall-bearer at a hundred of such funerals, the chances are that that man could supply only the most outstanding details—not the necessary intimate and fine ones that are required for the all-seeing eye of the camera.

"What kind of a dance was the minuet or the "cancan"— when you find out, teach it to the extras!" A new assignment, you see; I must be a dancing instructor!

"What kind of boats do the fishermen in the northern part of the Adriatic Sea use, in plying their trade?"

Sounds simple enough! But there are many errors into which the inexperienced may fall. It would be easy to find wrong information in many kinds of books and pictures—perhaps a photo of a fishing boat would show the only one of that type in the whole Adriatic! The story might use a whole fleet of them, and the technical director would be sure to be "called" sooner or later. Some one of the millions who see the picture would write in, demanding his discharge!

These problems do not come singly. In the last picture in which I assisted King Vidor as technical director, I had to design one hundred and forty different props, all Louis-Philippe style, besides fixing every detail in costumes.[1]

It's a wonderful life if you bear up under the strain!

1. *La Bohème*, M-G-M, 1926.

HERBERT BRENON
(1880-1958)

One of the first directors to gain a wide personal follow-ing, Herbert Brenon's background included journalism, vaudeville, and the operation of a small-town nickelodeon. His film career proper began in 1909 with Carl Laemmle's IMP Company (later Universal), for which he directed a noteworthy *Ivanhoe* in Great Britain and the spectacular *Neptune's Daughter* with Annette Kellermann. Brenon and Kellermann quickly jumped to the Fox Company and pro-duced on location in the West Indies one of the most elab-orate of early photoplays, *A Daughter of the Gods* (1916). Quarrels over production excesses and, surprisingly, Brenon's personal publicity, resulted in Fox editing the film himself and removing Brenon's name from the credits, a move which prefigured the studio suppression of directors —Stroheim, for example—a decade later. By the 20's Brenon had established himself at Paramount as a craftsman of the highest order with *Peter Pan* and *A Kiss for Cinderella*, and the original versions of *Beau Geste* and *The Great Gatsby*. Notable for their intelligence and controlled senti-ment, his films are especially strong in the richness of their performances. Pola Negri, Lon Chaney, Nazimova, and Norma Talmadge had some of their finest moments in Herbert Brenon's films, while carrying on uncontrollably elsewhere. Brenon here recognizes his success with tempera-mental performers, but never fully explains just how he managed to control them. One of the first great names *behind* the camera, perhaps he had no need to bump egos with the glittering personalities he was guiding. At any rate, his directorial success with the widest range of silent stars remained unparalleled.

MUST THEY HAVE TEMPERAMENT?

HERBERT BRENON

I wouldn't give a hang for an actor without temperament, for to me he could not be good unless he were temperamental. The amount and quality of temperament distinguishes a good actor from a bad one. Temperament is mood. And a performer, particularly of the motion picture variety, must be rich in moods. All the fine nuances of expression, all the delicate light and shade, the bold darkness and hilarious gaiety, are dependent upon temperament.

Temperament is more sensed than actually seen. I know that to many, the words "artistic temperament" bring to mind ranting and tearing of hair. Of course, some temperaments have expressed themselves in that way. Other natures have found an outlet in complete isolation from their fellow beings. Tears bring relief to some temperaments. Others turn to silence. And some to a forced, unnatural gaiety.

During my years as a director, it has been my pleasure, *my pleasure*, to work with some of the most temperamental stars on the screen. Alla Nazimova, Norma Talmadge, Percy Marmont, Ernest Torrence, Betty Compson, Richard Dix and many others. I find that the more temperamental an actor is, the easier it is for him to grasp all the subtleties of a rôle and imbue it with life, instead of merely playing a part.

But does this mean that these players go in for the outburst commonly associated with artistic temperament? Not at all. Such explosions belong to the lesser actors. In an industry like the motion pictures, stars drop out and disappear as suddenly as shooting stars in the celestial firmament. Yesterday, they were unknown, but today, because of some curious twist in their physical make-up, oddly slanting eyes, let us say, or a tantalizing smile full of that mysterious allure we speak of as sex

From *Motion Picture Magazine*, February 1926. Reprinted by permission of Macfadden Women's Group.

Herbert Brenon (left) with his cameraman James Wong Howe. They made nine films together in the late 20's.

appeal, they find themselves stars. They have little of dramatic ability, but they have exalted opinions of their power to act.

Such upstarts resent direction. They grow tempestuous, answer back when they are given orders, blow up, smash things if they can, call names if there is nothing on hand to break, and in general make a show of themselves. That's bad temper, nothing more nor less, and it need not have anything to do with temperament. *Need not*, I say, because temper and temperament are as intimately linked, and in the same way, as sleeping and breathing. You remember the little boy who pointed out that you could breathe without sleeping but you couldn't sleep without breathing. Just so with temper and temperament. You can have temper without temperament, but you cannot have temperament without temper. When marked artistic ability is coupled with it, temper is permissible.

Nevertheless, all temperament is not of the fiery kind. Not any more than all pictures are bright, or all music sad. There are light temperaments and somber ones, blazing as well as brooding ones. The temperament of an actor is the factor that decides in which field of drama he is to make his mark. I said that Richard Dix and Nazimova were temperamental. But no two temperaments in the world could be more unlike.

Richard's temperament is of the golden, cheerful variety. He radiates pleasantness. It is impossible to harbor any grouch when he is around. His nature is too sunny to permit anything like that. I remember one occasion when I was directing Betty Compson and Mr. Dix in *The Woman with Four Faces*. We had come to a standstill over one scene in particular, and Betty and I pondered over it, growing sorer every minute. Suddenly, a man in carpenter's overalls began pounding nails into the boards near my feet. Both Betty and I raised our voices higher. The noise increased, and so did our irritation. The fellow went on tapping. Finally, he raised his head. It was Richard Dix in the costume he wore for the picture. In the laughter that followed, good humor was again restored, and we could go on in saner mood.

Pola Negri is very temperamental, but she has her temper under tight control. She, like such other high-strung actresses as Norma Talmadge and Anna Q. Nilsson, resorts to tears if anything goes wrong. These three women I rate among the best on the screen today. It is a joy to direct them, they are so sensitive to impressions. But if any one of them is asked to portray a character in a way that she thinks is alien to the part, she will not be able to go on.

One thing I must point out in this treatise on artistic temperaments, and that is the exaggerated reports on the subject. You must have heard the incident of Pola and the peacock fan, or how another actress slapped a director, or any other spicy tales. Most of them are enlarged and elaborated versions of a simple, meaningless gesture. Have you ever played that game called "Scandal"? The players sit in a ring and the first one whispers a sentence to her right-hand neighbor. The sentence passes thruout the ring until it reaches the first one again, who recites the original and the garbled version, to show the vast difference. In a game it is funny. In real life it is apt to cause serious trouble. The movie studios are infested, from time to time, with sightseers, scandal-mongers, who pounce on an innocent little tiff. By the time it has been repeated about one hundred times, it may grow into a shooting or a knifing or Heaven knows what. And then it becomes known that the actress is the possessor of a terrible temperament.

However, in spite of all their faults, give me the one with the temperament. An actor without temperament is like a violin without strings. You can't play on either one of them.

HAROLD LLOYD
(1893-1971)

Unlike his chief screen rivals, Harold Lloyd did not have years of vaudeville or music hall success behind him when he entered films. He had neither a character nor a style, and certainly no fixed ideas on the proper nature of screen comedy. While the others may have taken temporary salary cuts when entering the new medium, they at least arrived as recognized comedians in featured comedy roles, and rose swiftly (and predictably) to new screen stardom on their own. Lloyd's background was completely unspectacular, bolstered only by sheer optimism and some insignificant theatrical work. His first film jobs were gained by hanging around the studio pens where hopeful extras would crowd each morning. His rise was the result of studying all aspects of film-making and exhibition, and carefully applying the conclusions to his own films. He makes no apologies here for the "certain standardization" in his comedies, because he knows this is exactly where their strength lies. Lloyd's films were completely mechanical constructions: once having established a screen character (and this, as he describes, was the work of several years), he hired writers and assistants to create material for it which varied so slightly from film to film that, "in a series of three pictures we can offer our whole bag of tricks." Not personally a brilliant comedian or a director of more than usual imagination, Lloyd displayed his great talent as a producer of his own comedies, a man who created laugh-provoking pictures and aimed them unerringly at the widest audience of any of the screen's best-known clowns.

THE HARDSHIPS OF
FUN MAKING

HAROLD LLOYD

During the early days of my screen appearances, I played a character called Lonesome Luke. It was thought then, as now, an obvious advantage for a comedian to have an established character in a series of pictures instead of essaying a new rôle with a new picture. In this way, though one becomes a sort of label, one is readily recognized as one first flashes upon the screen. Chaplin, Keaton, Langdon and I get this happy recognition at once. It is a tremendous help and advantage, but such recognition has its difficulties as well. They, sitting there in judgment, silently command that we had best be funny and get on the job at once.

But though the character was readily recognized, I didn't like Lonesome Luke. He was rigid, and gave very little leeway for development. He wore a little mustache, for no reason other than that Charlie Chaplin, who was already a big success on the screen, wore one, and therefore it was thought that all comedians had to wear a mustache. My other visible distinguishing bit was a pair of very tight trousers. After more than sixty Lonesome Lukes, I loathed the get-up and the character. I had not felt this way in the beginning, for naturally I was anxious to get on and I did what they wanted without resentment.

It did not bother me that I was somewhat of an imitator. Other comedians were doing the same thing. It almost seemed to be necessary. I figured out, however, that there isn't anything in being an imitator, even if you are good, which I wasn't. The imitator only advertises the original, and he alone benefits. Now, I wanted a sincere, serious character. I wanted to be on the screen a fellow who wouldn't be ridiculous, if a romance or the ordinary story of a boy and girl came along. I

Sid Grauman watches Harold Lloyd leave his hand, foot and eye-glass prints in the forecourt of Grauman's Chinese Theatre, 1927.

wanted to wear decent or at least appropriate clothes. When I took my ideas for a new character to the company I was working for, they were not at all sympathetic. "We," they told me, "have spent a great deal of money in making and advertising Lonesome Luke, and who is Harold Lloyd anyway?"

One night, in a film theater, I was watching a drama in which there was a minister—one of those friendly, broad-minded parsons, who is a man of the world and not merely of his parish. In one scene in the story, he jumped on a horse, overtook the bad man, had a rough-and-tumble fight and worsted him. Then he good-naturedly brushed himself off a bit and got back on his horse. This man wore glasses and appeared studious and dignified. He was also genial. The glasses, I noticed, in no wise interfered with the expression of his face. The mustache had always hampered me and, for me at least, prevented complete mobility. I kept bothering them at the studio until finally they allowed me to try the character I wanted to play. But they told me I'd have to be responsible, and that I could have no help. Accordingly, I wrote and directed as well as acted for a while. It was very good training. In those days so many pictures were made and they were turned out so quickly that they didn't bother with me, and I was thus enabled, without interference, to experiment and put over my character.

At first I did not get the glasses right; they were too big. In about the third picture I had them as I wanted them. They just fitted and did not even cover the eyebrows. I have worn them in every picture since and have never removed them even when, as in *The Freshman*, I played football. Now audiences expect and take as a matter of course my glasses, just as they expect to see my eyes through them. Never have we had a single gag in connection with them. A short time ago someone sent me a pair of specially constructed goggles that operate on the same principle as the automatic device which is attached to the windshield to wipe clear the glass. When a button is pressed, little arms come down and move across the lenses. We could have some fun with this, but I don't believe I shall ever try it.

Since those early days when I was concerned with what I should wear in the pictures, the film comedy, as all the world knows, has changed. Instead of a string of laughs, we now have plays and carefully developed stories. If we can have a theme, so much the better. *Grandma's Boy*, which was my first longer picture, had one that might be crudely stated as the triumph of mind over matter. This type of picture appeals more to me than a picture which is pure froth, like *Why Worry*. I like, however, to mix the pictures up and to do an occasional picture with no basic idea or theme. I feel in this way we can appeal to wider audiences. The older people like a picture like *Grandma's Boy*. The young boys and girls will take to *The Freshman*, and the children and those people who when they are in a place of amusement do not care for anything except pure relaxation, will like best *Why Worry* or *Hot Water*.

While we are working on a picture we perhaps grow very

enthusiastic and feel that we have in hand the best thing we have ever done. In more sober judgment, however, we ourselves often know honestly that it is not. It is not possible to make each picture better than the preceding one. If they are designed from slightly different angles, so that in a series of three pictures we can offer our whole bag of tricks and vary our appeal, then we have done what we aimed to do. And this will make for a certain standardization of comedies. Of course by this I do not mean that we create a rubber stamp or formula by which we make pictures. It is rather a standard of appeal from slightly different points, or a blending of average tastes.

If there is one thing of which I am proud, it is that exhibitors, recognizing that we have a certain standard, are willing to book the pictures without seeing them. There is another thing that is also typical of these comedies. For parties of children or even for a girls' school, *Grandma's Boy*, *Girl Shy* or any of the others are perfectly safe. A great deal of comedy can be obtained from off-color scenes, incidents or gags. It is giving up something from the producer's point of view to avoid such things, but we have always done it. There can be comedy enough and good comedy without offending the taste of audiences.

As a boy I was simply crazy to act. Ours was not a theatrical family and so far as I know no one connected with it has ever been of the theater, and the little town of Burchard, Nebraska, where I was born, was a long, long way from Broadway. When the family moved to Denver I could at least see an occasional play, and once I appeared with a travelling company that gave a performance of *Macbeth*. I was Banquo's son. This about finished me, and child though I was, I wanted to give up school then and there and become an actor. Only once did my desire to go on the stage lapse, and that was when I was in one of the five high schools in different cities that I attended. A fondness for gym work turned my thoughts to prize fighting. I did appear in the ring several times, but I am afraid I liked the lights and the crowds of people looking on much more than I did the science of the sport.

When I was eleven, we were living in Omaha. Walking

about the streets of this, for us, new town, I discovered one night on a downtown street a man with a telescope. I suddenly became interested in astronomy, and every night I appeared to listen to the spieler. For ten cents one might look at the heavens. I used to stand there and look at the charts, which cost nothing, and I took in every word of what I suppose was an extremely bad lecture on astronomy. Once a fire engine dashed madly through the streets, and the crowd thought a fire more vital than the stars. I wanted to follow, but I stayed to listen.

Much to my disappointment, the lecturer stopped, for it wasn't worth while to orate to an audience of one boy who didn't have ten cents anyway. A man who had been standing near began to talk to me, and asked me if I was really interested in astronomy. I was delighted at the attention. He told me that he had seen me there every night on his way to the theater. He was the leading man of a stock company that was playing in Omaha, and I was more than impressed, stage-struck kid that I was. It was John Lane O'Connor, a stock actor of a good deal of experience and popularity. I walked to the theater with him, and he told me that though he liked the company and Omaha, he had not found a satisfactory place to live.

I at once had an inspiration. We had just moved to the city, and because we were unable to find a house of the right size we had some extra rooms. I became persuasive, and sold him on the idea of mother's cooking. The next day he came to the house and rented a room. Thus began an association that was of the utmost value to me. O'Connor taught me a great deal, and, more important, his caustic tongue kept me, during what seemed to me like veritable triumphs, from becoming self-important. You can't expect a boy who has appeared before an audience and liked the job to be quite the same afterward. Someone needs to keep him down. In hero worship, I ran O'Connor's errands and took care of his clothes. When a boy was needed for a part at the theater he got me the job and he helped me with my lines and coached me generally. During that season I played a number of boys' parts.

But that stock company left Omaha all too soon. Frank Bacon, who made such a great hit in *Lightnin'*, was a member of that company. He wanted me to play with him in a one-act sketch that he had written for vaudeville, but mother decided that I must stay in school. When I arrived at the awkward age and was too old to play a child and too young to be a juvenile, I ushered, handed out programs, sold candy, was assistant to the electrician, though I knew nothing of electricity, and was for a time call boy. Later, in San Diego, I was assistant to the stage manager. I didn't care what I did as long as I was in a theater.

When I was seventeen the family once more indulged in its taste for wandering, and my education was continued at the San Diego High School. I at once got in touch with a stock company at the Spreckels Theater and played a number of small parts. Then my friend of Omaha, John Lane O'Connor, came to act in a San Diego stock company and remained behind to conduct a dramatic school. My days became very busy. I acted at night when I got a chance. In the morning I attended the San Diego High School and in the afternoon I assisted John Lane O'Connor at his dramatic school. The subjects I taught were Shakspere, fencing and dancing. This is not quite so bad as it sounds, for there were competent instructors in each branch. I merely assisted and helped the pupils with the groundwork. As dramatic schools go, I think this was a fairly good one, for O'Connor was an actor with a good deal of experience, and he had that rare ability to teach. Among the pupils of that school were quite a number of people who later became prominent in the movies, both as directors and actors. The school also sent several people to the theater.

The old Edison Film Company was making a picture near San Diego, and as ever in those early films, there had to be Indians. They applied to the dramatic school for some people to act as extras. I promised to send a class down, but I escorted them myself to the location and appeared with my pupils. I managed to get rather the best bit there was. It was a mistake. I was dreadful.

The dramatic school hadn't done very well from the beginning, and it soon disbanded. I found myself alone in San Diego with five cents. My father and brother had gone to Los Angeles, thinking that in a bigger city conditions would be better. I decided to join them, but I had no way of getting there. I spent my five cents for six doughnuts, on which I lived for more than a day. Walking the streets for hours, quite by accident I met a man who had appeared in one of the stock companies as an extra. I had let him take a few dollars. He had wanted to pay me back, but did not know where to find me any more than I knew how to reach him. I joined my father and brother in a cheap rooming house on Main Street in Los Angeles, where the three of us shared one room and ate when we could.

Finally both of them found jobs, though not very good ones, and I was engaged to appear as one of the students in a production of *Old Heidelberg* at the Morosco Theater. I learned a good deal in that stock company, particularly during the weeks that able actress, Florence Reed, played an engagement with us. My salary was twenty dollars a week when I worked. Often there would be no part in a play for me for a week or two, and to make matters worse, there were rumors in circulation that the stock company was going to close for a month or two. One night as the three of us sat in our one room looking out at Main Street, father suggested that I try to get some work in the movies. I was not altogether pleased with the suggestion. It seemed a comedown for one who had had experience in the theater, and especially for one whose ambition was as great as mine.

But things were so desperate and there seemed so little hope in the theater that I decided to try to get into the studios. It wasn't easy then, and it never has been for anyone without influence or acquaintance to get a chance in the pictures. It isn't even easy to get into the place where you can ask for work. Every studio has a gateman, and constant annoyance from both sight-seers and would-be actors has made these guards into a race by themselves. They can turn down heartbreaking cases as well as obvious fakers. I defy anyone, no matter who he is, without an introduction or a pass, to bluff his way into a studio. It is much worse than the stage door of a theater.

I was not a little like Merton of the Movies. I was ever at the gates of the studios, watching the people go in and out. I simply could not get in, but I went on hoping. I tried assuming an air of importance, and then I tried meekness. I endeavored to touch the sympathy of various gatemen. This was particularly useless. Just across the way from one of the studios was a little lunch room where people in make-up were often to be seen buying sandwiches and coffee. I could get in there, even though I could not buy. I mingled with them but was not of them. I overheard a good deal of conversation and absorbed much studio gossip.

One day it suddenly occurred to me that the ogre at the gate across the way never seemed to question these people when they returned to work. Obviously they were actors, for their faces supported quantities of the elaborate make-up which used to be thought necessary for film photography. They passed in and out in chatting groups of two or three. Now I had come prepared, in case I should suddenly be called upon to act, and I never was without my little black box of make-up that I used in the theater. While some of the fortunates were eating in the restaurant, I went behind the shack and put on a good deal of rosy make-up, which I thought was similar to what I had seen. I walked just behind a returning group and got past the gateman.

Of course this got me nowhere. It not only did not put me on the pay roll, but once inside I could not find anyone to listen to me. If sometimes my persistence and determination, which came from great need, would lead me to corner a director for a moment's talk, he would only tell me that I was not a picture type. I could never get anyone to look at the pictures in make-up that I had had taken. These were mostly of old men. In those days I thought that there was more art in playing characters and heavies. I particularly wanted to be a villain.

As I left the studio that first day I talked to the gateman and after a few times he and his companions got to know me, and I was able to get in without make-up, and I did not have to wait until after the fortunate employed actors had their lunch, to break into the studio.

At last a chance for a few days' work as an extra with the Edison Company came. "I used to be with you folks down in San Diego," I told them nonchalantly. Strange, but they didn't remember. I still remember, however, that first day's work on location. There was a great big table of food in a tent which was furnished by the company. Then again there were many waiting weeks, and finally I got a job as an extra at three dollars a day at the Universal Studio. One of the extras was Hal Roach, who has since become a producer of comedies and no longer acts in them. We were both engaged to support J. Warren Kerrigan, who was one of the early stars. He played, a year or so back, the hero in *The Covered Wagon*. Roach knew the casting director and was promoted to a part. Hal then persuaded his friend to promise me a part in the next Kerrigan picture. Roach himself never cared about acting. He wanted to be a director. In one film we were both to be crooks, and the director showed him how to do a scene. There wasn't much time spent in rehearsal, and Roach did not seem to get the idea right. The director said: "Let this other fellow try it." I was not backward and from my theater experience I knew what the director wanted. It was my first bit of luck. I was getting five dollars a day then.

Luck was not to last. It was decided that three dollars was henceforth to be the pay of all extras. I organized some of the people and went on strike. Our slogan was: "No work unless we get five a day." We didn't get any work. Roach had told me that as soon as he could get the money he was going to make a picture and have me in it as an actor. Fortuitously a little while later a distant relative of his died and left him two hundred dollars. With this we made a picture. Most of the scenes were exteriors, and most of them were taken in a Los Angeles park. We used a vacant house until the owner found out how we were getting our interiors. But we kept at making unbelievably cheap pictures, until Roach was offered a chance to make one-reel pictures for Pathé. He took me with him, at fifty dollars a week, and that seemed more money than there had ever been in the world. Bebe Daniels was the leading woman in those early pictures, and in all of them, to the number of sixty-odd, I played Lonesome Luke.

Though I was much impressed by fifty dollars a week and its great spending power, I had seen too many lean days to spend it all. I began to save, as I have always done since. Gradually my salary went up to one hundred fifty dollars a week, and the West Coast offices refused to give me any more, though my contract called for a renewal at three hundred. The business, they said, was changing, and it was getting so expensive to make pictures. I told them I wouldn't work. They were firm, too, and I decided to go to New York and talk to the main offices.

People have said that I have been lucky because I have never been forced into taking a disadvantageous contract. The real reason that I have not had to take just what has been offered me has been because I have persisted in the practice of living on less than I have earned. One cannot be independent by just living from one contract to another and spending all as one goes. When I went to New York to have my say with Pathé and find out whether or not I was to get three hundred dollars a week, I had already saved six thousand dollars.

It was my first trip to New York—that magical city of theaters, where actors' names are put up in electric lights. I got off the train and at once bought a ticket for a matinee to see Fred Stone. While I was looking for the theater where Al Jolson was playing I saw a movie theater on which my name was displayed. I didn't seem quite so lonely and quite so friendless. There was not a person in New York that I knew. There was no one that the family had known. We had never lived east of Nebraska, and in all of our wanderings in the West we had met few people of the sort who travel; in fact, our neighbors always looked upon us as very experienced and great travelers.

The next morning I called up the Pathé office and was surprised that they knew I was in town. I got an appointment at once, and went back to the coast with a salary of three hundred dollars a week. They even offered to pay my trip back. I refused.

With the making of the picture *A Sailor Made Man*, I felt that I had at last arrived somewhere. This picture was taken in San Pedro harbor in the United States ship *Fredericks*. Everyone was so fine that as soon as the picture was done I took a projection machine to the ship to run the film for the men. In the harbor at the time was a coaler, and the men of that boat were asked to come over on the Fredericks to see *A Sailor Made Man*. In the scene where I am put to work scrubbing the deck, one of the visitors, indulging in the friendly rivalry that always exists between the boats in the Navy, called: "You best do that for them, Harold; it sure needs it."

I liked that audience, and I like, too, the audience we get when we show a new picture for the newsboys of Los Angeles. They are so unrestrained and responsive. I sneak in at the back of the theater, not wanting them to know that I am there, and during the course of the show, they will often cry: "There he is; get him, Harold." The exciting parts never go so well as with such an audience.

There is another type of audience with whom everything that we do goes well, and that is the crowd which gathers around on a location. You cannot set a motion picture camera up any place in Southern California without having a good-sized audience almost at once. They have seen this happen again and again, but they will run for blocks to see the most trivial scene in the shooting. And they will laugh at a fall or almost anything else. We often encounter this same difficulty in the studio.

I am terribly afraid of anything that seems amusing when it is being taken. Somebody likes the thing, and we know him to have a sense of humor, or someone who has a reputation with us as being funny suggests a gag or wise crack, and we forget to separate the character of the man from what he says. The studio clown, however, is not a great help in the very serious business of making comic pictures.

When I am in the midst of making a picture, I never think of anything else, and I keep asking myself: "Is it any good? Is it exciting enough?" That is particularly important, but pictures cannot be all excitement. And I always worry whether there is sufficient distance to make the humor generally appealing. It is, of course, a trite observation that one man's tragedy is another man's comedy, but we must constantly have it in mind. The humor must be human enough to be understandable, but it must be sufficiently remote so that the suffering of the character will not arouse too much pity or sympathy in the audience.

I have appeared in over four hundred pictures, and yet I still find the question of timing and the pace very difficult in the making of comedies. They must begin at a good pace, but the pace may slow down a bit at times to permit, by way of contrast, certain quietly effective scenes. I remember as a boy how moved I was by the work of David Warfield in the theater. In the midst of great pathos in *The Music Master*, he would have a quiet comedy line. Those are the things that count with an audience and stand out in the memory. While it is our business to be funny on the screen, we gain greatly by a quiet moment or two or a little bit that is pathetic. Comedy in a drama, because it is something free or additional, may be slight. With us, it must be sturdy and robust, for comedy is our main reliance and the thing we have to sell.

I saw a Western picture not long ago in which the hero, very much in love and with his thoughts wandering in the open spaces, abstractedly put one spoon of sugar after another into his cup of coffee. This went as it always had, and has since. That wouldn't do in a comedy. We must have something more, and our gags must build up in proportion to our story, and they must be so placed that an exciting one is not followed by one less exciting. For instance, if some valuable china has been planted and it is broken in some amusing, characteristic way through awkward handling of a shy or embarrassed boy, that scene cannot be placed after a wild chase or exciting sequence in which the same character has at the risk of life and limb been in the street miraculously dodging traffic and other lurking dangers.

There are dangers, too, in the street where comedy is made. In the old days when four days was enough to turn out a pic-

ture, the process was not quite so terrifying. I think that if anyone who had never made a moving-picture comedy tried to do
so, he would soon become discouraged. The only reason we are
able to do it at all is that we have grown in the business, and
once one has made one comedy it is a little bit less hopeless to
go on. We build and change with a certain confidence that
comes from having done it before.

We are not dismayed when we find we are wrong. On the
picture I am working now, we have suddenly found that we
may want to change the ending. If we do, the whole story
must be changed and it will be necessary to go back and take a
great many bits over. Fortunately, all our sets are standing.
Otherwise I should merely exclaim the title of my new picture: *For Heaven's Sake*.

BUSTER KEATON
(1895-1966)

Buster Keaton and his screen character were never accorded the attention and respect bestowed by contemporary critics on his greatest rival, Chaplin. Keaton's unsmiling countenance seemed to distance those audiences charmed by the tramp's apparent accessibility, while his films never bothered with the appeals to pathos and sentiment that so warmed Chaplin's admirers. Keaton had to wait until the 60's for his rediscovery, but fortunately was still around to bask in some of the glory. Modern audiences delighted in his straightforward, non-sentimental style, and discovered in him a director as well as a clown, one with a remarkable command of the intricacies of silent film narrative. Keaton had always been fascinated with the mechanics of film-making, and in this article, which purports to discuss a thematic strain in his films ("Why I Never Smile"), he quickly veers to technical and mechanical questions. The story of the rubber fish is very revealing of Keaton's brand of screen comedy, and indicates how easy it was for this unique humorist completely to lose touch with his audience's sense of humor, leaving them stunned instead of laughing. Many of Keaton's finest scenes are similarly ambitious—as when he moves from one "film" to another in *Sherlock, Jr.*—and not very funny either. Of all the great silent comedians only Chaplin ever directed a drama (*A Woman of Paris*), but the evidence seems to indicate that it was Keaton who was the best suited, if not to playing Hamlet, then to directing it.

WHY I NEVER SMILE
BUSTER KEATON

I have never had a fan letter from the town in Kansas in which I was born, and the legend is probably true that the little village of Pickway was blown away in a cyclone. I was born under a tent during a one-day engagement of a road show my father and Harry Houdini had out. Mother and I were left behind in Pickway. Two weeks later we joined that tent show, and I have never been off the stage or out of the amusement business since that day, except for a year or more when I was at Camp Kearny and in France.

The show that I signed up with at the age of two weeks was called a Medicine Show, and Harry Houdini had the title of Doc. But it was an honest entertainment, and selling medicine was no more than an additional way of making money.

A butcher boy, as he is known in the business, walked through the audience selling bottles of medicine—I suppose the recipe was obtained from the Indians; they always were—that was guaranteed to be good for any kind of rheumatism. When the demand for medicine was dull, the butcher boy sold pop corn, peanuts and candy.

Houdini, I am told, did his famous needle trick and a few of his simpler handcuff stunts. He was not then, needless to say, the great magician, illusionist and collector of souvenirs and books of the theater that he is today. It was Houdini who dubbed me Buster.

Before I was three I toddled onto the stage. Before I was five I had make-up on. And before I was seven I was knocked about in a rough-and-tumble vaudeville act. I was thrown against the back drop, across the stage, and once, in New Haven, because some Yale students kidded my father and tried to break up the show, I was thrown out into the orchestra. It

From *The Ladies' Home Journal*, June 1926. Copyright 1926 by Curtis Publishing Company. Reprinted by permission of *Ladies' Home Journal*.

Buster Keaton between takes on *The Cameraman* (1928) his first M-G-M picture.

never seemed to hurt me, and I never met with an accident or even a bad bruise until I broke my leg making the moving picture, *The Electric House*, in which we used an escalator. I caught the toe of a large slap shoe—the type of shoe so often worn by comedians on the stage and in the pictures—in one of the steps, and the mechanism could not be stopped quickly enough. They often laugh at me down at the studio, and are often unnecessarily worried because I dsiguise myself and do a bad fall or a stunt that an extra has been engaged to do. Once I was in another studio looking on, and there was difficulty about an Indian falling from a cliff. I volunteered. Any acrobat or tumbler would understand there is no lack of modesty in mentioning this. One gets trained to falls, and some of those that look the most difficult are really quite simple, if one has been taught.

The Gerry Society in New York, and similar organizations

throughout the country that either prohibit or regulate the work of children upon the stage, could never understand this. They always expected to find me bruised and maimed. I appeared, I believe, before many different kinds of commissions, and in some cities before the mayor. In two states it was the governor who looked me over to see if I were being injured by the work that I did on the stage. Sometimes I was barred from appearing, but as our engagements were short, we would soon be in another town where the laws might be less strict.

In most cities and states, the laws specifically prohibited a child under sixteen doing juggling, wire work or acrobatics of any kind. This afforded a loophole for me, as I was not an acrobat. I did nothing except submit to being knocked about. When I went outside the theater, they used to dress me in long trousers, derby hat and hand me a cane to carry. In this way they fooled some people into believing that I was a midget. On the stage I was dressed as a replica of my father—a sort of stage Irish-workingman type, with overalls and red chin beard.

When my brother and sister were born, each of them in turn joined the company. If they couldn't walk, they were pushed onto the stage in go-carts. The act was at one time billed as The Four Keatons, though during most of the time there were only the three of us who actually worked. As this boy who wore the clothes of an old man and always felt old, grew older, he became too big to be used as the butt of his father. He could no longer be thrown around, and other things had to be put into the act, which was about played out anyway. One of our stunts was to burlesque the other people who played on the bill with us. They would often crowd around in the wings in the friendly, good-natured way of vaudeville people, and be much amused at the monstrous things we were doing in supposed imitation of them. We played with everybody in variety, and an autograph book which my mother kept for me is almost a complete roster of vaudeville as it used to be, of vaudeville as it was in the days when Tony Pastor's was not only a New York, but a national institution.

When I was twenty-one I got an offer to leave the variety stage and go into a musical show or a revue which the Shuberts were to put on at the Winter Garden in New York. It meant a good deal to me, for it was not only the first thing on my own, but it was a chance to do something really different. While I was waiting for rehearsals to be called, I met Joseph Schenck, who is now my brother-in-law, and he told me that he was making some two-reel pictures. He wanted to know if I wanted to try the movies. At the Winter Garden I was to get two hundred and fifty dollars a week. For pictures, I was offered forty. I had no more idea than anyone else at the time what the growth of pictures was to be. One feature of the films did appeal to me and that was that it would mean staying in one place for a while. I had been traveling on the road for over twenty years. I took the gamble and cast my lot with the pictures.

My first appearance on the screen was in a comedy called *The Butcher Boy*.[1] The scene was a general or country store. I entered to buy some molasses, but it happened that the two principal comedians were just then exchanging bags of flour with one another, across the store. I intercepted one with my head and was knocked out. Those early screen comedians aimed true and threw straight! I can remember that blow now. After I was picked up and brushed off a bit, I bought my molasses, only to discover that I had left the quarter in the bottom of the pail. Then followed a scene in which almost everybody in the store and myself tried to get the quarter. I became covered with molasses and my pan-shaped hat fell into the pail. As this scene did not seem to go right, it was taken several times. My first day in pictures, and it was for this that I gave up two hundred and ten dollars a week!

I think it was while I was working on a second picture that I was called to Camp Kearny, and after a period at that training camp, and eleven months in France, in which I was more useful, I am afraid, in camp entertainments than I was in the more ordinary part of soldiering, I returned to Hollywood to make a picture called *The Saphead*. This was a screen version

1. This was in 1917, and the film featured Roscoe "Fatty" Arbuckle and Al St. John. The omission of Arbuckle's name here is indicative of the impact of the scandal which destroyed his career in 1921.

of Bronson Howard's old play, *The Henrietta,* in which William H. Crane played his old part and I played Stuart Robson's part of Bertie, The Lamb.[2] After this, I began making two-reel comedies, in which I was featured.

The first was *One Week.* In this film I bought a portable house by mail and got the numbers mixed up, so that a downstairs door contrived to get upstairs and I, thinking I was walking into the garden, walked through it and dropped many feet. Even at this time the moving-picture comedy was getting to be more legitimate, logical and consistent; and the people were more human and less like the heroes of the comic strips. They were beginning to put things on the screen because they arose from the situation, as in stage plays, and not because they were supposed to be independently funny or because certain properties that could be used happened to be at hand. I was not in the films in the early custard-pie era, nor was I in the comedies that were wholly without logical development. I remember one old film in which there suddenly flashed across the screen a title: Then He Went to London. There was no occasion in the story why he should go to London, and no one knew who he was, except that he was the principal figure employed in the putting over of the comedy. The only possible reason for this journey was that they happened to have around the studio an English joke or gag which they thought would prove irresistible on the screen. Out here, in the making of comedies, we talk much about gags. A gag in comedy is what they call a piece of business in the theater. It is the handling of a property. It is not like a situation which arises out of the action, though it may help the action.

Today the comedy occupies a more dignified place in the amusement business than in the early days. It used to be a sort of after piece to a longer picture. Now it is often the whole bill. With this increased importance has come a different type

2. Another strange reference. While Robson had created the part of Bertie back in the nineteenth century, it was at this point connected in the public mind with Douglas Fairbanks, who starred in the 1913 revival and the 1915 film version, *The Lamb*—and who Keaton later claimed was responsible for getting Buster the role in *The Saphead.*

of comedy; space is now needed to work out logically and adequately a good idea or story. Formerly I did two-reelers, one right after another, and now it is an effort to get through two five-reel pictures in a year. This has not come from any slowing up. We work just as hard around the studio as we ever did, and we play our games of baseball no more frequently, but the old pace cannot be maintained. We have educated audiences, and they have gone beyond and demand more of us. We can no longer use the old, impossible gags that were inserted without rime or reason; anything served that was funny to fill in the time until the grand finale, and that was inevitably an elaborate chase, usually through the streets. I do not mean to say that the day of the impossible gag is over or to imply that these things were not funny. They were often screamingly so. I remember the finish of an early picture of mine called *Hard Luck*. For no particular reason I jumped from a great height. I missed the swimming pool, made a dent in the concrete alongside of it and disappeared into the earth. Then there was a title: Years Afterwards. It was the same scene, the swimming pool is covered with moss, but the dent into which I disappeared is still there. I emerge and then motioning with a sort of come on gesture, I am followed by a Chinese wife and two children. Audiences used to go out of the theater howling at that.

What makes the public laugh? Now, though I neither laugh nor smile on the screen, it is my business to get smiles and laughs, principally laughs, out of audiences. We can only judge by our experience, and by tests and observances of audiences in actual moving-picture theaters. Usually when a comedy is completed in a studio there are hurry calls for everyone who appeared in it and sets are put up again because it has been found necessary to retake early scenes. On the stage it is possible to form a certain routine for an act. If a thing doesn't go at a matinée it can be taken out at night. I do not care who the performer is, whether he is the humble supper chaser who gets the bad spots in a bill and plays three times, at least, a day, or the star act in the best position, he is influenced by his audience. The empty seats get you—and so do the occupied ones if they are not responsive. Now, in the films we are constantly without the benefit of an audience during the process of making our picture. It is an old story in Hollywood that the things we think are irresistible are the very things that the public can sit through in stony silence.

The property room in our studio is filled with rubber fish. They were made for what I thought was going to be the best gag that I had ever had. It was in the film, *The Navigator*, and I, in a diver's suit, was under the sea. A school of fish pass me, we will say, from east to west. Now, it was thought that it would be extremely funny if this school of fish could be held up, while a poor little lone fish that wanted to get from north to south could go through the traffic. I picked up a starfish, pinned it on my breast, and in the manner of a traffic cop stopped some of the fish, and then, when the lone fish had gone through the lane I had made, I signaled the waiting fish that they might proceed. They did. They were operated by a large steel contrivance which looked like a press capable of turning out an afternoon paper of large circulation. When this scene was exhibited in a try-out in one of the suburbs of Los Angeles, no one laughed. A minute or two later, still under water, I stooped over and washed some muck off my hands in a bucket that had been left on the bottom of the sea. The audience howled.

We tried two more small towns, and the same thing happened. They would not laugh. The gag was too intricate. Everybody in the audience was too busy wondering how the stunt was accomplished, for the rubber fish filmed beautifully and appeared very real. There was nothing for it but to cut out my favorite gag. It had taken days to do, for we were greatly handicapped, as there could be no communication between me and the cameraman in the diving bell, except by signals with the hand, and these, of course, were extremely clumsy. This stunt had kept me under water in a cold lake many extra hours and, exclusive of time, it had cost over ten thousand dollars.

It had always occurred to me that there was a good deal of comedy to be found under the sea, and I ordered a regulation diver's suit that weighed two hundred and twenty pounds. The only variation was that more glass was put into the front of the helmet. The face, even though it is not a smiling one, must be seen in comedy. That was the beginning of *The Navigator*. The story was built up from that diver's suit. We engaged a Pacific liner and anchored it off Catalina. But we found that when one walked on the bottom of the Pacific in a diver's suit, he stirred up so much sand that the films became cloudy and indistinct. It was necessary to have clear water into which we could lower our diving bell that contained the cameras. Someone suggested that we might use the sulphur tank at Riverside. We had to extend this, both in height and in area, in order to get part of the keel of the boat and our rather elaborate underwater setting. It must be made to look like the bottom of the sea. Though this tank had been for many years an object of admiration and a place for tourists, at twenty-five cents per person, to swim, it suddenly caved in when we got ready to shoot. Then we moved to Lake Tahoe, where the water was certainly clear and certainly cold.

It seems to me that we can get more comedy out of an original story like *The Navigator*, which may spring from no more than a diver's suit, than from a play or book that has already found favor with the public. We can sit around and discuss gags, and put in plot when it is needed and where it is needed. The idea is more important than the plot. We can also, when we build up and develop our story, put in a serious or pathetic moment or two. These, of course, are no more than the light and shade which make for the best comedy, whether on the stage or on the screen. It has been found in farces on the stage that there can be such a thing as too many laughs, that they can follow too close together for all of them to register. This is true with the elaborated screen comedy. Of course, the comedian's quiet bits or serious bits should not be held too long. They will seem dull. But how long a moment of pathos in a comedy may be allowed to run is like the timing of a gag. We can argue the question, work over it and experiment in the studio, but it is the audience that gives us the answer. We can merely guess and try things once, as the saying is. It is like the answer to the question: "What makes 'em laugh?" We don't know.

In a burlesque Western film, I, as a very verdant, green tenderfoot, got myself into a poker game with a villain in the bunk house. He cheats, and I tell him so in a subtitle. He pulls a gun on me and in another subtitle replies by quoting, inaccurately, from Owen Wister's *The Virginian:* "In this country, when you say that—smile!" Now, I never smile on the screen and never have. What was my character to do in this situation? In the studio, we thought this very much O.K. and highly comic—one of those happy accidents that turn up now and then to relieve the routine course of a carefully planned scenario. We had figured that the audience would know that I could not smile, and that they knew that my frozen face was as necessary to the character I always play as my flat hat and my necktie on a rubber, which pulls down and snaps back. But when the picture was projected in the theaters, no one laughed. I do not believe that this was because they were worried that I might be shot. Our mistake probably was that we had counted on something that was outside the picture at the particular moment. Perhaps they laughed when they got home, but in any event, the scene was a dud. Nor was there laughter when, with my fingers, I pointed up the corners of my mouth, making a sort of jack-o'-lantern grin. This is as near to a smile as I have ever been on the screen, and nobody laughed.

Long before I appeared in the films, I was used to pantomime and dumb show—always with a serious, expressionless countenance. In all the years that I played in the vaudeville theaters with my mother and father in the act billed as The Three Keatons. I never spoke, smiled or laughed. In this knockabout act, my father and I used to hit each other with brooms, occasioning for me strange flops and falls. If I should chance to smile, the next hit would be a good deal harder. All the parental correction I ever received was with an audience looking on. I could not even whimper.

When I grew older, I readily figured out for myself that I was not one of those comedians who could jest with an audience and laugh with it. My audience must laugh at me.

If ever I appear on the stage again, even if it is only for a benefit, I shall have no lines. But I am reluctant now to appear before a crowd of people, and nothing would induce me to make a speech. I am not sure that I approve anyway of personal appearances for moving-picture stars. It requires a type of showmanship which few of us have, and it is not our business to talk.

Once I was lured into attending the opening of a new theater in Philadelphia. It had been broadcast through the papers that a trainload of people, prominent in the theater and the picture world, was to arrive at the Broad Street Station to attend the opening of this very superior picture and vaudeville house. A mob of fans was waiting for the train. There was much smiling and bowing and many handshakes. I walked through the crowd in absolute seriousness until I heard someone say: "Stick a pin in him, and see if you can make him laugh." It was with no little apprehension and with a great deal of effort that I reached a cab outside the station. That night—how reminiscent those two words seem—I made a speech. Dumb show is best for screen people, if they must appear in public, especially for the comedian.

My serious, immovable countenance or pan face has brought me some amusing letters from film fans, and I find that they have some strange names for me. For instance, in Siam I am called *Kofreto*. In Cochin China my name is *Wong Wong*. In Liberia, *Kazunk*. And in Moravia, Czecho-Slovakia and Northern Hungary, I gather from my mail that I am referred to as *Prysmysleno*. In Spain they call me *Zephonio;* in Poland *Zybsko;* and in France, *Malec*. In Iceland, where business representatives tell me my pictures go well, I am dubbed *Glo-go*. No one as yet has given me authentic translations, but I imagine that most of these names of endearment signify null and void and their combined meaning, if totaled up, would equal zero.

ALLAN DWAN
(1885-   )

As the silent period drew to a close it became clear exactly what the narrative possibilities of the form really were. No longer did directors refer to written literature, the graphic arts, or some combination of the two as the ideal. Rather, the distinct limitations and advantages of screen narrative began to dictate its own material, whether in the form of original stories, or of adaptations from other media. Allan Dwan writes here on the proper handling of adaptations, how plays and novels must be conformed to the unique requirements of the screen. Of course the article is partly an answer to those who complained (and still do) about the manhandling of their favorite stories when they reappeared as photoplays. Dwan points out various types of changes that must be made (and it's significant that "good taste"—read censorship—is an important factor), giving specific examples to bolster his case. But one might wonder, then, why the films would continue to reach for alien narrative material if it was nearly inevitable that any adaptation radically alter the form and substance of the original. The answer was the voracious appetite of the beast itself. Although screenwriting was not yet the accomplished field it was soon to become, Hollywood in 1926 released 740 feature pictures, so the stories had to come from somewhere. More than most people, Dwan was acutely aware of this fact: over his fifty-year career he was associated with some 800 pictures, fully half of which he directed himself.

ADAPTATIONS
ALLAN DWAN

The advantages and limitations of the screen as a story-telling medium, as compared with the novel, short story, or drama, have formed a subject of endless discussion ever since motion pictures came into their own as an artistic medium.

Similarly the fact that a screen play, taken from a play or novel, varies in movement, action and often in plot details from the original version, without varying however from the theme, is another subject that is little understood outside of the technical circles of the motion picture world.

As a matter of fact it is the desire of producers and directors to adhere to the original plot and plan of a novel or drama as closely as possible, and at the same time have a workable *pictorial* story. But the written and pictorial mediums differ greatly—a fact that is never taken into consideration by the theatre patron.

A novel may be "strong" and deal with a somewhat unpleasant theme without leaving an unpleasant impression on the mind of the reader. It is a study of life, rather than a portrayal of it. This is due to the reflective quality that is possible in writing, and is due also to the deft shadings of language. An author can lighten his touch, can leave a hiatus, or he can describe mental processes or psychological situations.

But a picture must be *pictorial*. There must be something to photograph every minute. Something must take place every second. Action—and I do not necessarily mean spectacular or violent action—should be the essence of the screen tale.

The screen's possibilities are essentially narrative, and do not partake of reflective or introspective processes. The screen can't describe a situation. It has to *show* it, or else suggest it, partly by photography and partly by the use of words—that is, by a title. There is no way in which the screen can devote a

From *The Motion Picture Director*, June 1926.

Allan Dwan (in eyeshade) with the moving camera apparatus he used for Gloria Swanson's *Stage Struck* (1925).

reel or half a reel to the thoughts of the hero or heroine, the way a book can devote a chapter or two to the thoughts of its characters, their emotional and psychological reactions within the mind.

As a result, if a literal translation of a novel were attempted on the screen, in many cases a very different tone, in fact a different story, would be the result. The impression left on the mind by the screen play would be greatly different from the impression made by the novel. Unpleasant effects would be heightened to an impossible point, and a frank story handled in a deft way would become brutally vulgar if adhered to literally in its pictorial translation. This is because the screen methods are pictorial and visual, the appeal is directly through the eye

155

rather than through the channels of thought. Pictorial art reaches a vividness of effect which a novel seldom attains.

To point out what I mean, let me use a frank example. A novelist may write a subtle story of a fallen woman in her surroundings, a story with the remorseless hand of Fate as its theme, and a sense of pity as its reaction. Let me ask you whether you could take such a story, scene for scene, surrounding for surrounding, event for event, and translate it literally to the screen without having a revolting picture, brutal and utterly repulsive to the picture-goer, and entirely lacking in the deft and subtle qualities of the author's written tale? It *is* quite possible to tell such a story subtly on the screen, but it would have to be done by using the screen's own methods, by changing plot and surroundings and scenes, even though the theme remained the same.

This emphasizes one phase of the problem which is encountered when book material is considered for the screen. The illustration is purely general and represents a type of story that presents difficulties that are practically prohibitive of literal translation.

A more concrete illustration of the many seemingly insignificant items that crop out in the translating of a story from the one medium to the other may be found in the adaptation of Rex Beach's powerful preachment against the narrowness of reform—his latest novel, *Padlocked*, which I directed for Paramount.

In the motion picture world it has long been recognized that Rex Beach instinctively writes in terms of pictures. Translation of a Rex Beach novel from book to screen involves few if any major changes such as so often have to be made in the works of some of our best fictionists. We all recall *The Spoilers* as a particularly vivid illustration of this point. Both in its earlier creation and in its more latterly screen presentation, the fundamental story is virtually unchanged.

So it has been with *Padlocked*. Basically the story is screenable material. And yet certain changes have been necessary in bringing this novel to the screen, each for a very definite reason, and I am frank to say that I think the picture version is just as strong as the novel, and that it drives home the theme of the story just as hard.

For instance one very fundamental change that has been made is in the specific talents of the heroine. In the novel Edith Gilbert, a high spirited modern girl of seventeen, the daughter of a small-town bigot, is a talented singer. In the picture Lois Moran, who is herself an accomplished dancer, portrays the character as a cabaret dancer.

The reason for this is found not in the fact that Lois is a dancer, but in the simple little truth that the human voice—or any other voice for that matter—doesn't photograph on the motion picture screen, but the rhythm of the dance does. Following the characterization of the original in this respect would have gained nothing and lost much in realism, charm and human appeal.

As it is the change does not affect the theme of the story in the slightest, although this one change may have caused several other minor changes. The fact that Lois is herself a clever little dancer adds materially to the realism of the part and the screen story rings true and sincere.

Again in the scenes where Gilbert's bigotry and narrow-mindedness—his humiliation of his family—finally brings his wife to the breaking point, the action of the story is changed to make the death of the wife—as played by Florence Turner—accidental rather than deliberate suicide. In the screen version, instead of deliberately turning on the gas in her room, she is made to faint, following a quarrel with Gilbert (Noah Beery) and falls, accidentally opening the gas cock.

There are many obvious reasons why this scene had to be changed. It is one thing to read this sequence as described in the flowing language of the author and quite another to see it reenacted on the screen in all its grim reality. Insofar as the story itself and its development is concerned the result is practically the same. If anything the later action is improved.

Upon the death of his wife, Gilbert brings Belle Galloway (Helen Jerome Eddy) into his home as a "comfort" to his daughter. Belle is characterized as a smirking, hypocritical woman reformer who has aided Gilbert in his reform work.

Here the action on the screen follows the action of the book. Edith reacts at once to Belle's being brought into the house, knowing her to have been one cause of much of her mother's unhappiness, with the result that she leaves home and goes to New York where she becomes a dancer in a cabaret.

In the novel Edith became a singer through the influence and patronage of Jesse Hermann, a wealthy Long Island patron of the arts, with whom Gilbert has clashed over the question of the purity of the theatre. This episode has been eliminated in the film as not being essential to the screen version.

Similarly in the novel Norman Van Fleet became enamoured with Edith's voice as heard over the radio, without having identified her as the cabaret singer. This angle has been eliminated by the change in Edith's professional talent, and on the screen Van Fleet (Allan Simpson) is attracted to Edith by her dancing in the cabaret and Edith responds with sincere love. At the cabaret she also attracts the attention of Jesse Hermann (Charles Lane) who sets about to develop her talents, and who angles for her, using as his blind Mrs. Alcott (Louise Dresser) a woman who moves in best society but is a former mistress.

All of this follows the story in a general way. Edith is lured into the Hermann home by Mrs. Alcott, Van Fleet is led to misunderstand by the cynical comment of his companions. Edith goes back to the cabaret and Van Fleet goes to Europe, disillusioned, as he believes.

In the story Edith innocently takes refuge with a girl friend in an apartment that is raided by the police, because of immorality charges, and is brought into court. She has about convinced the judge of her innocence when Gilbert and his new wife appear. Edith refuses to go home with them, and denounces Belle. The latter prevails on Gilbert to have the girl committed to a reformatory. The complications of this situation have been eliminated in the film version, in which Edith is arrested in the cabaret on a warrant sworn out by her "mother" charging her with being a wayward minor. She is brought into court and Gilbert wants to take her home. Edith repudiates Belle as her "mother" and the judge, with Gilbert's consent, commits her to the Home of the Good Shepherd, a quasi-reformatory, for three years.

Edith finally is paroled in Mrs. Alcott's care through the influence of Hermann, and is taken to his Long Island home, where she looks upon him as a friend and benefactor.

In the novel Gilbert is left wallowing in his marital unhappiness after he is made to see how Belle Galloway has helped him to wreck his home.

In the film version he goes to New York and enters Hermann's home just after Van Fleet has arrived. Edith believes he has come to take her back to the reformatory and faints. He carries her away, but he actually is taking her to freedom and trying to make amends for what his bigotry and narrow-mindedness have caused in the past. He takes her to Europe, where he and she become true friends, and there, through Gilbert's connivance, Van Fleet again finds her and—well the picture ends in the manner that all good pictures are supposed to end.

CECIL B. DE MILLE
(1881-1959)

Although the title of this article, "The Public Is Always Right," might at first seem the sort of philistine sentiment that one could expect of Cecil B. De Mille, the real significance is not so simple. De Mille looks over the past thirteen years of film history and finds, as did Thomas Ince before him, that the number of years involved is slight, but the amount of change involved enormous. Credit for this should not go just to the film-makers, but to the audiences who by their power at the box office have directed the general course of film history in first one direction, then another. Film-makers may come up with advances in technique, new twists of style, or whole new genres, but it is the public that has final say on their validity. And De Mille argues strongly against the ever increasing power of production executives, distributors, and other non-creative types to mediate between the film-maker and his audience. Two years earlier he had broken a decade-long association with Paramount over just such difficulties, and formed his own producing company. Like Griffith, Flaherty, and Stroheim, De Mille had to fight the executives for his freedom at some point, and moving into his own studio was a temporary solution. But the venture collapsed with the coming of sound, and De Mille was once more thrown into the lap of Paramount and M-G-M. That he flourished there while those others were destroyed has long been taken as evidence of De Mille's hopeless commercialism, but a more fruitful interpretation would acknowledge the resilience and flexibility that allowed him to survive at all.

THE PUBLIC IS ALWAYS RIGHT
CECIL B. DE MILLE

Almost anyone who does creative work reaches a point in his career at which he is ambitious to do something different from the accepted order of things. He is not content merely to go on either repeating himself or doing in his own way what others in the same field are doing. But this adventurer will meet with a great many discouragements, for the people who control the markets where artistic endeavor is sold have, from the beginning, evinced a desire to play safe and to do those things which will probably make money because they have already made money. This is particularly true of the theater and, because of the greater financial risks, even more so in the making of moving pictures. "You can't do that; the public will never stand for it," is their oft-repeated slogan.

My own slogan would be that the public is always right. But the way to the public for the film producer is a tortuous one. The man charged with the responsibility of creating a feature picture in Hollywood, or wherever the studio may be, is selling his product directly to the public—at least, it is the public that buys. But before the finished film reaches the consumer who registers his approval or disapproval at the box office, many people, some expertly critical and some critically expert, will see the picture and argue with solemnity its chances of success. Of course they do not know.

No one knows what the public wants. But the chances are that the man who had the original inspiration, who was present at all the conferences, who determined upon the treatment, who worked on a cogent development of the story and then translated it into photographic material and created it on the screen, knows more about its appeal to the public than the

From *The Ladies' Home Journal*, September 1927. Copyright 1927 by Curtis Publishing Company. Reprinted by permission of *Ladies' Home Journal*.

Cecil B. De Mille instructs Estelle Taylor in the proper worship of the Golden Calf during filming of *The Ten Commandments* (1923).

executive who comes in fresh—but late. His opinion may be sound, for it is based upon experience gained from contact with exhibitors and the trade in general, but the residuum of that experience is often inimicable to anything new. In this way there can be no progress.

After studio executives have seen a production, salesmen, whose duty it is to sell it to the theater owners, and often certain theater owners are given a chance to express their opinion. The result is that everyone feels he alone knows just what the public wants; and the hitherto happy producer—happy because he has had the serenity that comes from interest in doing his job as well as he could—becomes a harassed business man. But even he may not be right, for every now and then the fashions in what the public wants will change. When I was in the theater it used to be said that the styles of plays which were popular changed every twenty years. In the movies the cycle would be shorter—probably not over ten years—for so many more pictures are made in one year than there are plays put upon the stage. The public will like one type of entertainment and then forget about it and like another. Of course there are a few staples. The Western picture seems to be one of these, and a thoroughly good comedy or a sheer melodrama will always find public appreciation, but still the popular taste will change frequently. At first we had all low-life pictures and then we had all high-life pictures. For a time there were nothing but modern pictures, and then we were swamped with costume pictures. At one time nothing but the native drama was liked; then stories with a foreign background found favor to the exclusion, to some extent at least, of the native drama. We went in for spectacle on a large scale and forgot about the intimate or domestic stories where the characters' emotions reacted in a room and not in a coliseum or a palace.

Originally, as almost everyone will recall, the moving picture was supposed, since it was the people's entertainment, to represent what might be called just the average, everyday sort of folk. The poor working girl was usually the heroine—she was seldom higher in the scale. She might marry a rich man and get out of her class, but the story was over when that happened. I remember the howl that emanated from the chorus of unhappy pessimists and headshakers when in one of my pictures we tried the experiment of moving uptown to high life. But then, every innovation has come into the pictures over someone's outraged protest. And the exceptions to "playing safe" are successful often enough not to stultify all progress! And it is the public that is right.

It was a theory that died very hard that the public would not stand for anyone dressed in clothes of another period. The supposed Western clothing was all right, but the Civil War was as far back as one was supposed to go. That period was known to movie audiences from the very beginning; it was not considered "costumes." It used to be stated positively that people would not enter a theater if they learned from the stills and billing outside that the picture was not modern. In a picture which I made some years ago, I got around this objection by staging what we call a vision. The poor working girl was dreaming of love and reading *Tristan and Isolde*. The scene faded out, and scenes were depicted on the screen that the girl was supposed to be reading. Of course there is a parallel between her story and that of Isolde, and the same girl played both. The vision fades and we see the girl reading again. Her lover comes in, takes up the book and throws it down with disgust and says, "Why do you read such things?" Thus a bit of a costume picture was put over on the man who bought the picture for his theater, and there was no protest from the public.

The same method was used in *For Better, For Worse* to get over a religious feeling. The heroine and hero are saying good-by and she sends him off to the Great War. Again the scene fades and we see the same two in the clothes of centuries ago. The heroine sends her lover off to the Crusades. And thus religion got onto the screen in a popular form for the first time. To introduce many other things that were slightly different, this same method has been used again and again. It is practically the only way in which anyone can get a fairy story on the screen. There is, I suppose, no type of entertainment that more terrifies the business people than the thought of a fairy story.

When Douglas Fairbanks produced *Robin Hood* it was immediately successful and attracted a great deal of attention. The production won many prizes from exhibitors and other non-Hollywood bodies. The theater owners then turned to the producers and demanded to know why the costume pictures had been so long kept off the screen, forgetting that they had been partly responsible for keeping it from the public. When several years ago I talked with Mr. Lasky about doing a religious picture, I myself felt that the public was perhaps not quite ready for an entire picture devoted to Biblical episodes. I did not have the courage to spend nearly two million dollars on one. Therefore there was a modern story to *The Ten Commandments*, which so many people—and this includes a great many of the professional critics—did not like. I, however, believe that it was Miss Jeanie Macpherson's modern story that made this picture a success and that it is the modern story that continues to make its appeal to audiences.

All the spectacle that went into the beginning would not have been worth the film required to record it, had it had no response in the second part or had it not influenced thought and action of the characters. Spectacle, for spectacle's sake, is not only not worth what it costs, but it can be a positive detriment if it is not hooked up with human action. Some of the German and other foreign pictures which have gone out of their way to introduce spectacle illustrate this very thoroughly.

Having been reluctant to spend two million dollars on a religious picture because I thought the public was not ready, I have recently spent more on a picture which is wholly religious. *The King of Kings* does not contain any story or a suggestion of a story that is not actually in the Four Gospels.

The decision to film this great story was not the result of any success that the Biblical part of *The Ten Commandments* may have had. It is a story that I have always wanted to do in some medium. I used to think of it in the terms of the theater. I am merely going back to my boyhood, for I was brought up in a most religious household. My father had intended becoming a clergyman. He was teaching at Columbia College, studying very hard himself and trying to save money that he might continue his education. It was my mother who turned him from this study to the theater.

Having a father who was associated with David Belasco in the writing and putting on of plays, it was not unnatural that both my brother and I should turn to the theater. I wanted to be an actor and I think I was fairly good. There is, however, some lingering difference of opinion upon that point.

When I was first approached to go into the pictures I hesitated a long time. It didn't seem to me that the then new industry had given any indication of great possibilities.

When I had finally made up my mind to have a try at film direction I was cautioned that I should find things very different. I did.

My first picture was *The Squaw Man*, a melodrama with scenes in England and in our own West, which William Faversham had played in the theater. Some years later—I'd be willing to say many years later, for to me it marks so long a time, and so much happened in between—I did this picture over. The difference between the two versions was very great. Coming from the theater, I naturally directed as I had known direction in the theater. I always visualized a proscenium and had the characters enter and exit as on a stage. Always they were facing an imaginary audience. We took many groups, and the grouping was that of the stage.

Now, of course, in a group scene the camera must be a certain distance away, and the result is that only physical action will show. The distance from the camera to the objects or people to be photographed is always measured. I have found that what is called acting will count for nothing beyond fifteen feet. This is one of the things that trouble people who come from the theater. They do not appreciate that so much is going to be lost. The eye of the camera will not get things that the boy in the top gallery of the theater would see. From fifteen feet down to seven the actor may act and his acting will be recorded. From seven to four and a half feet the workings of the human mind can be depicted upon the screen—that is, if the actor has it in him. Here is a place where the good screen actor has a great advantage. It is difficult for the actor from the theater to overcome his training and his reliance upon a certain distance between himself and the spectator. And incidentally all this is not so simple as it may read.

Of course, between the filming of the two versions of *The Squaw Man* the whole industry had changed and the mechanical differences were literally tremendous. But the difference in direction and acting was great also. Because of our group method of placing the characters we lost all possibility of getting over shades of meaning. We did not know what the word "subtle" meant in those days. To illustrate this: When, in making the second version, the two leading characters were on opposite sides of the set, we photographed them where they were, then separately with the camera nearer, showing what each was thinking. Then they became attracted to each other, and in a separate "shot" we see them walking and then in a close "shot" we see them together. In the earlier version of *The Squaw Man* they merely walked across a supposed stage. In the simple movies of the early day this was all right, for it was all pure action. We knew that the boy loved the girl from the beginning and that the bad man would make it uncomfortable for them for as many feet as he dared; and the villain was always so made up that he couldn't have been mistaken for a good man by anyone.

I looked at both of these films the other night and was forcibly impressed not only with the great strides the industry has made in the past thirteen years but with the thought that there is a great compensation for working in the films.

One's work is never lost. Great stage spectacles or finely mounted plays can live only in memory or in inadequate flashlight photographs. I can any night in my house project any of the films that I have ever made.

It was thought in the early days of the screen that an emotion could be depicted by rapid movement and by jumping about. And the actors used to get themselves into that hectic state where they felt scenes. Twenty years ago, when I was in the theater, I should have said that to act a scene well one must feel it. I have changed my mind about that, as the result of having directed many screen plays. If you feel a thing too much yourself you are probably not going to make anyone else feel it at all. When the onlookers particularly like a bit of acting and consider it tremendously effective, the chances are that that is good acting for the purpose of the theater and that it will not look well on the screen. And actual crying is not so good as simulated crying on the screen.

Though family life has changed and the old-fashioned pleasures are seemingly no longer enjoyed as they were, there is the compensation that a great many more people can be reached today because of the radio and the movie than ever before. When formerly I used to dream of staging *The King of Kings* on a platform of some sort with spoken lines, we could, even if the work had been done as well and as reverently as might be, have reached but a comparatively few people. With the film we can go everywhere.

From the start of *The King of Kings* I have never had any idea except to put the actual story on the screen. We show this in episodes that do not depart from the text. I do not mean to write that I have not read between the lines, but such "reading between the lines" doesn't mean what is usually understood by that phrase. As an illustration, there is in Matthew xvii, 14-17:

> And when they were come to the multitude, there came to him a certain man, kneeling down to him, and saying,
>
> Lord, have mercy on my son: for he is lunatick, and sore vexed: for ofttimes he falleth into the fire, and oft into the water.
>
> And I brought him to thy disciples, and they could not cure him.

In our film we first show the disciples failing to cure this boy.

In the making of *The King of Kings* we have made use of the great paintings of the world. What better source of picture making could there be than pictures? Ordinarily I have found that Doré was the best source of inspiration. The photographic quality of this master's drawing seems to me peculiarly akin to the needs of the movies. When I work I compose a scene in exactly the same way that it would be drawn or painted. I do this not by moving people about in the space between the camera lines arbitrarily but by looking through the lens of the camera. This gives me a top, bottom and side, just as there would be to a canvas. I originally think of this in black and white, just as anyone who paints begins by drawing his composition before he puts on color. When the people have been placed I turn to the cameraman and tell him what kind of lighting is wanted. We paint with lights as a painter uses his brush. The cameraman will know what is required when he is asked for Rembrandt's, Vandyke's, Reubens' or any other painter's lighting, or for a Corot effect. Then there is the problem of applying color, if the picture is to be done in colors. But that is a very different and a very complicated problem. I do not know that I approve of a whole picture done in colors. I think it is more effective if held for decoration or heightening of certain scenes which are formal or cameolike in their place in the story. Intimate action, where a red-and-blue check cravat might distract attention from the face upon which thought must be registered, is not only difficult to handle but may prove dangerous to the story. And yet some of the loveliest things that I have seen anywhere have been bits in color films. Sometimes they have been so lovely and the spectator has been so thrilled by them that he has even missed the real drama of the scenes.

The director of a picture must also consider in his composition the faces and the personalities of his players. He cannot change them at will as the painter may. Therefore, he must consider well in advance and choose slowly. In selecting the actors for *The King of Kings* I was guided by the principle that the greatest story ought to have the greatest cast possible. Some of my associates think that I have misspelled a word and that what I really meant was the greatest "cost." Nevertheless, I have engaged actors to play bits who are really stars. Among the extra players will be found people who usually play good parts and even leads.

As a producer, I have found that there is some fatality about my trying to save money. I usually waste time—the most important and costly consideration in the making of a movie. But still, one must worry about costs or others will do it for one. Neither state is particularly gracious to the producer.

After having directed, personally, fifty-six films and supervised the making of some two hundred and seventy more in thirteen years, I wonder sometimes why the making of a motion picture always seems a life-or-death job. We take it more seriously than most men do their life's work. Perhaps there is some reason for it. The two great civilizing influences that exist in the world today are a little round lens, the eye of the movie, and a round disc, the microphone of the radio. Neither has been with civilization very long, and yet they have already given evidence that they possess the greatest educational power and that they can be the agents that will bring different peoples with different creeds and of different races together.

In all this contemporary ado about the American film, one fact is lost sight of and that is that the films must be made somewhere, and naturally they reflect the country that they are made in. There would be an outcry from somewhere wherever they were made.

Years ago, in a picture which I directed called *The Cheat*, the villain was a Japanese. There was a good deal of comment because at that time nations were just beginning to take the screen seriously and they were awake to the great potency of this influence. Today it is not safe to choose the nationality of your bad man wantonly. Mexico is tired of supplying the evil-doers for border dramas, and there have been cases where American films have been interdicted. But this does not apply to Mexico alone; other nations have protested, and it is far safer to have your hero and bad man of the same race and nation. When *The Cheat* was done the second time, and by another director, the villain became a Hindu.

But one need not internationalize a mother and father's concern for a sick child. What does it matter if the house that mother and father live in is of Spanish architecture adapted to Hollywood? The mother and father will be understood by primitive mothers and fathers everywhere, and there will be no thoughts of hatred or of war against the people of the nation where that film was made. It is the politicians, not the people, who resent the American film.

And we who are in the making of the films must take this great trust seriously. We have not always done so. And there has been much talk of censorship. We have had some of it, and the great natural power of the movies has been almost throttled by it. Sometimes such regulation can be amusing, though it is always aiming at the very existence of a great force of potential good. A ban was put upon *The Ten Commandments* in one of the provinces of India because the boy Pharaoh strikes Moses with a whip. It was held to be bad to show a great prophet being hit. And this was a government edict, not for the British Empire or for India but for one province! But such things will be forgotten, as will be the attitude or type of mind which makes this narrowness possible. The movie and the radio will bring people together. They will make for unity and for a certain great oneness in the world. Ultimately it may even be oneness with God.

ERICH VON STROHEIM
(1885-1957)

Budgetary restrictions and producer interference were the constant complaints of Erich von Stroheim, and the following piece on *The Wedding March* is no exception. But more than just the usual catalogue of grievances, we are given here a direct insight into one of the director's most characteristic obsessions. The single element of the story which he focuses on might seem a strange one (the brief sequence in which Fay Wray goes to confession), but the importance he gives to it is revealing. Stroheim was a devout practising Catholic throughout his public life, and his films are filled with the ritual of that Church, often incorporated for ironic or metaphoric effect. This in itself was strange because his true background was Jewish, a fact he managed to suppress throughout a myth-shrouded career. His concentration on the scene in this article is completely out of line with its importance in the film: "a confession scene, the first time on the screen" would hardly be the drawing card he claims. Yet in his only contemporary writing on *The Wedding March* this is the scene he is moved to discuss. As usual with Stroheim, a later postscript gives the story an even more ironic twist. When he was allowed to recut *The Wedding March* at the Cinémathèque Française in the early 50's, he at most altered a shot here and there, or the arrangement of several shots within a sequence. But the "confession scene" he ruthlessly truncated, relieving its originally overawed piety and improving the pacing considerably—yet another of the many minor mysteries of Stroheim scholarship.

THE SEAMY SIDE OF DIRECTING
ERICH VON STROHEIM

There has been much talk, to-day, of the waste of money in motion pictures. Most of the accusation is thrust upon the director's shoulders. That, at least, has been my experience. But the extravagance is committed long before the director enters the scene.

This is one of the follies of the industry. Take, for instance, *An American Tragedy*. Two or three companies buy it. When I say "it," I mean, most often, the title. Let us say $97,000 is paid for it. That is but the initial expense. It is like buying a car without spare parts. Then there is the expense of adaptation, script, continuity, and so forth, which aggregates approximately an additional $75,000. That is before the picture is begun. Then the director with vision, who wants authentic details, surroundings and general atmosphere, is watched with a hawk-eye. He is lucky if he can enforce his own interpretation, incidentally the reason he has been engaged.

My greatest handicap has been the fact that when I started directing one of the publicity men thought that since motion pictures impress people with the huge sums entailed in the making, it would be a capital stunt to advertise the amount of money I was spending. And so, this publicist chose Forty-second Street and Times Square, New York, as the target for all hungry eyes, and each day, with the help of his widely imaginative mind, posted the latest figure, increasing the numbers in leaps and bounds. The result was most harmful to me in the industry, for while the producers were pleased to boast of their extravagance, they privately resented it.

A human characteristic this and not unlike incidents that arise in one's own family. I recall when a very young man, a student in the Austrian army, boots were the most fastidious part of my uniform. I used to order six pairs at a time, instead

From *Theatre Magazine*, November 1927.

Writer-director-star Erich von Stroheim spends a few minutes with his family between takes on the Corpus Christi sequence of *The Wedding March* (shot in 1926).

of one, so that I would not be compelled to wear the same pair until they grew shabby, at the same time keeping them all in good condition. While my father, well able to afford the expenditure, proudly beamed at my well-groomed appearance, he ranted and fumed at my extravagance, just the same.

How can a director be expected to turn out an artistic work if he is ever conscious of money—of an amount he is supposed to spend. The holes in the motion picture industry are not in the prodigality entailed by the director, but in the salaries paid to stars for months and months while they are not working, merely because their contracts call for salary. A director has many "white elephants" on his hands, too; often the producer's relatives. Sometimes he is given one of these prize purchases that is no more suited to the motion picture than a violin. If the director should change the story very obviously, as he often has to because of the difference in vehicles between spoken and silent drama, he is severely criticized.

I must record a word of sympathy here for the smaller director. He is usually watched so closely on the financial budget that he daren't begin to express himself. He is rarely given the wherewithal to make a picture that would turn out to be "big." He is limited to time, expense and also usually given poor actors with whom to work. In that way he is forced into a snag. His work is grouped with the less important, and eventually he is classified as "just an ordinary director," with the result that when a producer has a big story on which he can spend freely and which calls for an excellent cast, to whom does he naturally turn? To the man who has already made a "big" picture. That forces the "smaller" director into a rut, from which he can rarely extricate himself.

A director should no more be limited to the time and money spent on a picture than an author or a playwright. Neither of the latter can be told that he must write something within forty days, and see to it that the properties involved should not exceed $10,000. In the same way it is utterly impossible for a director to be told that he must complete a picture in a given time and see that it does not cost more than $ . . . . . A capable director is not necessarily content with a scene after it has been shot five or six times, or after he has spent the scheduled four days on it. Perhaps one more shot, or another day would give him the desired result; does that not justify his delay? After all, no director enjoys retakes any more than the producer does the additional expense, but if he feels that he has not achieved the desired result, that in itself is assurance something better is possible, and that he can give it. What we want is better pictures, but restraint will never produce them.

Art in the motion picture profession is not protected. In *The Wedding March* I have a confession scene, for which picturization I was given permission by the Pope. It is the exact ceremony of the Catholic Church. The producer and other officials of the company were so proud of the picture that they invited other cameramen, directors and various people of the industry to a pre-view. The result, another picture, a less imposing one, that was able to be sandwiched in by another company, with a confession scene. Since the picture is but a small one, it will be out and shown before mine appears, with the selling point "a confession scene, the first time on the screen." Directors must be protected from such things.

The best motion picture actor is one who has an inborn talent, lack of self-consciousness, and has traveled from gutter to throne, but been engaged to act while still in the gutter. If not in reality, then through imagination, through great reading. Whether he or she be a tragedian or comedian, each must possess a keen sense of humor. Besides, I must like them personally to be able to direct them. There cannot be a smooth product where in the making jolts or breaks tear the threads.

HARRY LANGDON
(1884-1944)

That Harry Langdon's once high-flying career came to so abrupt an end should have surprised no one. First, his comic style was so idiosyncratic that it seems a wonder he ever achieved widespread recognition at all. Infantilism as the root of a comic character has inborn limitations, and sound would inevitably have dealt it a death blow. But more important, when success was achieved Langdon dismissed his collaborators and foolishly attempted to run both the creative and financial sides of his operation himself. A failure at both ends, he personally ground his career to a disastrous halt, but not before producing some of the most personal and perplexing works of the American cinema. After firing people like Frank Capra and Harry Edwards, Langdon was left with a personal vision unhindered by the commercial sensibility of the Sennett-Roach studio style. The films he made on his own, *Three's a Crowd*, *The Chaser*, and *Heart Trouble* (1927-28), wallow in obsessions so misogynistic as to make Laurel and Hardy seem running dogs of the women's movement. But as Langdon drifted completely away from his audience he became ever more involved in his own study of comic theory. To hear a silent clown casually allude to a theory of comic automatism (which is just one of the things Langdon does here) comes as no little shock. But more surprising still is the fact that his films clearly function as illustrations of these theories. One day our critics will get around to Langdon, but until then we have to content ourselves with his handful of peculiar comedies, and with cryptic statements like this one on the "tragic business" of screen comedy.

THE SERIOUS SIDE OF
COMEDY MAKING

HARRY LANGDON

There are few more tragic businesses in the world than the making of funny pictures.

There is the tragedy, for example, of working for weeks, sometimes months, on a sequence which the producer expects to be extremely funny, only to find that it fails to evolve even a ripple from the audience. In the producing of any big feature comedy this situation is certain to arise at least once. The producer and the star often find that their most cherished material is not funny when transmitted to the screen and the result is a tragedy not only for the audience, but for the makers of the picture.

I am convinced that comedy is much harder to achieve than drama. There is more worry, more disappointment, more genuine heartbreak. A comedian must realize that it is his duty to make all people laugh—the rich, the poor, the bereaved, the sick. He must attempt to reach all of these with a message which will make them forget their woes, and cause them to laugh. There is a great deal of tragedy for the producer in facing this realization every time he starts to make a picture.

Comedy is the satire of tragedy. Serious matters repeatedly turn to comic as they pass through a morbidly active conscience. Most deliciously comic moments on the outside, are full of sad significance for those who realize the sinister characterization of the situation.

A man walks into a ballroom and forgets to put his suspenders on. To him it is a tragedy, to an audience it is comical. A despondent man goes up to leap to death from a high building; his coat catches on an awning and he dangles in midair. It is tragic to him, but the audience screams. A man is in love, the girl rejects him for another. That is tragedy, but the things the comedian does are funny. A man buys a new hat, it blows off

From *Theatre Magazine*, December 1927.

and a horse steps on it. It is a calamity to him, but a howl to an audience.

Have you ever analyzed why you laugh at these things? It is the concentration on the physical, as opposed to the spiritual.

Any individual is comic who automatically goes his own way without troubling himself about getting in touch with the rest of his fellow beings. It is the trifling faults of our fellow men that makes us laugh. A comic can make us laugh, providing care be taken not to arouse our emotions. To view comedy is delightful, but to partake of its ingredients, might leave a bitter taste.

Systematic absentmindedness, like Don Quixote, is the most comical thing imaginable. The four greatest stimuli to laughter are rigidity, automatism, absentmindedness and unsociability.

John Bunyan said: "Some things are of that nature as to make his fancy chuckle while his heart doth ache."

One cannot give himself up to tears, yet there are few comedies in which tragedy does not play its newly developed rôle. Comedy at its best, has always pointed a moral. It has not set out to do so, but instead, has assumed seriousness as the foundation of laughter.

Tragedy frequently stalks behind the scenes during the making of feature comedies, more so, perhaps, than during the making of dramas, for an essential element of successful comedy is thrill, and thrills are seldom obtained without some actual physical danger. During such moments there is no hilarity in the producing company. There seldom is for that matter. I have often thought a comedy "lot" is the saddest place on earth and comedy constructionists are, as a rule, the saddest people. You will find them, without exception, a serious-minded group of men, seldom smiling and not at all given to outbursts of mirth. This, however, is beside the point.

Every man in a comedy company dreads to make thrill scenes. So often a man's life hangs on a bit of invisible wire, or his ability to conquer the instinctive fear of danger. A slip of the foot may mean actual peril to a comedian during such moments—but it is always good for a gale of glee from an audience.

During the filming of *Tramp, Tramp, Tramp*, nobody in the

company wanted me to hang on a fence at the edge of a steep cliff. There was no one else to do it, so I had no alternative. You can be quite sure there was not a laugh in the crowd back of the camera while this stunt was being done. The cliff dropped precipitately for several hundred yards with nothing to break the fall. When it was finished I was greatly worried about it, because there hadn't been a titter from the crew. Usually, you know, you can judge whether your stuff is funny by the reaction it gets from your impromptu audience. When I got off the fence I met nothing but blanched faces and silence. On the screen, as you know, the stunt proved tremendously successful. Audiences laughed.

During the filming of *The Strong Man,* a trick cannon exploded as I pulled the lanyard to fire the final shot of the scene. In the noise, the smoke and confusion, I didn't even know there had been an accident. When the smoke cleared away, we found that one piece of the metal cannon had grazed the back of my head, struck a musician a glancing blow in the cheek and buried itself in the wall of the stage. On the screen this scene was a scream.

The enjoyment of comedy, just like the enjoyment of tragedy, is the result of the feeling of remoteness from the situation caricatured.

FRANK CAPRA
(1897-   )

Any true understanding of Frank Capra's great comic features of the 30's and 40's must certainly take into account his early days as gag writer at the studios of Hal Roach and Mack Sennett. Comedy was being carefully moulded to character in those last days of the silent fun factories, and Capra learned lessons here that served him well years later in the most personal of his mature features. He had been trained to style comedy directly to the personalities of men like Harry Langdon, a trick he later employed in giving box office stars like James Stewart, Gary Cooper, and Cary Grant three completely individualized comic masks in the films they made for him. The fact that they fit these stars so well helped create that believability, warmth, and good humor that seem so typically Capraesque. At the time he wrote this Capra had just broken into feature directing with *The Strong Man* and *For the Love of Mike*. He had left Sennett to work as writer and director for Harry Langdon's own company, but their relationship was ill fated: Langdon (an early believer in Capra's own "one man, one film" dictum) bounced his director in an effort to gain full personal control over his films, and Capra was thrown to the jaws of poverty row, a fate he escaped only by turning his own life into a veritable Frank Capra movie.

THE GAG MAN
FRANK CAPRA

The gag man is the newest institution of the motion picture studios. So new is he, in fact, that his fame—if such it is to be—has not yet reached the public, and his efforts, which are a large and essential contribution to practically every production, are unrecognized by the millions whom they entertain.

The gag man is the expert in humor—visual humor—who creates laughs where there were no laughs before. He relieves the tension of the sternest drama with a humorous incident; he carries forward the development of a plot with a series of comedy episodes that replace what would otherwise be dull, though essential, sequences. He is the apt story teller, who uses action, rather than words, as his medium.

Gag men, though it is only recently that they have been recognized as such, have been important factors in motion picture productions since the birth of the art. Formerly, every studio worker—the star, supporting players, directors, scenario writers, title writers and others—contributed to the construction of the gags. Within the last few years, a few of these impromptu fun-makers, realizing that their natural aptitude for gagging made them more valuable to producers in this work than in their previous fields, became specialists. And, so, the gag man was born.

The field of the gag man—this newly conceived specialist—was, at first, limited to comedy production. Gag men, rather than writers, or, better, writers who were also gag men, were the scenarists at the Sennett, Roach and Christie studios. Their method of working differs with the varying policies of the several producers. Usually, however, an initial conference is held for the purpose of outlining a simple, skeleton plot, which is essentially humorous in its conception. With this plot as a basis,

From *Breaking into the Movies,* edited by Charles Reed Jones, New York, 1927.

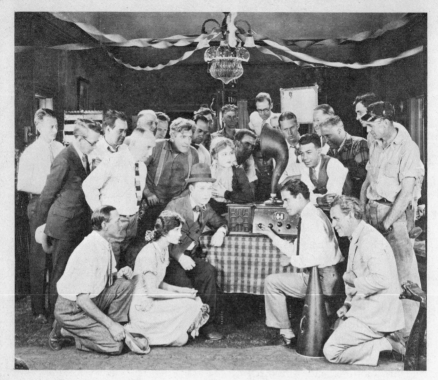

Frank Capra dials in the Dempsey-Tunney fight as Harry Langdon and other members of the cast and crew of *Long Pants* (1927) are glued to the radio.

the gag men work collectively to develop the comedy incidents that work in smoothly with the running narrative of the story. Further conferences between the gag men and the director result in the elimination of many of the gags that are not generally accepted as feasible.

The original story is then adjusted, as may be necessary to fit the selected gags, and these are developed and polished by the combined efforts of the staff. In the production of comedies, to which this immediate discussion is confined, it is usual for one or more gag men to be active on the set throughout the making of the picture. His purpose, obviously, is to co-operate with the director in the staging of the gags and to suggest such new ones as may occur to him as the story is developed.

The recognition of gag men, as such, by comedy producers soon became general with the development of the system that is outlined above. The importance of his work was appreciated to such an extent that it was not unusual to reverse the general order of story preparation and work out plots to embody series of gags which had been worked out independently. Gag men—still continuing their all-important work of gagging—became comedy scenarists and directors. And, what is more important, the term, "gag man," attained a definite standing in the industry.

Producers of feature productions—dramas or, so-called, comedy-dramas of five reels or more—had been for years making what they now recognize as unreasonable demands on their scenario writers. Every director and every production executive demanded "comedy relief," and this comedy relief, all too often, was not forthcoming. Your comedian, whether he be a clown, a monologist or a gag man, is a specialist, and it is not to be expected that a man who has trained himself in the intricacies of photoplay writing should be able to qualify as equally proficient in gag construction.

The failure, a perfectly natural failure, of the scenario writer in a field outside his own opened new precincts to the gag man. His advent in feature production was, at first, in the nature of an experiment. His ready adaptability proved his worth and showed beyond a doubt that he can be a constructive influence in the making of every type of photoplay.

There is a general demand for gag men today. No good gag man is out of work. Unlike almost every other studio worker, he may be busy fifty-two weeks of every year. He has no "vacations" between pictures, because he is needed by every studio for every picture. He does not have to wait until his type of production is being made, because there are very few types of photoplay that do not require his constructive services.

The great need for gag men today has made the field an open one. I do not mean that anyone may become a gag man, but I do know that the qualified man, outside the industry, has a better opportunity of breaking in as a gag man than as a worker in any other production capacity. If you are confident that you have the ability to create gags, the Mack Sennett studios, the Hal Roach studios and many others will possibly give you a chance to display your talents.

Untrained, inexperienced men who can convince others of some initial comedy ability are accepted regularly by these studios for, perhaps, a four weeks' trial at about one hundred dollars a week. If their first efforts show any promise at all, they will be retained on the studio staffs, advancing in salary and position as rapidly as their aptitude warrants.

There is a limit, of course, to the potential earnings of the gag man, but the limit is high enough to make the goal an end in itself. No gag man earns less than one hundred dollars weekly, and several earn ten times as much, which is, perhaps, the limit. In considering the opportunities of the gag man, or his limits, it is well, however, to bear in mind that he will usually earn his salary, whatever it is, every week of the year.

Many gag men have gained public recognition as directors and scenario writers. These two fields, which may prove more highly remunerative in weekly salaries, are open to established gag men. From gag man to scenario writer or director—I have chosen the latter—is a natural step and, quite often, an advisable one. It seems, however, that it would be decidedly inadvisable under any circumstances for a person to lose his identity as a gag man since—I repeat because it is so important—in no other branch of the profession is the supply of talent so much less than the demand.

No specific training can be suggested to one who aspires to a career as a gag man. The essential qualifications are a matter of natural aptitude or innate talent; they cannot be acquired through any amount of study or practice. Many factors may contribute to the development of your talent, but the talent, itself, cannot be caught.

A general education or, for that matter, any type of technical education, is not essential to a gag man. But the value of education as a broadening influence is beyond estimate in any work, and it is an interesting fact that college graduates predominate among the new-comers in the studios. This, of course, is, to a large degree, a reflection of the fact that the man of education has the first call in every business and profession.

Short story writers, playwrights and newspaper columnists comprise the majority of the gag men. Many of these, attracting attention in their former work, have been sought after by motion picture producers. Their training in these other fields undoubtedly enhanced their value as gag men, just as working as a gag man will make one a better gag man. Their experience, however, did not qualify them as gag men; rather, the abilities that establish them in other fields qualified them, also, for comedy construction.

An obvious question that will be in your mind as you read this is: Is there some minor studio job I can take as a stepping stone to gagging? Definitely, the answer is no. There is no place for untrained workers in motion picture production—no place, that is, except among the gag men, who offer talent instead of experience. Every studio worker is a highly trained specialist. The carpenters and electricians, for example, are specialists within their own trades, attending duties for which average carpenters and electricians would be incompetent.

If there is any short cut to fame and fortune in motion pictures, it is as a gag man. Here you may jump to the top overnight, after the short probationary period, which is long enough to show you whether you have the stuff that makes gag men.

EDWIN CAREWE
(1883-1940)

In 1927 Edwin Carewe advised aspiring film directors to provide themselves the widest possible dramatic background, one particularly strong in acting and writing, and, if possible, "a long background of training in the studios" as well. Such wisdom would have been echoed by many of the directors of the period, who saw no point in the fancy "photoplay study" courses that had existed since the earliest days of film. How could any formal schooling hope to train one for so complex and harrowing a profession, they wondered. And indeed, not until Francis Ford Coppola was the graduate of any film school to achieve a breakthrough success in Hollywood. Carewe was using himself as a role model, at least in general terms. Years on the legitimate stage (coupled with a period spent roaming the country as a tramp) provided him with the broad background he demanded of would-be film-makers. In 1914 he broke in with the old Lubin Company and managed to maintain a surprisingly low profile until the late 20's, when he directed a series of ponderous literary adaptations. *Evangeline* (1929) was probably the most successful, visually dazzling in its picture of the scattering of the Acadians, but the others (including *Ramona* and two versions of *Resurrection*) were ill advised. His decision to cast Dolores del Rio and John Boles as Russian lovers in the 1931 *Resurrection* was so misguided that it effectively ended his association with the major studios. He spent his last years working on poverty row projects and religious pictures and, like many directors of his generation, was never able to establish himself in talkies.

DIRECTORIAL TRAINING
EDWIN CAREWE

Motion picture direction, like other angles of the movie-making profession, is far from standardized, and it is well-nigh hopeless to formulate any definite precepts regarding it that might be of value to ambitious youth outside the industry.

As is the case with every other business of magnitude and influence, the better movie jobs require a wealth of background and a rigid training in the fundamentals,—and this is more true today than ever before.

The film industry has grown so rapidly, and is still making such rapid development, and there are such constant changes in the technique of photoplay construction, that it requires an alert, pioneering mind, in the first place, to grasp the spirit and essentials of picture making.

I cannot conceive a successful school for training directors any more than I can conceive a successful academy for scenarists, actors or other artisans of the profession. The nature of film-making forbids any extensive theorizing, and actual first-hand training in all its details and intricacies, if I may be pardoned the generalization, is probably the first and foremost requisite for the uninitiated who aspire to direct pictures.

Many directors of the past and present were recruited from the ranks of the actors and many of the future artists of the megaphone will be likewise drawn from the successful actors of today. A keen sense of the dramatic is a required attribute of a successful director, and a good actor usually is possessed of this talent to a marked degree. An experienced actor before the camera is in constant contact with the methods of film-making, and, if he is an intelligent fellow, he is bound to absorb a certain amount of directorial detail. If he applies himself and makes an earnest effort to learn direction, he is in a fine spot to

From *Breaking into the Movies*, edited by Charles Reed Jones, New York, 1927.

Edwin Carewe directing Count Ilya Tolstoy (eldest son of Leo Tolstoy) in a bit part as an old shoe-mender on *Resurrection* (1927). Robert Kurrle and Al Green at the camera.

prepare himself for the future when his dramatic talents may lose their box office power. I could name many directors of excellent calibre who were graduated from the make-up box to the megaphone.

The writing end of the movies has probably provided the next highest number of directorial successes. A good director has an inherent "story mind," a trade term, and one that is much misunderstood. By a "story mind" is not meant a man who can write particularly, so much as one who knows a good story, can visualize it in terms of celluloid and dramatic technique, and can transpose his ideas into logical and effective screen drama. A brilliant writer often makes a mediocre or inferior scenarist, although I believe that the greatest screen writers are those with a facile gift for expression as well as apt "plot minds." Many capable writers achieve success in their fields of endeavor because of the beauty of their descriptions. It is for this reason that so many of our "best sellers" and great works of fiction fail so miserably, when simmered down, to make effective photoplays. Beauty of writing cannot be transposed successfully to the screen. The spirit of a great story, its dramatic situation, and its plot context, are the elements which make a graphic celluloidic success.

I would say that the greatest directors are those who possess keen dramatic senses plus vivid "story minds" and that, furthermore, the successful directors of the future will all have these two qualifications more than anything else. The scenarist and the director are working more and more in harmony than ever before as the progress of movie-making continues. Their work is closely akin. In the old days, a director paid little attention to his scenarist, and less to the scenarist's script. Often a picture was made with total disregard of the manuscript, the director following out the plot sequence only, and injecting his own dramatic situations and "business" as he went along. Today, and the trend persists, a director and his scenarist work in close relation not only before the filming begins and during the production of the picture as well. The two are in constant conference and, before the "shooting" begins on a story, the director has a polished manuscript before him which has the entire approval of both the writer and the director, and which he can adhere to, with minor exceptions, feeling certain of the results for which he aims.

In all my best pictures, I have had the capable cooperation of my brother, Finis Fox, the scenarist. He was my closest co-operator in the production of *Resurrection*, for which he wrote a masterful script from the original novel by Count Tolstoy, and our success in adhering to the spirit and text of this great story was in no small measure due to our close relationship before and during production. We have worked in similar relationship on my current screen drama *Ramona*, a beautiful love story, based on Helen Hunt Jackson's immortal romance of early California.

There are many items of direction which only experience can drill into one, such as details of lighting, photography, settings, closeups, dissolves and countless other technical tricks. The directors of the future may come from the ranks of the observant cameraman, the electrician, the script clerk or the prop boy. The motion picture industry is an amazing business, and directors have risen from the lowest ranks of the profession. And they have come from all walks of life.

The really successful directors, however, have all had a long background of training in the studios, close to the cameras and scripts.

It would be difficult to advise a young man where to begin in this ever-changing, fast-moving business of movie-making. It would depend entirely upon the young man's abilities and his educational background and training. If he has a gift for writing, together with an imagination and a sense of humor, I would advise him to begin in one of the writing departments of a big studio, preferably the scenario end, if he can establish himself there. If he has a strong personality, and executive ability, he should try for a position in the production department. If he is an actor, I would suggest he get all the work possible before the cameras, if only "extra" or "atmosphere" parts. If all of these avenues are closed to him, I would suggest any number of other positions, easier to obtain, but laden with opportunities for advancement, such as property hand, script boy, electrician's assistant and cameramen's aide.

Any position which will place a young man in the environment of the studios, closely identified with actual film production, is almost certain to lead him to advancement, if he is worthy and has ability.

The movies are a challenge to youth. There are no time-honored precedents, rules and regulations governing the making of motion pictures to damper the enthusiasm of a pioneering spirit or a man with new ideas. In no other business are new ideas so welcome as in this amazing and fast-growing film art. A director may do a thing one way today and do it entirely differently tomorrow. He need not follow a beaten path and do something this or that way because it was done this or that way by someone before.

A barber from Podunk or a school teacher from Oskaloosa may crash his way into the film plants of Hollywood with some fresh ideas and blaze a new and highly successful trail in movie-making. And I might go out on the lot any day and encounter one of my former prop hands or script clerks with a megaphone, directing a forthcoming "epic" of the screen.

After all, there are no formulas for "breaking into the movies" or "becoming film directors."

TRANSITION TO SOUND
(1928–1933)

FRED NIBLO
(1874-1948)

Fred Niblo was an ex-vaudevillian who entered films around 1916, directing his wife in a series of pictures for Thomas Ince and learning the craft of film-making from the master himself. He established a reputation in the early 20's with his direction of such Fairbanks swashbucklers as *The Mark of Zorro* and *The Three Musketeers*, and continued throughout the decade to work with some of the silent screen's most notable stars, including Valentino, Garbo, Gish, and Talmadge. But his most famous film was of course *Ben Hur*, the extravaganza that nearly swamped newly formed M-G-M, inheritors of the project from the classically mismanaged Goldwyn Company. Niblo took over the film while it was still on location in Italy and worked for months in Europe before M-G-M brass ordered the whole unit back to Hollywood. It is somewhat ironic to hear Niblo, director of one of the first "runaway" productions, complain about too many foreign locales in American pictures, and perhaps he is having a little fun here at the reader's expense (*Ben Hur* is not mentioned!). It should also be kept in mind that the other films he mentions, those with foreign talent and locales, are actually Hollywood back-lot productions and not foreign-made at all. But Niblo does put his finger on one of the major changes sweeping Hollywood at the close of the silent period: romantic costume epics had had their day and were inevitably giving way to a new form of screen realism further promoted by the coming of sound.

AMERICANIZING THE AMERICAN PICTURES

FRED NIBLO

To direct an American picture is a favorite ambition of mine. For the last four years I haven't handled a single film that doesn't advertise Europe, Asia or points west! Since 1923 I haven't had the opportunity to show my own people in pictures. Steamship companies and tourist hotels in a dozen countries really owe me royalties.

Why not America—just for a change? Some of my recent locales are South America, India, Holland, Spain, England, Jerusalem, Italy, France, and Austria, in addition to a few mythical kingdoms. Some directors prefer stories of distant lands, but I would gladly try my hand at an American story in preference. If I ever have the pleasure of doing another American drama it will probably seem more foreign than the other nationalities I have learned to consider my own. Eight stories in as many countries make me feel like the proverbial "Man Without a Country."

Such an overwhelming number of foreign films suggests the question of why our public patronizes them. Your average fan will answer that romance is synonymous with foreign spheres. In the broader sense, romance is the elusive, that something which always evades. Many in every audience dream of visiting Europe, and enjoy seeing these dreams realized on the screen. After a day of confinement and routine affairs, the stenographer and clerk go to the neighborhood picture-house to be lifted out of reality into the glamorous whirl of entertainment. The girl will admire the *chic* French gowns and handsome Italian count, while the man admires the hero's athletic skill and daring. They revel in foreign flavors. Similar situations may be equally as interesting in an American story, but they become triply romantic when placed in a foreign setting.

Because of this popular demand, an all-American cast is an

From *Theatre Magazine*, May 1928.

On location off the Italian coast during the shooting of the raft sequence of *Ben Hur* in 1924. Frank Currier and Ramon Novarro stop for a bite of lunch with director Fred Niblo (right).

unknown quantity in movietown. The English tongue is becoming a lost art in Hollywood. Russian, Swedish, and German interpreters are regularly employed in the studios. I have yet to direct one picture in which other nationalities are not dominant. Take, for example, my present feature, *Leatherface*.[1] Vilma Banky is Hungarian; Ronald Colman, English, and Nigel DeBrulier, French.

Lillian Gish is the only American in *The Enemy*, featuring English Ralph Forbes, Swedish Karl Dane, and Viennese Fritzi Ridgway. Norma Talmadge is the native daughter in *Camille*, with Mexican Gilbert Roland, French Rose Dione, and Russian Michael Visaroff.

The Temptress stars Swedish Greta Garbo with Spanish Antonio Moreno and Italian Roy D'Arcy: not one of Yankee descent. *The Devil Dancer* is another instance. Polish Gilda Gray

1. Released under the title *Two Lovers*.

plays the title rôle with English Clive Brook; the rest of the cast is principally Chinese.

Romance need not be limited to foreign spheres. The purpose of the photoplay should be to paint true pictures of American life, as well as the life of any country foreign to ours. I maintain that we would more wholesomely inspire an American audience by showing their co-workers on the screen. Otherwise, the picture industry will be restricted to mere entertainment, rather than entertainment which is inspirational.

After dwelling in marble halls with royalty, the average worker receives an abrupt jolt upon leaving the theatre. His world becomes that of the street car, drug store lunches, and eight-hour drudgery. The stenographer also realizes that no knight on a white charger is going to rescue her from secretarial duties; films are outside the ken of her daily existence. She dismisses them from her mind during business hours.

Most movies offer no practical inspiration translated in terms of everyday experience.

Studio experts agree in their prediction that American pictures, locales, and screen characters will be on the ascendency within the next year. Metro-Goldwyn-Mayer studios, for example, announce many American stories on their new schedule, as well as crediting thirty-four within the past season.

Realism is surely being realized on the screen.

Mr. and Mrs. Everyman will be the stars of the future—The Epic of Everyman.

King Vidor has captured and kept for us the new thought in his *Crowd*. The hero is a twenty-five-dollar-a-week clerk. The girl is a typical typist. They fall in love, marry, become parents, fall out of love, are reconciled, and don't go on living happily ever after. In other words, they're just humans. This picture begins where the average story ends. The bank cashier in the audience will appreciate the characterization, because he didn't get a raise either.

Mary Pickford reflects the new spirit in *My Best Girl*. Mary isn't an heiress in disguise; she doesn't win a beauty contest. The girl clerks it in a five-and-ten store and ends by marrying the boy she loves.

But so long as motion pictures are made, there will be foreign films, though, happily, our national stories gain steadily in popularity. Native pictures strive for a world market and must have universal appeal, including other angles beside the American.

JOHN FORD
(1895-1973)

Although John Ford was later to become the most honored of Hollywood directors (by film-makers as well as critics) his reputation in 1928 was modest at best. While he had proved himself a commercially responsible director, only two or three of his films had won more than passing notice, and pre-1929 Ford, according to Andrew Sarris, seemed to deserve "at most a footnote in film history." But 1928 proved to be a pivotal year for many of the directors on the Fox lot, including Raoul Walsh and Frank Borzage as well as Ford. The importation of F. W. Murnau and his production there of *Sunrise* sparked a terribly self-conscious effort to emulate the dramatic new style of the German UFA studios. The "UFA Style" of lighting, acting, and camerawork infiltrated the films of the most un-self-conscious directors, darkening them with warning shadows and expressionist angles. Ford's great success of 1928, *Four Sons*, was even shot on the leftover *Sunrise* village set. So it is not surprising that he seems particularly concerned with the most important trends in 1928 film-making, the growing internationalization of production style and the rapid approach of talking pictures. Compared with the carping xenophobia of Fred Niblo, Ford's attitudes of internationalization seem remarkably well balanced, but his prediction that talkies will liberate the cinema from narrative material is downright visionary. Nostalgic and sentimental as any good John Ford film, these romantic and often disjointed 1928 "musings" nonetheless bear traces of many key themes that were to obsess his later years, "man's unceasing search for the something he can never find" being only the most obvious.

VETERAN PRODUCER MUSES
JOHN FORD

The world that has its Seven Wonders has, too, its seven stamping grounds of civilization: the Tartar City of Pekin, the Kremlin at Moscow, the Acropolis at Athens, the Alhambra at Granada, the Campagna of Rome, the Hradschin at Prague and the Eyub Cemetery of Stamboul. Within their walls or over their pavements has swept the tremendous torrent of migrations which have summed up into the history of mankind. To them tribes and peoples have brought tribute of cult and culture. From them peoples and tribes have taken tribute of wealth, material or inspirational. They have been pre-eminently the market places of the earth, rising for centuries above the level plains of the commonplaces of event. Through those long periods of their establishment no other monument of man's migratory spirit has arisen to contest their supremacy until the last decade. Then, with the World War over, there began the most remarkable hegira the world has ever witnessed. Westward and eastward the creative artistic brainpower of modern civilization has been making pilgrimage to a town on the California coast of our own United States of America, until today the eighth great stamping ground of the world's relentless horde is Hollywood.

If you believe this statement far-fetched, you have only to stand upon Hollywood Boulevard at almost any hour of the day or night to realize the character of this amazing invasion. English, Irish, Germans, Hungarians, Russians, Italians, South Americans, Mexicans, Chinese, Japanese, Hindus, Persians, Scandinavians, Egyptians, men and women from almost every country on the globe pass in such numbers that you soon pay no more attention to them than to native Americans. If you still believe their coming casual, you need only live through a

John Ford (with pipe) directs Judge Charles Bull in the part of Lincoln for *The Iron Horse* (1924).

day in the director's office of one of the motion picture studios to find that each and every one of the pilgrims has come to Hollywood out of the motive that has brought people to the other stamping grounds—the wish to barter brains for fame or fortune. Every one of them has something to sell, a play, a personality, an idea. In ten years Hollywood has become the great mental marketplace of the world.

The reason for its remarkable development is, of course, the growth of the motion picture industry. Written in the universal language of visual imagery, the pictures have made appeal to the creative artistic impulses of almost all peoples and to almost every class of society. No man has been too high-brow to scorn the medium of motion pictures for his ideas, no man too humble to be denied the chance of success in this most modern medium of a world-old desire to tell a story. In order to understand its extent, however, one must have known Hollywood from its none too distant inception as a studio town. Only by remembering the place as the laboratory of a tentative, though never timid, project can anyone realize the amazing attraction adventure still has for humanity. To those who have the steel of ambition in their minds Hollywood is a magnetic hill pulling them up its slopes, sometimes to rewards, sometimes to failures, but always to trial.

When I came to Hollywood twelve years ago the motion picture industry was comparatively new. Colonel Selig had brought a studio out here because of his thought that a longer period of sunshine through the year would make picture-taking less of financial risk. Other producers had followed him, but the making of pictures was still a matter of hazard, both of life and money. Nearly all the pictures were either absurd comics or wild thrillers. My brother, Francis Ford, was directing one of the latter, and in it I made my last histrionic appearance.

The action of the picture demanded that I walk upon a fifty-foot trestle while the cameras ground record of my progress. No one had informed me of the plot of the story, and, when I saw an engine advancing upon me from the other side of the trestle, I turned tail and ran for life. In frantic disgust the camera men and my brother yelled to me an order to return. I went back, facing the demon locomotive. Just as it came down upon me they shouted the cry to jump. I looked down from the trestle, saw the gulch fifty feet below me—and jumped; but I had ruined the picture irretrievably, for on the verge of taking the fatal plunge I had remembered my good Catholic training and piously blessed myself. The words of brotherly counsel administered when the rushes showed my piety convinced me that I was not destined to be an actor, and so, as speedily as I could, I got a job in the directing department.

If I hoped to leave hazard behind in leaping from the trestle of acting to the gulch of directing, I was speedily disillusioned. It was, however, a different kind of hazard that I found at the director's end of picture production. It was the time of real pioneering in picture making. The great trail blazer of the

films, David Wark Griffith, was swinging the axe of his fron-
tiering, devising methods, securing effects that were to make
pictures a real artistic medium as well as a stupendous industry.
Those were the times when first nights meant something beyond blare and lights and noise. To those of us who were fortunate in working in Griffith's influence they meant the revelation of inspirational genius. The showing of those early
pictures in the old Philharmonic Auditorium in Los Angeles
meant more to the film industry and to the making of Hollywood than all the spectacles of inauguration that Hollywood
promotes in these later days and nights.

Not for a moment would I seem to imply in this statement
of the value of that pioneering that the motion pictures have
ended their pioneering. All art is fluid, and no phase of it more
so than the development of motion pictures. Technic that is
daring today will be outdated tomorrow. The quality of uni-
versality in pictures is in itself a pitfall, for the director who
strives too hard to represent humanity by rubbing down the
rough edges of racial and personal traits is likely to make his
work drab and colorless. The picture likely to attain great and
wide success must have its theme of universal appeal but its people vivid. It is my belief that it should be true to its setting—for
instance, that Germany should be represented by the sons,
since it is essentially a man's country, but that Ireland, being
matriarchal, should be visualized as Mother Machree.[1] This
could not, perhaps, be carried on indefinitely, but it is certain
that the relationship of background to character and picture
development will be increasingly important in the future of
the film.

The question of background has become something of a
problem with American producers just now, because of the
fact that nearly all the foreign outcry against American motion
pictures has been inspired by the belief that it is the background of the American pictures that is luring immigration
toward the United States. A current story declared that the
Russian leather supply is being exhausted because of the de-

1. An allusion to two of Ford's 1928 releases, *Four Sons* and *Mother
Machree*.

mand of Russian peasants for leather shoes, a luxury with which most of them became acquainted through the sight of them in the pictures. Whether or not this is true, it is certainly true that the European peasant, or miner, or tradesman or craftsman sees on the screen pictures which show an average standard of living in the United States much higher than that of his own land, and becomes imbued with a desire to give himself and his children the advantage of such a standard. That is the political reason for the ban on American pictures in so many countries of Europe.

All such bans, however, are transitory in view of the possible future of the pictures. We are only at the beginning of the use of pictures as factors in education. There is no doubt of the value of pictures in visual education nor of the effect of them upon the child mind. Tests of the receptivity of the child mind to motion pictures have shown the enormous possibilities of screen portrayal. There is no reason why history should not be taught younger children almost exclusively by this method. We should regret intensely, though, the use of visual education without the corresponding development of auditory imagery, for the pictures are just now on the threshold of one of their most important developments, the use of sound as well as of sight images.

With the same capacity for experiment in the adaptation of sound to sight that he has shown in all his work, William Fox has been working on the use of the movietone. The synchronization of the instrument recording sound with the movement in the picture is practically perfected, but the field of its artistic possibilities is not yet furrowed. It will, I think, revolutionize the casting of films, for inevitably a different type of actor and actress will be required to vocalize the roles. It was, you may recall, by her voice that the true princess made herself known. It will also give to motion pictures the chance to project symphonic qualities for the creation and holding of a mood, so that pictures will no longer be limited to pure and simple narrative for material.

Just as in all art, however, the simple story will always remain the most effective. Morality may be a relative term, but the producer who plans his product upon that relativity makes an artistic as well as a financial mistake. The continuation of the broad scale of production at the Fox studios through a time of near panic in Hollywood has been no accident but the logical result of William Fox's policy of refusing to countenance filth in the pictures made in his studios. The pictures that people remember for years are not the spectacularly sensational films, but the heart-interest stories of plain people interpreting vital emotions.

Because almost every one in the world has at least one story, and because he believes that his story may win the golden prize of production, Hollywood is bound to remain the Mecca of the ambitious as long as the pictures remain the broadest medium of expression. Just as Greeks and Romans and Tartars and Moors and Cossacks and Turks and Huns have left their imprint upon the places that stand memorial to their passing, so the historian of the future, looking back upon our high-speeding, high-powered civilization, will choose as its focal point Hollywood of the hills, pointing to it as crossroads for Orient and Occident, as market square for brains and beauty, talent and genius, the ballyhoo bazaar of a whirling world. Because, however, I have lived in that Hollywood for twelve years, seeing and feeling the heartaches, the joys and the sufferings that are the lot of every mother's son of us, I shall have to tell the truth, however disillusioning it may sound, that Hollywood is, for all its Kleigs and cameras, all its parties and bootleggers, all its gayeties and extravagances, a human city. Knowing it for what it is, a town of success and failure, of aspiration and achievement, of doubt and despondency, I have come to feel that the other seven stamping grounds have been in their times no more and no less than this town of mine, not high monuments of man's accomplishment, but turbulent plazas of man's unceasing search for the something he can never find.

EDMUND GOULDING
(1891-1959)

This is one of the first extended analyses of the possibilities of the sound film, actually pre-dating the appearance of the first all-talking pictures. Edmund Goulding, a British actor who came to Hollywood as a writer and had been directing since 1925, was sent by Adolph Zukor to New York to investigate the Fox-Case sound system and to direct test footage. His report shows an astonishing sensitivity, describing the application of off-screen sound, interesting new possibilities for camera movement, and a number of asynchronous tricks that were too radical to ever be adopted. Goulding's own talkies were interesting, though hardly remarkable, and his career is best remembered for such well-mounted studio classics as *Grand Hotel* (M-G-M), *Dark Victory* (Warners), and *The Razor's Edge* (Fox). While his best films are often considered "actors' pictures," he also possessed a peculiar visual style which seems to have been unique in Hollywood. Goulding had an aversion to seeing his characters walk out the edge of the frame, and whenever possible had the cameras follow them until they literally disappeared from "sight" through a doorway or behind an obstruction. While his camera crews often found this an absurdly theatrical form of staging, in reality it opened up vast areas of off-screen space and gave his pictures an extremely solid and naturalistic geography. Goulding has never had many critical defenders, but any Hollywood director with so distinctive a handling of screen space, and so prophetic a grasp of sound possibilities, is certainly deserving of further study.

THE TALKERS IN CLOSE-UP
EDMUND GOULDING

By lack of sound, motion pictures have lost more than their producers or spectators have been conscious of. Silence implies the loss of fifty per cent of the observer's logical emotional reaction.

Among other things which silence must have eliminated has been the sense of fear. If that is roused while the other faculties are assuring safety, it is one of the most fascinating of all psychological experiences.

No producer or director of a motion picture ever has truly thrilled an audience with actual fear by showing them the silent drama. The eye is not afraid. Fear comes through the ear or sense of pain.

The picture has suffered for the lack of sound exactly as the radio now suffers from the lack of sight.

With the sound and sight picture it is about to happen. With all the various perceptive powers of auditors engaged and functioning with completeness the situation will be startlingly changed.

Complete conveyance of complete ideas will be more than a mere novelty. It will bring about a change in human life. It will be an upward step in racial development, which is dependent, absolutely, on the arts of communication.

And with the speaking motion pictures now at hand, with its capacities for producing reactions on the human mind far more vividly than those of the old, silent pictures, the industry has a new necessity for thought along these lines. It can forestall restrictions by wise procedures now or by unintelligent methods, it can bring new and almost endless troubles on itself.

The sound picture is a possession almost of the ultimate.

Now, the whole will be presented, for the story, being seen

From *National Board of Review Magazine*, July 1928. Reprinted by permission.

Edmund Goulding (under tripod) directs Joan Crawford in *Sally,
Irene and Mary* (1925). John Arnold mans the camera as sideline
violinist provides a mood-inducing accompaniment.

and heard, will be fully sensed for the first time in human history. This theatre of the future will completely picture human
life. The world and all its human mind and soul reactions, every
detail of its drama—its tensity, throbs, holiest emotions and
worst iniquities will be, not merely thinly imitated, but will be
reproduced in actuality, including sound! What an inconceiv-
able vaudeville is now being born! No audience in any theatre
on earth ever has had the great train tragedy presented to it
in the full force of its true terror; ever has had complete conception of it and a full emotional reaction. Now, with the machinery at hand for such full presentation, we must be cautious
even while we are bold and enterprising. Neurologists and psy-
chiatrists can tell you more of this than I can.

They probably will!

I have heard a salesman say: "This film will knock them out
of their seats——" No silent film ever has actually done that.

But tomorrow, he may be right!

My months of actual experimentation and observation have been full of illumination for a man who has been, in turn, scenario writer, playwright of the spoken drama and director of the motion picture and so forth. I do not believe that the talking pictures now to be seen in New York City, with the exception of the news reels, give much of my indications of the talking picture's possibilities. I scarcely think they indicate, at all, what it will be.

Actually, they are but silent motion pictures accompanied by synchronized, but wholly mechanical and artificial sounding voices or instrumental music. Their novelty may be called the only element which invites attention to them. They are scarcely even samples of that which is to come. They are old-style movies with a little sound superimposed upon them.

The clever craftsman in sound pictures will set a camera at a sufficient distance from a scene so that it will record the conversation which may be in progress as diffused, not emphasized —virtually showing pantomime accompanied by indefinite sound.

The camera will move forward and back, according to its mood. It will move in a spirit of inquiry. Only when it wants to hear what is said will it move up for its sound close-up. The drama will proceed accompanied by all the vague subconscious sounds of life from the song of the bird to the wash of the waves and the sigh of the wind. Nature's obligation to her own drama.

The roaring mob in the street will be heard and not "cut to." The distant choir in the church will chant the entrance of the star. Pantomime will be carried to its ultimate, as it is now (or should be) in the silent picture, and only when dialog is indispensable to story progress will it be heard. This will not complicate, it will simplify. Short sentences will characterize the new dialogue.

The new director will be more DeMaupassant than Dickens —terse, tense, succinct.

The eye hates to be teased. The ear revels in it. Sight and sound are now wed in illusion. The soul of Beethoven moving with those of Shakespeare and Rembrandt supplying the complete drama.

Sound negative will soon be made cheaper than silent negative, because there is at once eliminated one of the great elements of waste in picture manufacture. Overhead lost through delay in decision and lack of pre-visualization.

The producer will select a story. The sound picture scenarist will adapt it. When the director is assigned he will engage a cast and rehearsals will begin. At the end of a week or more the producer, accompanied by his engineers and studio technicians, will witness a rehearsal in a specially designed small theatre. He will hear the dialogue, watch the action in much the same way as a stage producer now watches his final rehearsals. He will see his picture before it gets to the plant. He will criticize, change, and express himself generally, to return again to another rehearsal when his directions have been carried out.

Meantime, the engineers and technicians of the studio will work from a prompt copy of the script made during rehearsals by the scenario writer from the director's mechanical design and prepare sets with metronomes set in positions indicated and so forth.

Thus, when the producer, satisfied with his dress rehearsal, sends his director and company to his plant to manufacture a commodity known as a sound motion picture, he can be reasonably certain that nothing but a technical accident can delay the expensive schedule of actual making.

For a long time yet they will make a silent picture of a subject at the same time that they are making sound pictures. A great many of the silent scenes will be shot on the sound sets. The added scenes necessary will be shot probably after the sound picture has been completed. The same director will probably do the two jobs.

Most of the best men associated with picture making have developed a subconscious technique and are not bothered about anything much outside the story problems, so that when the story problems are solved as they would be in these cases, the silent picture will not present any difficulties. It will be purely a matter of organization.

Thus the sound picture will be made to schedule and should alterations and additions be found necessary after its completion they will be attended to, again after proper rehearsals at which the producer will decide if justifying the cost involved.

For the present, however, the producer of sound pictures will operate principally on short stuff, comedies and dramas in small equipped studios in New York. As his confidence grows and he absorbs a more definite knowledge of technique and engineering while engineers and technicians get more knowledge of pictures and while the personnel of the speaking theatre become more expert in motion pictures, and vice versa, the larger talking picture will emerge.

The problem before the industry, taxed as it is to the limit, and with great efforts confronting it in connection with its present obligations to manufacture silent pictures already arranged for, with every good man in demand and assigned, and with other activities rather firmly set in old and well established molds, will be how to, slowly and with safety, efficiently yet economically, change the gearage of its huge machine, readjust its personnel, find new intelligences and make whatever changes may be necessary without untoward cost or dislocation.

The new intelligence, whether drawn from the present personnel or brought in from elsewhere, must be of the best. Men of past achievements must work almost as students at the new task, but because of their past achievements, these students probably will want high prices during the period of their education, which, coupled with their loss from the productive work of making silent pictures, will be something which the producer must cope with.

There is a real cause for worry there. His personnel is an expensive one. His expensive student may not be effective in the new medium and so his loss of time from the old one may prove to have been wholly ineffective; endeavors to make good in the new line even may harm his usefulness in the old. But there is this about it. This process may bring to an end a lot of high priced accidents.

For his acting talent the producer of sound pictures will be able to draw from the speaking theatre and vaudeville. His demand will be enormous. It will be like asking an extensive blood transfusion from one very old gentleman.

In acting talent, the new actor will bring with him to the screen a new kind of voice. The fallacy of voice training will soon be discovered. The pompous, grandiloquent actor will be a nuisance. Grand sayings in sound pictures will be as utterly ridiculous as they usually are in actual fact.

The soft, insinuating voice of an Elsie Janis, the attractive utterance of a Whispering Smith, the characteristic gruff shout of a policeman, voices which can imply so much more than their words say, will be sought-for treasures. Voices will be effective more because of their color and implication than because of any mere sound quality. Only when talking motion picture projection has been developed to a perfection not as yet attained will the quality and tone of the voice, its graded richnesses and tonal picturesquenesses be of interest to the public.

The girl who in a close-up can sing a soft lullaby to her baby and whisper—"Good night, my darling," in such a way that the camera might be listening in through the key-hole—she will be the new star.

Vocal tricks, screams, sobs, snores, laughter, will be among the valuable tools for story telling.

First will come the one-act play and the short story made by the small units of the principal companies. They will not be longer than two reelers, and plenty of material will be found ready. To these small producing units will be sent from time to time, in interchange, from the silent production companies, directors, cameramen and actors, its new group profiting by the discoveries of its predecessors on the job in the producing studios, which for a long time to come will be virtually experimental laboratories.

There will be many new theories, and discussion of them will wax fast, furious and fierce. Nobody will be wholly right, few will be wholly wrong, between the lot of them great things will be created.

The technique of the new form of scenario writing will develop quickly because the art of the writer of the spoken-play already is developed as is that of the silent photo-play. The welding of the two should not be difficult, and intriguing possibilities exist in the idea. The sound picture dramatist will struggle to develop the high art of expressing a maximum amount of drama with a minimum of words.

Retrospects in pictures have recently been called old-fashioned. To dissolve back from a present time scene to one of a past time, necessary for an explanation, has been held to be an inept thing in the modern silent picture. But we must remember that seventy-five per cent of all human conversation deals with retrospect. Thus, admitting the ineffectiveness of silent drama retrospect, we find the films of the old order suffering another severe handicap to be added to the one already mentioned due to their inability to produce upon the minds of their spectators the impression of fear. With these two elements missing from their drama they are handicapped indeed.

And here, again, the speaking picture promises to show advantages. Consider character in a witness box being asked to describe what happened on the night that he dined with Mr. and Mrs. Greene, which was the night that Mr. Greene murdered his wife.

In the new sound picture we dissolve from the witness box, as the witness commences his narration, to the home of Mr. and Mrs. Greene before the crime, and there show the scene which the witness in the box has begun to describe before the dissolve into the home, of the Greenes, where we watch events unfold as the witness' voice drones on, descriptively—mechanically, calm, telling of the same events which we are witnessing.

There is the witness being shown in by the butler, there he is as he stands listening tensely, his attention caught by sounds of quarreling while waiting for his host to receive him; there he is, later, as he notices the diamond dog collar of Mrs. Greene, which consequently was found to have been covering a bruise caused by Mr. Greene's earlier attempt to strangle her.

Throughout this action the voice, as of the witness in the chair, continues. It will be as if both the witness box and the actual crime in course of perpetration, were simultaneously visible. Here is the perfect retrospect.

Picture-making, in the new era which is dawning, will be a sounder, simpler thing than ever it has been before. The two-reel business and almost the feature business will start all over again.

The present strain for material, though new material always will be in demand, will be alleviated or brought to an end. Scarcely anything has been made in silent pictures that cannot successfully be remade in sound pictures, not merely because we shall be adding sound, but because the old tales will have a new dramatic value; they will be different.

The high spot of the speaking picture will not be the high spot of the silent picture. With the introduction of the use of sound in pictures will come a change not due so much to the mere addition of sound but to a new dramatic form which the use of sound will both permit and inspire.

The infant industry has taken the ribbons from her hair. She has put away some of her bright toys—she is growing up. She may have a child, one day, and the child's name may be Television, but that's another story.

F. W. MURNAU
(1888 - 1931)

The modesty of this piece, in which Murnau claims that "I do not know how to make pictures," must have seemed strange to his Hollywood co-workers, who found him demanding and egotistical, a man who felt he was the greatest director in the world, and willing and able to prove it! The predictions that he makes are interesting, but television, 3-D, and the specialized "art house" movie theater were already topics of wide discussion. Rather more important are his references to characteristic Murnau preoccupations and the weight he gives to each. The idea that films will bring about a universal brotherhood and thereby "end war" was a subject he wrote about more than once, and stems from the "international language" days of his German period, and his association with writers like Carl Mayer. He feels it important to defend his use of dramatic camera angles, and boasts proudly of the new moving camera equipment that has been created for his latest film (*The Four Devils*). Perhaps most interesting of all is his desire to direct a film in which background settings would be reduced to an absolute minimum and would serve no dramatic function whatsoever. Murnau was of course the director who moved the silent German film away from the studio constructions of *Caligari* days, as early as his 1922 *Nosferatu*, and eventually ended his career with the completely non-studio production of *Tabu*. But all of his hopes and speculations went for nothing. Unlike the films, Murnau himself had no future, dying tragically in a freak car crash only a few years later.

FILMS OF THE FUTURE
F. W. MURNAU

What is the future of the motion pictures? Alas, I am not an oracle!

If I could answer you I would be, perhaps the most important man in the world, for the screen has as great potential power as any other existing medium of expression. Already it is changing the habits of mankind, making people who live in different countries and speak different languages, neighbors. In the future it may educate our children's children even better than books. It may put an end to war, for men do not fight when they understand each other's heart. I am of the opinion that as a world force, the screen has possibilities beyond imagining.

It is very strange to me that we have a generation born and grown to manhood since the motion pictures were invented, and yet so far, no great Poet of the new art has arisen. All great arts have had great artists born to understand them as no other men can, and the motion picture is the single art expression of our age. Do you smile at that and think: "This man, Murnau, is a foreigner and all foreigners are a little odd!" But when a genius in expressing the heart and soul through that tiny strip of celluloid comes to us some day you shall see that I am right in calling the motion pictures an "Art."

Such a one is growing among you now, perhaps many such, for singers know more about song than silent men, a painter must be born and not made, and there will be great geniuses of the screen who will know instinctively what the motion pictures can do that no other form of art can do. Now we must use novels, stage plays, short stories, history as a basis for our film plots. But in the future scenario writers will think screen ideas, and dream screen dreams. The directors of the future will realize that the motion picture is a separate art that has

From *McCall's Magazine*, September 1928.

Comfortably seated on his camera dolly, director F. W. Murnau poses with his cameramen and assistants during the production of *Sunrise* (1927). Manning the two cameras at left are Karl Struss and Charles Rosher.

nothing in common with the stage and can express fine shades of thought and feeling that are impossible to the spoken drama.

When this Poet of the pictures comes to Hollywood he will not be met at the station by bands and flowers. He may have a hard time getting by the studio gatemen, and a harder time convincing the makers of the movies that he can show them something new and worth their while! That is natural. Always men have shrunk from the idea of change.

But when he does make his way inside the studio gates he will find some one at last who will listen to him. And from that moment the motion pictures will change until perhaps we shall hardly recognize them as the same things we make so clumsily today.

For many years the "movies," as I have learned to say since I am in America, have not developed a great deal. People said, "we must do this and that because we have always done this and that." The audiences learned exactly what to expect. Pictures in the past have too often been made by a formula, so much of scenery, so much love making, the good rewarded, the villain punished, everything finished off very neatly. Too often pictures have made the world banal instead of revealing new heights and depths in life. One would think to look at them that there were only beautiful women in the world and young men with broad shoulders and flashing eyes!

I think that pictures of the future will show *persons* rather than screen personalities, humanity instead of popular movie stars. In *Sunrise* some of the critics were severe with me because of the ugly two-colored wig I allowed Janet Gaynor to wear. They complained that it extinguished her beauty and made her almost plain. They did not guess that that was exactly what I was trying to do! I wished Janet to play, not Janet Gaynor, the screen beauty, but a poor stupid little peasant girl. I had to submerge her physical beauty to emphasize the beauty of her heart. It was a difficult thing, trying to suppress that little actress' loveliness! But to me, beauty is not going to be the chief requisite of the stars of the future. They must photograph well, naturally, but it is their sympathy, their understanding of the heart, and their ability to show that understanding that will be important.

The chief change they made in the movies for a while was to spend more money, and then still more money on pictures—big sets, elaborate historical costumes, mob scenes, the destruction of property, spectacles, "epics." They advertised as the great reason for going to see their picture: "It Cost a Million Dollars," until people perhaps came to feel that they were not being treated fairly unless they saw a city burned down or five thousand extras all in wigs and costumes on the screen at the same time. That, I firmly believe, is not what the pictures of the future will have to do.

I think that audiences are getting tired of crowded sets and involved plots. It is like eating too much cake. I think they would like to see something simple and real. I think that in the film of the future the story itself will be more important than splendid sets and costumes. One of my dreams is to make a motion picture of six reels, with a single room for setting and a table and chair for furniture. The wall at the back would be blank, there would be nothing to distract from the drama that was unfolding between a few human beings in that room. Some day I shall make that picture.

The motion picture of the future will not cost so much. It is the mechanical end of picture making now that is holding us back. Forty percent of a director's time is spent on getting the machinery of the studio arranged as he wishes. By the time he comes to the actual making of the scene where he needs all his creative ability, all his power of the imagination, he is already tired from his struggles with wood and iron and canvas.

The camera, that is different. They have experimented with the camera. It will do many strange and fine things now, almost as much as I can ask of it. But one must keep a large and expensive cast waiting for hours while the lights are moved about. Then when at last the scene is being made perhaps a tiny bulb blows out, or a screw comes loose and there is a five thousand dollar a day cast held up again while the trouble is repaired.

The present machinery of the studios will not be enough for the director of the future. Even now I ask that they make me especial equipment so that I can get my camera where I want it. The picture I am working on now is a circus story and naturally the camera must not stand stock still in one spot in such a gay place as a circus! It must gallop after the equestrienne, it must pick out the painted tears of the clown and jump from him to a high box to show the face of the rich lady thinking about the clown.

So I have had them build me a sort of travelling crane with a platform swung at one end for the camera. My staff has nicknamed it the "Go-Devil." The studios will all have Go-Devils, some day, to make the camera mobile.

They say that I have a passion for "camera angles." But I do not take trick scenes from unusual positions just to get startling effects. To me the camera represents the eye of a person, through whose mind one is watching the events on the screen. It must follow characters at times into difficult places, as it crashed through the reeds and pools in *Sunrise* at the heels of the Boy, rushing to keep his tryst with the Woman of the City. It must whirl and peep and move from place to place as swiftly as thought itself, when it is necessary to exaggerate for the audience the idea or emotion that is uppermost in the mind of the character. I think the films of the future will use more and more of these "camera angles," or as I prefer to call them these "dramatic angles." They help to photograph thought.

I think that some day in the near future there will be many different kinds of movie theaters, just as there are many kinds of theaters of spoken plays. There will be houses that show films made especially for young people. There will be others devoted entirely to talking pictures. There will be places where the program picture of today will be shown, intended only to entertain and amuse. And there will also be theaters, not very many perhaps, but a few in every city where the very highest type of films may be seen *and where nothing else will be shown.*

The Chinese have an ancient proverb, "A picture is worth ten thousand words." Yet I think that this new invention, the talking picture, is here to stay. Those who saw that great drama of the air, *Wings,* at the early previews without the movietone attachment, and later at the regular performance with the roar of the motors, the whirr of wings, the tattoo of machine guns will admit that the sounds increased the intensity of the action.

There will be, before long, motion pictures in which the characters speak their lines from beginning to end. Perhaps before these words are printed you will see such a picture on the screen. In some ways the spoken words will hamper the picture. For one, the action will be slower, for one can represent a long conversation by pantomime in a few feet of film.

I do not think that all pictures will become talking pictures. There will be silent drama as now, except that it will have developed into its perfect form, a film without a written title.

Pictures may be made understandable without captions which interrupt the rush of the drama. I have proved that myself. *The Last Laugh* had only one title when it was shown abroad, and I have never heard of anyone who did not understand its meaning.

Color pictures are another future development of the screen. There will be occasional movies in natural colors just as there are tinted prints to put upon your walls as well as etchings.

There will be other technical changes in the next ten or twenty years. The three dimension movie will be the usual thing instead of the occasional effect. I produced an appearance of depth in the marsh sequence of *Sunrise* by a trick arrangement of lights and shadows. Other directors have experimented with sets in which the floors rise and fall, and the lines of doors, ceiling and furniture slant sharply according to the laws of perspective. But there is a simpler and less expensive device already in preparation which I may not explain now, but which will produce the same illusion of depth and distance as the old-fashioned stereopticon slides.

Perhaps too, there will be a radical change in the way motion pictures are projected. I understand one producer is experimenting in a method of showing a picture without a screen so that it looks as though the characters themselves were present in the room in which the audience sits! Television and the radio may bring the movies of the future through the air into your own home at the turn of a key.

But to me as a director the most interesting difference between the motion picture of today and that of tomorrow lies, not in the mechanics of the studio or theater but in the treatment of stories and the work of players.

They call me a "mental director" by which they mean that I try to make the players understand the minds of the characters they are asked to portray, so that they will know their very thoughts. I talk to an actor of what he should be *thinking*, rather than what he should be *doing*.

I do not merit such a high-sounding name as "mental director." I am feeling my way as we are all doing, among the rapid changes that are coming into the motion pictures. No one really knows how to make pictures yet. I do not know how to make pictures. Developments of the future will make our present day efforts appear as the play of children, as the stuttering of an unsure tongue.

PAUL FEJOS
(1898-1963)

A director of eccentric and undisciplined talents, Paul Fejos spent a good deal of his life as a research biologist and anthropologist. In his lighter moments he directed plays in New York, films all over Europe, and was for a short time the top director at Universal City. Fejos had won considerable attention with *The Last Moment* (1927), the first feature-length experimental film produced in America, and Carl Laemmle, Jr., felt he was just the man to handle Universal's most important productions: he was given the run of the studio. The films he directed there display a dazzling sense of camera dramatics, filled with dizzying wipes, multiple superimpositions, and vertiginous camera movements. *Lonesome*, the story of a romance that blossoms at Coney Island, has been hailed by French historian Georges Sadoul as one of the most important precursors of neo-realism; *Broadway* was an early musical designed around a mammoth camera crane and a spectacular "cubistic" nightclub set that filled the world's largest soundstage. But Fejos' sense of narrative was weak, and he ignored his actors to concentrate completely on camera effects. When he was passed over for direction of *All Quiet on the Western Front*, Fejos slipped out of his contract and eventually returned to Europe, where he ended his film career as a director of anthropological documentaries, and then returned to scientific research as director of the Wenner-Gren Foundation. While the confusions of the transition to sound have completely obscured his American career, any survey of that period must eventually come to terms with his rare, inconsistent, and definitely eccentric Hollywood films.

ILLUSION ON THE SCREEN
PAUL FEJOS

Millions go every night to the motion picture theatres of the world. They go there always seeking the elusive mood of a child listening to a fairy tale; seeking, in other words, the photoplay, which will for a few brief hours lift them out of the monotony of their own humdrum existence into the enchanted realm of make-believe. Children listening to fairy tales imagine themselves to be the Prince Charming or the enchanted Princess of the story, for there begins the endless road that leads to romance. First came the minstrel, then the play and now the motion picture—for all of them are but fairy tales grown up, their tellers and their audiences nothing more than the adult searching for the childhood ideal.

The motion picture has the broadest appeal of all forms of entertainment because of its scope, the biggest stage to play upon. Out here in Hollywood, over in London, Paris or Berlin, we who tell the tales revel in them no less than those who hear and see them, for, after all, the flower of fairyland is in spinning the yarn. Those who listen are necessarily limited by what others have to tell, while those who make them up are bounded only by their imaginations.

And now, as the latest contribution of science to the world of make-believe, we have not only the motion picture at which to look, but the music to hear; not only players to see, but their voices now come to our ears. This new sound picture should be neither of the stage nor of the screen, but quite a different manner of expression, although one somewhere between them.

The future of the talking picture obviously embraces the furthest limits of the screen. For never could an audience be an actual participant of a play upon the screen. The talking pic-

From *National Board of Review Magazine*, June 1929. Reprinted by permission.

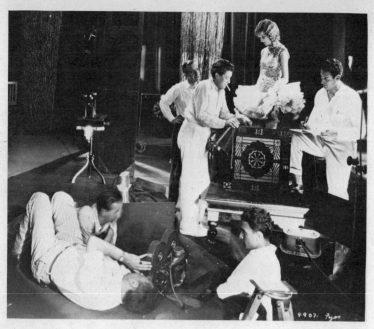

Paul Fejos (with megaphone) adjusts a prop for Mary Philbin while cameraman Hal Mohr lines up a low angle shot for *The Last Performance* (1928-29).

ture, however, will in its perfection accomplish the making of the audience a party to the dramatic conflict.

The sound picture, at the present time, is so new as to have no standard whatsoever by which its limitations can be judged. When it is perfected—as in time it undoubtedly will be—it may prove to be so plastic as to be the ideal medium for the picturization of our fairy tales, making them so realistic that they accomplish to the ultimate the purpose for which they are told. In the audible picture, it is certain, there is no line of demarcation between the characters and the audiences such as is inevitably formed by the footlights of the stage, nor is there the spectre of unreality, or uninterrupted action, such as the titles of a silent picture.

Even in a silent picture, the camera is the audience. What the camera records is the audience's point of view and a picture can be made in such a way that the camera, instead of merely witnessing the action, enters into it.

It is the enormous dynamics of the screen, as compared with the confines of the stage, which should thus enable audiences to participate in the doings of the characters.

Nor is the achievement of this objective a lowly goal for which to strive. For an hour where dreams come true is worth years of strife in the present mad scramble for wealth; nothing could be closer to the pursuit of happiness than the fantasy produced by a few thousand feet of realistic bits of photography.

Talking pictures are a medium characteristic of America, where the prevailing, dominant motive is speed. In Vienna, the atmosphere of Marie Therese still prevails, life tainted with sophistication; in Berlin generals on horses are still the mood. Statues of them everywhere. The talking picture, however, must develop its own technique. There must be new plays, sound pictures even as there were motion-picture plays. The stage play, the musical comedy, the operetta will not fulfill the articulate picture's destiny.

Herein lies the real future of the screen, for the sound picture, whether we welcome or regret it, is here. It has captured the approval of the multitudes.

Of color photography in connection with sound pictures I am inclined at the present stage of development to be skeptical. So far, reality in color has not been approached. The real medium of sound pictures, I believe, is in black and white. As yet color films have only succeeded in transferring the prismatic hues which belong on the teacups to the screen, making of men and women not human beings but painted dolls. That is a start, however.

There is no doubt that the perfect photoplay—perfect mechanically and technically, that is, though not of necessity perfect in illusion, which really is the only perfection—should include in its projection complete naturalness of voice and sound, color and depth. Voice and sound are already so nearly natural that perfection can only be a question of a short time. Color and depth, however, are a different problem. Of them, possibly, the third dimension will be the most difficult to achieve, although it is possible even now to obtain an illusion of depth simply by photographing the principal object beyond a second focusing object, the latter nearer the lens.

In the light of what has already come to pass in the motion picture field, we who make pictures come to discern, dimly perhaps, the perfect picture and to strive toward it as the possibility for an amazing medium of illusion.

MONTA BELL
(1891-1958)

When sound arrived, Paramount reactivated its Astoria studio to take better advantage of the Broadway acting and directing talent it was hoping to use in talking pictures. Jeanne Eagels in *The Letter* and the Marx Brothers in *Animal Crackers* were two of the films that resulted from this scheme, a project supervised by an ex-Chaplin gag-writer named Monta Bell. Bell's first theatrical experience was gained with various stock companies in the Washington area, after which he drifted into publishing there, and in New York. Here he met Charlie Chaplin, who assigned him to ghost-write the Chaplin memoir "My Trip Abroad." As part of the Chaplin group, which also included Harry d'Arrast and Mal St. Clair, he was exposed to Chaplin's meticulous style of comedy construction and complete immersion in all aspects of film-making. He worked for various studios before being assigned to Paramount's east coast operation when sound arrived, a position no doubt intended to take advantage of his experience in stock. Bell, who never quite achieved first-rank success as a director, is usually dismissed by historians as one of the many Lubitsch imitators of the period (although his *Man, Woman and Sin* has achieved at least some cult support). In this article his thoughts on the proper uses of the dialogue film seem strikingly modern. He prefers a trashy, but highly styled melodrama like *Alibi* to a more respectable, literate, and ultimately static photoplay such as *Madame X*. His pre-release support of Mamoulian's *Applause* is similarly adventurous. But despite such an apparent grasp of the potential of the talkies, Bell claims a preference for the silent film, an attitude shared by his mentor, Charles Chaplin.

THE DIRECTOR: HIS PROBLEMS
AND QUALIFICATIONS

MONTA BELL

I feel like an amateur in my own business. In other words, with the advent of the talking pictures, I find myself back in the ranks of the amateurs who, while very keen, are also approaching something new with more or less trepidation. Not that my years of experience as a motion picture director have been wasted. Far from it. I believe that the director of silent pictures is far in advance of his brother-director of stage productions, as we both approach this new medium.

But I am certainly not kidding myself about it. I know that I must adapt myself to something new just as rapidly as the entire motion picture industry has adapted itself. For, in the short space of one year, every picture company in America, in embracing the lusty new infant, "the talkies," has changed its entire program and its entire method of working.

A year ago I came East to the Long Island Studio of Famous Players, knowing nothing whatever about sound. To date I have learned a little and I am hoping before another year to feel more sure of myself. At the time I came East I did not like talking pictures. I do not like them today. This, however, is personal taste. I do not know whether the public likes them or not. I do not believe any one can tell that, because the public is just being fed talking pictures and as long as that is their enforced diet, they are going to take it.

If some one company had the courage—perhaps it would have taken a very rash courage—to hold aloof from the hysteria that brought these things about so rapidly—to produce only silent pictures during the year, I am not sure but that they might have found considerable market for these same silent pictures. However, that is past. Talking pictures are here and here to stay.

I had some theories at the time I came East. My theories prin-

From *Theatre Arts Monthly*, September 1929.

Courtroom dramas were especially popular in the early days of talkies. Here director Monta Bell (center) poses with Leatrice Joy on the set of *The Bellamy Trial* (1928-29).

cipally were that we were still making motion pictures; that if we continued to keep that fact in our minds and use sound and spoken dialogue where the effectiveness of motion pictures would be enhanced, we were on the right track. I believed that a year ago. I believe it today. I think that the best talking pictures I have seen during the past year are: *Speakeasy*, *Alibi* and *Bulldog Drummond*. I had nothing to do with any of these pictures. I simply say I believe they are the best ones that have been made, not because of the quality of their stories or expertness of their dialogue or acting, but because all three were moving pictures. I believe that the prescription is right even though some of the elements are not. In other words, that if the dramatic quality inherent in *The Letter*, in *Madame X*, *Gentlemen of the Press* or *Close Harmony* were equally evident in *Speakeasy*, *Alibi* and *Bulldog Drummond*, I think we would approximate talking pictures that would hold their own artistically in any season, even five years hence.

It is interesting to note that a year ago, before I had ever seen a sound studio, I wrote an article for the *North American Review*[1] on talking pictures. I am quoting some things from that article simply because after a year of intensive experience with the new medium, I find that my beliefs have become convictions.

"There is no getting away from the fact that that which the eye sees is the chief attraction of the screen. After about fifty feet of a 'picturized' overture I begin to get restless. My eyes get tired of the same figures scraping the same violin bows.

"Good directors will avoid this monotony by making the screen continuously interesting. If a Beethoven symphony is being played, the picture may be telling Beethoven's story or revealing what he had in mind when he composed the music. Then the eye is entertained while the ear is being satisfied.

"Realization of this fact will lead to the use of many new and interesting camera angles. While a ballet is being played, for instance, the camera can be dodging about, catching a glimpse of dancers, of bounding legs, of billowing skirts. There will be scenes from behind, from above, from various angles—the idea being always to keep the eye pleased while the ear is being delighted.

"To be specific, let us suppose that Miss Gertrude Lawrence is singing a song. Just to see Miss Lawrence singing becomes, after a while, wearisome to the eye if not to the ear. Not that Miss Lawrence is not attractive or that her singing is wearisome. But we have been so trained for action that involuntarily we weary of one set figure. If, instead of showing her standing in front of a camera singing for ten minutes, the camera should steal away, give us a glimpse of the chorus behind her, flit here and there, while her voice is coming from the screen only to

1. "Movies and Talkies," *North American Review*, October, 1928, volume 226, pages 429-435.

conclude with Miss Lawrence in some captivating expressions, then we would have something to hold the attention.

"To the director, the most interesting possibility of the talking or synchronized picture is that of presenting a complex situation, such as that of hearing the voice of one actor and of seeing the face of another. The reaction of the person addressed is frequently of more importance than an impression of the person speaking.

"Take this one very simple illustration. A man goes to the telephone and picks up the receiver. A voice on the other end says, 'I'm sorry, but your wife and child have just been killed.' We hear the voice without seeing the speaker. What we do see is the husband to whom this tragic news has been brought. That, to the director, would be something worth while. It has real dramatic interest. You can feel the grip of it; and out of this simple little illustration may come a thousand variations."

Almost all the pictures we have turned out in the Long Island Studio have leaned toward the stage formula. This was the obvious thing for us to do. In the early stages of talking pictures the producers and the public wanted them to talk, so we let them talk and at length. Much too lengthily. We are beginning to see now that this type of picture does not move; therefore it doesn't hold. We are appealing very definitely to one sense—the sense of hearing, but we are neglecting the visual side of pictures. This must stop and we are already taking measures to stop it.

At the moment, at the Long Island Studio, we are making a picture called *Applause*.[1] This picture has been designed, prepared and is being executed as a motion picture. In it we will use dialogue and sound effects to heighten the movement of the picture. I do not believe we will have a single unnecessary speech. All lines spoken shall be for the purpose of furthering the story. Because of this fact, there are perhaps fifty percent more titles[2] than would be used in the same picture if it were

1. The "we" in this case certainly should include director Rouben Mamoulian.

2. For many years into the talkie period the word "title" was used to describe the actor's spoken dialogue, as in the director's command to "speak the title."

silent, but no more than that. I believe the mixture is right and I am hoping that this picture will be a model.

As I said before, I believe the silent picture director has an edge. The silent director has always been more important than the stage director, because the silent director carries the entire burden, whereas the stage director, once his project is in shape, turns it over to the actors and they carry on. The stage director, being hampered by lack of sets, of necessity has to confine his work to dialogue and see that lines are spoken properly. This, of course, is of vital importance and it is a trick or an art that the silent director must learn.

On the other hand, whereas the silent director has only to acquire the knowledge of the reading of dialogue, the stage director must master hundreds of tricks with the camera, with the film, with cutting and editing which he has never before been up against. Some of the stage directors are going to do this but their success depends upon the rapidity with which they can absorb these things.

These are a few points applicable to the two classes of directors starting at scratch. Now, these directors, both stage and screen, must meet and solve unusual problems with which neither class is familiar. Here again the picture director has an edge, because in the past he has had to be more adaptable.

One very vital attribute that talking picture directors must have in the future is a knowledge of costs and how to eliminate expenses. If the director is adroit enough to know when to use his silent camera, for instance, he will save his company many thousands of dollars. If he can know and make quick decisions as to what can be effectively re-recorded rather than recorded directly, he will save time and, again, money.

It is possible, in talking pictures of the type that I believe will come forward this year, to shoot two-thirds of a picture silently, even though of that two-thirds, more than one-half will have sound when it finally reaches the public. Some of this sound will be put on the film later. Some of it will be dialogue that is actually taken in close dialogue shots and the sound-track run over longer shots that have been made silently. The director who can master this and make quick decisions as to his shooting will be invaluable.

Please don't think I am overlooking the fact that quality is paramount. I am assuming quality and simply saying that, of the two directors who have equal ability, the one adroit enough to make himself adaptable will be by far the most valuable. In fact, I almost believe that a director can have a shade less of quality in his work, if he is adroit enough to use both sound and camera where they are most effective.

I have always considered the director a writer; in other words, a person who writes with pictures, rather than with words. The day of the script-holder is past. A director in these days should be able to take a short story, novel or play and write the adaptation himself. To do this, he need have no knowledge of writing whatsoever. Every word in his script may be misspelled. Every sentence may be grammatically incorrect and it can still be a great script. Do not think I am eliminating writers or their importance from the art of picture-making. As a director I have always wanted to work with a writer. I find that the two of us are mental punching bags for each other. In many instances one was the complement of the other. So I am not minimizing the importance of the writer. If the writer can put a screen story on paper properly, he can also put it on the film. In other words, with a bit of the executive ability necessary to handle people, he can be a director.

FRANK BORZAGE
(1893 - 1961)

While the most advanced works of the European cinema from the late silent period onward fairly flaunted their self-conscious artistry, the best films of Hollywood tended to adopt a completely opposite strategy. Invisible craftsmanship hid the efforts of actors, designers, cameramen, editors, and directors so that no creative seams were to be seen and the illusionistic qualities of the medium were allowed full sway. "The finished picture should bear no sign of consciousness and no sign of effort," wrote Frank Borzage, and should concentrate on "the struggles of the characters," instead of some more abstract concept. The director of *Seventh Heaven* and *Man's Castle* had little use for undisguised artifice, but knew perhaps better than anyone how to create masterworks of romantic sentiment out of the phony tinsel of the Hollywood studio. At the age of nineteen Frank Borzage parlayed a few years in stock and repertory groups into a promising movie career, first as a romantic lead, then as actor-director for such companies as Santa Barbara's Flying A. The unaffected sincerity and warmth that would characterize his finest films can be seen in his earliest silent features, and by the coming of the talkies he was established as the screen's finest director of romantic melodrama. In retrospect he seems, with Leo McCarey, the only director who was consistently able to create affecting and believable characters in the most sentimental of Hollywood situations.

DIRECTING A TALKING PICTURE
FRANK BORZAGE

The first duty of a director is to tell a story. The art of narration is important. A good director should be able to hold your interest in conversation. Some people are naturally good story tellers. Others are not. I believe it is possible to develop latent ability as a story teller, but it cannot be wholly acquired.

To make a really good picture, a director must have a good story. Players who can act—Photography—Sound Recording—and settings are all important, but the story tops the list.

It takes a very bad director to entirely spoil a very good story; but a director, no matter how skilled, can achieve little with poor material.

It is one of the duties of a director to make his picture financially successful; which is another way of saying he must please his audiences. An "arty" picture usually is misnamed. Real art can be understood by you and I and by everyone else.

The effect of a picture should be unified. If the unity is of time and place as well as action, so much the better.

Every good story is based on a struggle. Complications help and better most stories. A character study, or a tableau is not a picture and a director must avoid the false trails that leave such a film product upon his hands. Suspense, clues, dramatic forecasts and all the other arts on the story teller's shelf can be used with effect.

Even with talking pictures I believe that the story should be developed as far as possible through scenes. Audiences prefer the action of characters, to a steady exchange of conversation between the players.

The audience must be credited with intelligence. It is not good to "hang out signs," so to speak, pointing out this development and that. The average audience follows the events swiftly and skillfully and does not have to be led by the hand.

From *How Talkies Are Made*, edited by Joe Bonica, Hollywood, 1930.

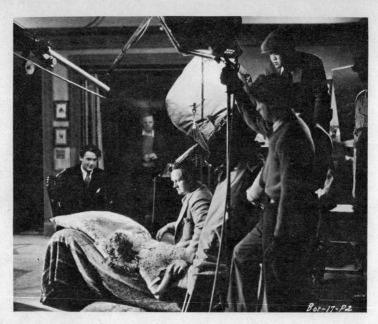

Frank Borzage directs Marian Nixon in a close shot for *After Tomorrow* (1932) as Charles Farrell (left) looks on. At top of picture James Wong Howe can be seen at the camera, which is wrapped in a silencing blanket to muffle its noise.

I believe in letting the audience do part of the acting. Let the audience read the players' minds and experience some of the emotions of the characters on the screen. The story that is too obvious and the portrayal that is too obvious lack the artistry which conceals real art. The finished picture should bear no sign of consciousness and no sign of effort.

When you go to a theatre, and, looking at a picture, are made to forget the screen, the theatre and the unreality; when you live through the struggles of the characters in the story, you are witnessing real motion picture art.

Many persons contribute to the making of a motion picture: Author, Scenarists, Dialogue Writers, Cameramen, Art Directors, Sound Men, Players and Director. But it is upon the shoulders of the Director that the responsibility for the picture's success or failure rightfully rests.

The efforts of all the others fuse in the Director's hands. He must, therefore, have an understanding of the problems of all these persons. He must understand their work and have their point of view, never forgetting, of course, the point of view of the audiences for whom the picture is being made.

A good Director plans his work out well ahead. Before he walks upon the set each morning he knows exactly what ground he is going to cover during the day. He has practically memorized the "sides" (dialogue) of each player. He has mapped out all the bits of "business" (action) so that there will be no need for last minute delays—no waits for the suddenly discovered need of rearranging the set and its lighting; of additional props from the property room; or unexpected changes of costume. He must understand human nature so that he may aid his players in presenting true to life delineations.

A Director should have some of the qualities of a leader, the ability to make decisions that are right most of the time, and the quality which inspires confidence in those about him.

He must have a world of patience and resourcefulness to overcome obstacles without too much deliberation.

He must have a lot of co-operation and some luck.

There probably aren't many such persons this side of heaven.

WILLIAM CAMERON MENZIES
(1896-1957)

William Cameron Menzies made his greatest mark in film as an art director, but while most art directors are content to limit themselves to the graphic problems of set design, he took upon himself a far wider range of visual responsibilities. In fact he sketched out beforehand every set-up for his most important films, constructing his settings so that they could only be photographed from the angle he demanded, with the lens he prescribed. In so doing he was dictating to the director, cameraman, and actors, and always had the complete authority of producers like Selznick to back him up. It was understandable that he should soon turn to direction himself, and that his own films should be strongest in terms of sheer visual style—*Chandu the Magician* and *Things to Come* are only two examples. But he was too valuable as a "production designer" (the title Selznick gave him for *Gone With the Wind*) to remain a mere director. There are only a few films actually directed by his own hand, but the number in which he had a large (perhaps the largest) creative responsibility is imposing. Menzies' designs were at their best when a bit of fantasy was involved, as with the Fairbanks *Thief of Bagdad* or in *The Beloved Rogue*, but he was equally at home with more naturalistic studio projects such as *Tom Sawyer*, *King's Row*, *Foreign Correspondent*, and *Around the World in Eighty Days*. Menzies was not of primary importance as a director, but any man who designs the look and feel of each frame of his productions has earned for himself an even more distinctive title: in this regard he is certainly one of Hollywood's true *auteurs*.

PICTORIAL BEAUTY IN THE PHOTOPLAY

WILLIAM CAMERON MENZIES

As an art director I am interested in the photoplay as a series of pictures—as a series of fixed and moving patterns—as a fluid composition, which is the product of the creative workers who collaborate in production. As soon as the writer commences work on the scenario the composition of the picture begins. When the art director receives the finished scenario he begins to transpose the written words into a series of mental pictures. As he reads the script he visualizes, as nearly as possible, each change of scene, collecting in his mind the opportunities for interesting compositions. He sketches his settings with an eye to the action that will transpire and the emotional effect that is desired.

The director, when he places his characters and guides their movements, is composing pictures—still pictures and moving pictures. The costumer, the designer, the set dresser, the decorator, all contribute to the final composition. And last, but not least, the cameraman in the direction of his lighting and the determination of his different points of view, photographs the composition, to which many have contributed.

The photoplay as a pictorial art is unique in a number of respects. First of all, it is not an individual art, but rather is the product of a number of minds. The painter who paints a picture usually works alone, and his conception is his own. He alone is responsible for the color, technique, craftsmanship, and the spiritual something that he accomplishes. But the screen composition is the collective result of a number of minds working together. Secondly, our art is based on certain mechanical inventions, and is greatly dependent upon its mechanical and scientific resources. A piece of canvas, a dab of paint, and a few boards, often gives us a stage setting. Two or three of these and

From *Cinematographic Annual*, edited by Hal Hall, Hollywood, 1930. Reprinted by permission of ASC Holding Company.

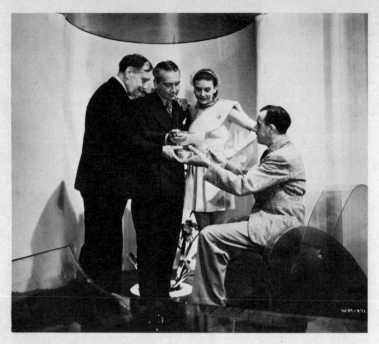

Author H. G. Wells, director William Cameron Menzies, actress Pearl Argyle, and cameraman Georges Perinal confer on the set of *Things to Come* (1935-36).

the requirements, as far as the settings are concerned for the stage play, are satisfied. The screen, on the other hand, offers many mechanical considerations and complications. Finally, other arts may or may not have universal appeal, whereas, our art *must* appeal to all the people. Our pictures are viewed by a larger and more varied audience than any other pictorial attempt. But this does not necessarily preclude the possibility of artistic achievement, for the truly great artists have been made great by the masses.

The photoplay of today reflects the tastes, habits and sentiments of the times. The pictorial beauty of the modern photoplay is an indication of the more general appreciation and the greater demand for beauty that is characteristic of modern life.

Automobiles are advertised for their beauty of line and color as much as for their mechanical efficiency. Henry Ford advertises beauty of line and color. This is true also of household furniture, and practically everything we use. The portable typewriters which you use are no longer just plain black machines, but they are now offered to you in various colors and designs. The manufacturers have suddenly awakened to the commercial value of beauty and are exploiting it. I think that the motion picture, through its representation of beauty in clothes, furniture, automobiles, and other features of our life, has been a vitally important factor in stimulating this new respect and appreciation for beauty that is noticeable. I know for a fact that many designers and illustrators see motion pictures for the inspiration and pictorial ideas they get from them.

The pictorial history of the photoplay is a history of the development of the public taste for beauty on the screen. This taste has been developed by tasting. One artist, in his efforts, has outdone the other, and the public continues, as always, to demand more and more. The artist who succeeds today must be able to give a wee bit more than his predecessors. Through cumulative progress the motion picture, with its tremendous resources, physical and human, will continue to blaze the trail for all other pictorial arts, and will assure our recovery from what has been referred to as "the ugliest age in history"—1850 to 1900.

In the earliest pictures, little, if any, attention was given to background. These were the novelty days, when the mere seeing of movement on the screen was sufficient to satisfy the public. The background was whatever happened to be behind the object or person photographed. The next step was a sort of travelogue background, using natural settings. As the pictures were done with a limited personnel, and in a short time, the backgrounds were not very carefully selected. In fact, it was quite usual for a company to go into the country in the morning with a camera, a couple of horses and an actor or two, and return in the evening with an epic of the period.

With the coming of stories demanding interiors the first sets had to be devised. These were originally, either a borrowed stage set, or a painted canvas backing. All the wall furniture, such as bookcases, pictures, was painted on a flat surface. Even vases with flowers, and chairs against the wall were painted, the only objects not being painted being those in the center of the room in actual use in the action. The company making the picture usually painted a trademark in a conspicuous place on the wall. For instance, Pathé used its rooster trademark in this way.

The sets were made of light framework and canvas, so that when an actor entered and closed the door the whole room, including the painted furniture, would shake. Usually these sets were set up outside and were lit by sunlight, giving a peculiar outside effect to a supposed interior. In addition the cameraman often had to pan up the camera to avoid showing the grass or dirt floor, and if a wind happened to be blowing, the actor almost had to hold his hat to keep it from blowing out of the scene. These early sets were designed principally by scenic artists or head carpenters, and often were planned or sketched on an old envelope, or the stage floor. In fact, an early designer of my acquaintance used to design his sets on the palm of his hand if nothing else happened to be handy. These early sets merely filled the requirements of entrance and exit; but in some cases they were surprisingly well done. The advent of the open stage did not help matters much, for, though the lighting was controlled by diffusers, or large overhead awnings, which could be rolled back and forth, the lighting throughout the scene would be continually changing with the movement of the sun.

As lighting equipment developed, the glass stage was abolished or darkened in, and all lighting was artificially created. At this time, artists and architects began to take a hand in designing sets. Texture, effect and composition began to be considered, and efforts were made to please the newly awakened taste of the public, which was growing more discriminating, now that the first novelty of the first motion picture had worn off. Gradually through the efforts of illustrators, painters, stage designers, architects, and commercial artists—all of whom had tried their hand at movie design, the set of the present day was evolved.

The set of today is neither a purely architectural nor a purely artistic product. It is an ingenious combination of art, architecture, dramatic knowledge, engineering, and craftsman-ship. It combines in just the right proportions theatrical license with the reality of good architectural pattern. Simplicity and restraint are its chief characteristics. Simplicity is absolutely necessary for the audience must be able to grasp the whole scene and its meaning at a glance.

The orientation of exterior sets so as to take best advantage of the changing position of the sun presents many interesting problems. Your geographical location is a large factor in deter-mining how you will lay out your set. You wouldn't do it the same in New York as in Los Angeles. It is usual to lay out a set to the south because back light is much better. Of course if you are going to shoot on the set all day you have to bear in mind the changing positions of the sun in relation to the chang-ing action on the set. The declinations of the sun must be con-sidered. I put up a set for Valentino's picture *The Son of the Sheik* which was supposed to be a desert palace or something of the sort. We didn't shoot the picture until three months later and had forgotten to take the changing declination of the sun into consideration; and the result was that the lighting was terrible—it was a complete back light, whereas we arranged it for a beautiful cross light.

It might be interesting to you to know how pictorial accom-plishment has gone from one country to another. The original artistic pictures were mostly French, and for some time French cameramen and art directors were almost alone in the field. Then the Italians did *Quo Vadis* and *Cabiria*, which were among the first artistic productions. Mr. Griffith made *Intol-erance* and *Broken Blossoms*, which for settings and photog-raphy created a new era in pictures. With the war America had the field mostly to herself and for several years most of the progress was here. After the war Mr. Lubitsch's pictures such as *Passion* made in Germany, along with the lesser ones such as *The Golem* and *The Cabinet of Dr. Caligari*, were very daring and different experiments. America again forged ahead with such pictures as *Ben Hur*, *Robin Hood*, and *The Thief of Bagdad*, which Germany followed with *Variety*, *The Last Laugh*, and *Faust*. In the last couple of years America seems to

be leading again in artistic pictures such as *Seventh Heaven,
The Street Angel,* and the very interesting work in *Our Danc-
ing Daughters. Sunrise* was made in America, but by a mixed
German and American staff.

I would like now to discuss the importance of setting to the
dramatic effect. First of all, the setting may be negative as in
the old days when the background was often an irritating dis-
traction. The setting may be neutral, in which case it neither
adds to nor detracts from the effect. The setting may be designed with an eye to the intended effect, and may, in such a
case, become a very important contributing factor. The setting
might even become the hero in the picture, as would be the
case, for example, in the filming of such a subject as *The Fall of
the House of Usher.*

The art director and the cameraman, with their many mechanical and technical resources, do a great deal to add punch
to the action as planned by the director. For example, if the
mood of the scene calls for violence and melodramatic action,
the arrangement of the principal lines of the composition
would be very extreme, with many straight lines and extreme
angles. The point of view would be extreme, either very low or
very high. The lens employed might be a wide angled one,
such as a twenty-five millimeter lens which violates the perspective and gives depth and vividness to the scene. The values
or masses could be simple and mostly in a low key, with violent
highlights.

In a scene such as the one to which I have just referred, when
the tempo of the action is very fast, there are usually rapidly
changing compositions of figures and shadows. For idyllic love
scenes, or scenes demanding beauty, the values and forms are
usually softer, the lens is diffused and the grouping and dressing graceful and lyrical. In the case of pageantry such things as
scale and pattern, figures, rich trappings against a high wall,
through a huge arch are demanded. In comedy scenes the composition may be almost in the mood of caricature. In tragedy
or pathos, or any scene photographed in a low key, the setting
is often designed with a low ceiling, giving a feeling of depression.

The set itself causes a laugh. I recall in Corinne Griffith's picture *The Garden of Eden* a place where a couple starts an argument after they are in bed and every time they sit up to argue they turn on the light. There was a man living across the court and he noticed the light going on and off and thought somebody was signaling and began to flash his light on and off. Then other people saw it and did the same. We made a miniature of the complete side of a hotel and all the windows were flashing lights. It caused a great laugh.

Thus we see that the design of the setting and lighting may become a very important element in the securing of any desired emotional effect, and this explains why, in many cases, authenticity is sacrificed, and architectural principles violated, all for the sake of the emotional response that is being sought. My own policy has been to be as accurate and authentic as possible. However, in order to forcefully emphasize the locale I frequently exaggerate—I make my English subject more English than it would naturally be, and I over-Russianize Russia. An interesting thing happened when I was working on a Spanish picture with Miss Pickford quite a few years ago. We had to have a Spanish city near Toledo and I put the Campanile of Toledo in to make it authentic. As you know, Madison Square Garden in New York has copied this campanile, and so many people recognized it and asked what Madison Square Garden was doing in the picture, that I had to change it.

It might be interesting for you to go through the routine of the art director's work from the moment he receives the script. In the first place, although not customary, it is of great advantage to the art director to know something of the story as it is being constructed. Very often he will have many valuable suggestions to offer. Now, what I am describing is my own method. Except for some slight variations, I think most of the art directors follow the same method. When reading the scenario, notes are made, and if there is sufficient time, rough sketches of the separate scenes are prepared. After consultation with the cameraman and director and the incorporation of their suggestions, the art director works up his sketches into presentable drawings. He considers such things as point of view, nature of the lens to be used, position of the camera, and so forth. If he is concerned with intimate scenes, he concentrates on possible variations of composition in the close shots. If he is designing a street, or any great long shot, he considers the possibility of trick effects and miniatures, double exposures, split-screens, travelling mats, and so forth.

When the drawing is finished the director, cameraman, and designer confer again, and when all interested are satisfied with the drawing, it is projected through the picture plane, to plan and elevation.[1] However, this process reproduces the composition line for line, and retains all the violence or dramatic value of the sketch, even with changed point of view. The finished plan and elevation is blue printed and sometimes transposed into a model and turned over to the construction department.

From then on the artist's main interest is the supervision of the texture and painting of the set. Texture is a rather interesting subject. All our straight plaster textures are cast in sheets nailed to a frame, and then pointed or patched with plaster. Brick, slate roofs, stone work, and even aged and rotted wood are casts taken from the original thing, made in sheets and applied. That is, if we have a stone wall, we get in a lot of stone and build up a wall about six feet high, put the plaster cast on it, and peel it off like you do a cast from a tooth. You can cast any number of pieces of wall from that. The painting is usually done by air guns, and in many cases the light effects are put on by expert air gun operators.

As much as it's possible, now-a-days, everything is shot on the lot. Forests, ships, country lanes, mountains, canals, and all, are built up and tricked so that what, on the screen, may cover miles of ground, in reality only occupies a few acres of the back lot, or a few hundred square feet of the stage.

Sometimes we have to resort to optical illusions. In the *Thief of Bagdad*, Douglas Fairbanks wanted to swim under water to find a pearl or something, on the bottom of the ocean. We took a set and cut out seaweeds of buckram, and had a series of

1. That is, an isometric drawing is produced which shows the true elevation of walls, doorways, windows, etc. in order to assist in planning camera positions or movements of actors around the completed set.

them hanging down in several places. A wind machine was put on so that seaweeds flapped, but as the scene was taken in slow motion, they undulated when shown on the screen. The camera had a marine disc over the lens and was turned over. Mr. Fairbanks was let down through the scene and went through the motions of swimming under water. The scene had the appearance of water and gave almost a water feeling. It was a very interesting effect.

In this same picture we had the problem of photographing Mr. Fairbanks on a flying magic carpet. We got a ninety foot Llewellyn crane and had the carpet suspended on six wires. There was Doug hanging on six wires he couldn't see. They were each guaranteed to hold four hundred pounds, but he said, "I would like something more than a guarantee in a place like this." When the beam was started, the carpet would be left behind a little until the slack was taken up and it gave us quite a thrill each time it was started. We also had to arrange for a travelling camera (which by the way is another thing that an art director is involved in), and had a platform built for the cameraman which travelled with the crane. That was the first travelling shot. Of course today they have complicated machinery for this purpose. For instance in *Broadway*, they had equipment for moving shots which cost thousands of dollars to build. The Fox company has a lens they can use to bring a person from a long shot up to a closeup which saves a great deal of expense.[1]

As an illustration of the advance made in this matter of getting trick shots, I might mention my first experience in pictures. When I got out of art school I went to see George Fitzmaurice to get a job, and he tried me out. The studio where his pictures were made was in Fort Lee, New Jersey, across the river from New York. For one of his pictures he wanted a close-up in a tropical setting. Now here in California there are

1. This early zoom lens can be observed in a number of films of this period, notably those of Paramount. It would seem that Menzies refers to the ability of the zoom shot to inexpensively mimic the action of a costly camera movement, but this technique was not widely adopted until the late 1960's.

plenty of palm trees and you would have no difficulty, but in Fort Lee, New Jersey, there is nothing of the kind. The only thing I could find was a couple of palm leaf fans. I stripped them down to palms and to secure my effect, stood on a chair in the sun, waving the palm leaves so that the shadow was thrown on the wall back of the actors.

So you see the motion picture technician must have great ingenuity. He must have a knowledge of architecture of all periods and nationalities. He must be able to picturize and make interesting a tenement, or a prison. He must be a cartoonist, a costumer, a marine painter, a designer of ships, an interior decorator, a landscape painter, a dramatist, an inventor, an historical, and now, an acoustical expert—in fact, a "Jack of all Trades."

A word about the cameraman and the importance of his work. The development of photography has kept pace with that of the set. The cameraman has brought his work to a fine art. His equipment has become much more complete, and he too, has become a specialist. He does the actual photographing, which means that he has been handed the results of the previous workers, and through his photography he has great possibilities for good as well as harm to the picture. His responsibility is a grave one and the art director can often aid him by properly designing the sets. The cameraman must see that the star is photographed to her best advantage. Close-ups are the most difficult because the accentuated dramatic action and their composition and lighting must be perfect. He must see that the desired pictorial effect is obtained from the scene as a whole. He must take infinite pains with his lighting and his composition, and he must carefully watch the development of the film. Many times the cameraman, after a twelve hour day, has to go over to the laboratory and watch his negative and time its development himself because if the negative is overdone or underdone, his photography will suffer. You have to be careful that the film is neither too light nor too dark, or it scratches when run and then after it has been run six or eight times it is full of scratches and oil. If it is in a medium key you don't see it so much. If extremely low or extremely dark, it is full of holes and flashes and everything else.

Not only must he do these many things, but he usually has to do them under pressure of time. He must select his compositions with very little previous study. He must light for continuous and changing movement, rather than for one beautiful picture. He must sacrifice for visibility many lovely light effects in low keys. He must remember that the film will be run many times, and by projectionists of all sorts, so that what constitutes beautiful soft photography in his projection room, may look very poor when handled by the projectionist in some small Arkansas village for instance.

The advent of the talking picture, as you realize, disturbed the craft in all branches of motion picture production. The addition of speech has, possibly, made the reliance on pictorial values a bit less vital. History seems to be repeating itself. Just as the novelty of movement on the screen was sufficient to hold the first audiences, so the novelty of hearing people talk on the screen was at first important enough to satisfy the curious audience. Pictorial beauty, so far as the first talking pictures were concerned, was noticeable by its absence. The public soon began to feel this. There was something lacking, and that something was that pictorial beauty that was in a very subtle manner an important element in the silent picture.

The talkies are no longer a series of mere pictures of people speaking lines, but are rapidly bringing back all of the values, all of the beauty, of the silent motion picture, with sound and speech as a supplement. *In Old Arizona* was probably the first talking picture that did not ignore pictorial beauty. I think that this accounts, to a great extent, for its tremendous success. Several others have had some pictorial interest, but the ultimate in a finished, artistic talkie has yet to be made.

The acoustical demands in connection with the production of talking pictures have had a very noticeable effect on the design and the construction of the settings. Too much plain hard surface cannot be exposed unless of a very soft and absorbent texture. We are making very many of our sets of cloth, or a very porous wall paper. Hollow, tunnel-like cavities must be avoided. Also, the set in talking pictures, must be lit for long shots and close-ups, which are shot at the same time. There are fewer sets, but more of what might be called single shot effects. A set prepared for a short and long shot looks almost bare to the eye, but when seen on the screen it has a habit of muddling together. For instance, if the pieces of furniture are close together they look like one mass and you cannot tell what it is. Therefore you have to use them sparingly. The arrangement of the set must also be different for different lenses. A wide angle lens will throw the thing back, which will simplify it and give it depth and you can naturally have more furnishings; but a narrow angle lens will jam it all together and consequently you must have a greater distance between the furnishings in the set.

I think that the addition of speech has been a great step forward. And, with the addition of color, stereoscopic perspective, and possibly a variety of shapes to the screen proportions, we will have attained almost reality itself. The subject of stereoscopic perspective on the screen has been brought up thousands of times. Many think it is impossible because everyone cannot look at the screen from the same focal point. I was talking to an eye specialist from Johns Hopkins University and he seems to think he has got it. If he has, it is a tremendous thing and will change the proportions we are now using.

As I have suggested here the pictorial quality of the motion picture rests largely with the public. Douglas Fairbanks spoke a great truth when he once said: "Better films will come when appreciation for better films is developed. It is appreciation and criticism which guides the artist."

The producers, like many other manufacturers, have awakened to the fact that beauty is efficiency, and that good art is usually good business. They have found that the public is no longer satisfied with the settings, costumes, lighting, and groupings of last year, or yesterday. They have learned that pictures must be well composed, for a well composed picture is one at which the audience can look at and see a lot with ease. The eye and the attention of the spectator is attracted to the right point and directed in accordance with the demands of the story.

Somehow the idea has crept into many minds that the artistic picture is destined to be unpopular. However, I think that if you will look at the matter fairly you will find that where artistically composed pictures have failed, they have done so not because of beauty, but because of lack of some other necessary attribute.

SLAVKO VORKAPICH
(1895-   )

Film historians differentiate two parallel schools of montage, that of the Soviets and that of Hollywood. The Soviet tradition, primarily distinguished by the writings and film work of S. M. Eisenstein, is seen as intellectual, objectively analytical, and perhaps overly academic. Hollywood montage, romantic in the extreme, is written off as a series of wipes, dissolves, flip-flops, and superimpositions, and laid at the feet of Slavko Vorkapich. In reality Vorkapich's theories, as articulated in the late 20's and early 30's, were quite similar to Eisenstein's, although leaning more to a subjective analytical technique grounded on physiological rather than intellectual principles. In this paper Vorkapich describes his theory of effective "cinematography" without once using the word montage. Only later did this term, by then used generically to describe certain stock visual effects of "pure cinema," come to be associated with his own much more thoughtful work. Born in Serbia, Vorkapich was an art student who arrived in Hollywood in 1921 and quickly developed an interest in the special nature of cinema. His early writings led to a collaboration on the pioneer *avant garde* short *Life and Death of a Hollywood Extra* (1928) and then to jobs at the major studios creating "montage sequences." These set pieces might be realistic (the *San Francisco* earthquake), symbolic (the opening of *Crime Without Passion*), or vast encapsulations of time (the opera career of Jeanette MacDonald in *Maytime*). After the war he devoted his energies mainly to teaching and lecturing in Europe and in America, where his most vocal recent disciple has been William Friedkin.

CINEMATICS: SOME PRINCIPLES UNDERLYING EFFECTIVE CINEMATOGRAPHY

SLAVKO VORKAPICH

Cinematography, considered as a medium of expression, is comparatively new. It is still experimenting and groping in its search for self-knowledge, in its attempts to find its own way of telling expressively what it seeks to convey. It is hybrid insofar as it imitates or borrows from literature, stage, painting and music; it is unclear and undecided as to its proper style and form.

If, in the old Socratic manner, we ask ourselves a few questions and try to answer them, we may find a clue leading to the solution of the problem.

What fundamental means of expression do we find in the art of painting?—Lines and colors.—And in sculpture?—Forms, volumes.—In music?—Tones.—That is clear. But how does cinematography express itself?—In pictures.—So does painting and photography. Evidently the answer is not satisfactory. So again we ask: What kind of pictures?—Motion pictures.—There, in that one word—*motion*—we have perhaps our clue.

The present article is an attempt to investigate in that direction and to see whether the proper language of cinematography might not be the language of motions.

We shall approach the subject, in a summary way of course, from three different angles: psychological, aesthetic and practical.

II

As soon as the child begins to see, its attention is attracted by anything that moves. There must be something interesting in those vague changes of light and shade and those indistinct

From *Cinematographic Annual,* edited by Hal Hall, Hollywood, 1930. Reprinted by permission of ASC Holding Company.

shapes that float across the baby's field of vision. Things are a little out of focus perhaps, nevertheless they are exciting because they—move.

For a while the child is only a passive spectator; it watches with curiosity whatever appears on its limited screen, but soon it demands to take active part in the general movement of life. You have to pick it up and carry it around.

Now the panorama swiftly changes: walls, windows and the objects in the room merrily pursue each other around for the entertainment of the little creature. The pleasure of visual change is enhanced by the travel through space of the child's own body. The instant you stop the movement, the baby voices an energetic protest. Obviously there is a keen delight in motion both visual and bodily. The latter is perhaps some pleasant physiological sensation caused by the displacement of the body's center of gravity. But if this is done too violently, as in sudden dropping for instance, an emotion of fear may be produced. Motion, as we see, can be a source of pleasure and also of pain.

With the growth of the child its interest in motion increases. The perambulator, the wooden horse, the seesaw, the swing, the merry-go-round, etc., provide a large variety of motions. These motions have the power to quicken the feeling of life, to produce exhilaration and provide entertainment.

And we never outgrow our infantile interest in motion. From the cradle in childhood to the rocking chair in old age we find in dancing, sports and travel a variety of bodily and visual motions invigorating, entertaining and soothing.

Amusement places thrive on motion. Advertisers use it to attract buyers: barber-poles gyrate, windmills revolve and electric signs do a dervish dance every night.

Modern psychology teaches that our primitive emotions can be sublimated and our reflexes conditioned. In other words, and in the present case, we may create pleasure and entertainment by suggested motions. By merely seeing motion on the screen our minds, conscious or subconscious, may be made to react in a similar manner as in active participation.

III

If we approach the subject from a more aesthetic and philosophical angle we may find arguments which speak in favor of the motion picture as a new form of art.

The existing arts are divided in two groups: *one static and spatial, comprising architecture, sculpture and painting with their subdivisions; and one dynamic and temporal: music, poetry and drama.*

The motion picture is *both*, spatial like painting and temporal—dynamic like music.

This double characteristic harmonizes with the modern scientific concept of Space—Time. It is within the power of the cinema to create its own space and time. It can tie fragments of several different objects, situated in distant points of space, into one organic unity; it can stretch one tragic moment into unbearable suspense. This ability of the motion picture to recreate, expand, contract and transform space and time to its own purposes makes it very much in keeping with the theory of Relativity.

The aesthetic terminology, whenever it attempts to speak of vital values of any work of art, is compelled to use words which are really descriptive of the qualities of motion. In such static arts as sculpture and painting we look for the "flow" of lines, "rhythmical" arrangement of forms, "movement" in composition, etc. In music we find tempo, beat, rhythmical pattern, movement, etc. All these concepts are intrinsic attributes of actual motion. With the motion picture camera at our command we can now have all these not only figuratively but literally. The power of the cinema to embody the principles of rhythm makes it a truly dynamic form of art. And the modern age being a dynamic one, its logical medium of expression should be the motion picture.

Motion is energy visualized, therefore motion is a symbol of life itself. Immobility is death. And yet, there is no immobility—within every atom the infinitesimal electrons keep on whirling.

Our world is infinitely rich in color, form, sound and motion. All, except the last have been used by man artistically to express his thoughts and feelings. Although the oldest of arts—dance—is an art of motions, it is very limited in its scope. It uses only the movements of the human body and of drapery. Now the cinema offers possibilities, almost unlimited, of creating symphonies of visual movement, by using a tremendous range of motions from the violent sweep of a tornado to the delicate drooping of an eyelid.

IV

To treat the subject from a practical angle without actual demonstration is rather difficult, especially for the present writer who is not a writer but a man used to thinking visually. However, we shall attempt to make a few observations.

The majority of the motion picture public seems to prefer pictures of action to those of mental subtleties. This is natural and perhaps closer to truth and the logic of the medium; for action is motion in a broader sense. But, for purposes of cinematography, the meaning of the word "motion" should be limited to only a certain type and certain views of actions. There are objects and persons which "photograph well," and there are motions which "cinematograph well," that is—expressively. As there is in music a difference between tone and noise, there is in motion pictures a difference between any kind of movement and—shall we say—cine-motion.

In almost every motion picture are to be found moments in which there occur some particular movements imbued with such intense life and power that they seem to carry us along, regardless of the meaning and the specific point of the story. What is there obtained perhaps accidentally should be sought, studied and used consciously.

The insistent emphasis on motion in the foregoing discussion may have created in some minds the wrong impression that the perfect picture would be the one in which the camera constantly perambulates and the actors wildly gesticulate or perform a sort of breathless ballet. Nothing of the sort. We must remember that an essential element of rhythm is—*pause*. Also, cinematically speaking, motion is not only actual movement but also certain types of *visual changes*, namely: lap-dissolves, fades, changes of focus, changes in iris, rhythmical cutting, etc. The last mentioned is one of the most important elements of expressive cinematography. A sequence of scenes—even static in themselves—cut in definite lengths in such a manner that we rhythmically feel each jump from one scene to another, has sometimes the capacity of creating a feeling of intense vitality.

There are two opposite methods of being expressive: by using a strict economy of means or by piling up a wealth of impressions. Some scenes demand a simplicity and directness of style, while some require an abundance of images. Into the latter method belong the "camera angles." By making the camera mobile and omnipresent, in other words, by shooting the same scene from different interesting angles and by showing a variety of views related to the scene at hand one could make it more vivid and impressive and perhaps save it from possible dullness.

Now to come back to actual motions. Space does not permit a thorough analysis, so we must be satisfied with some general remarks and a few examples.

Like lines, colors and sounds, different motions have different emotional values. In the graphic arts horizontal lines usually suggest rest, peace, serenity; vertical—dignity, strength; curves—fluidity, warmth, femininity, etc. Something similar is to be found in motions.

The following examples should not be taken as formulas for effective picture making, but merely as general observations. The golden rule is that there is no rule. We know that in any form of expression the values of individual elements are greatly affected by their correlation.

If, for instance, we open a picture with the camera perambulating into the scene we may create the effect of drawing the audience into the picture and thus making it participate intimately in the story from the very start. The reverse motion, receding from the scene, may be effectively used at the end of a picture. This would create a sensation similar to those produced by the last diminishing notes of a musical composition.

The ascending motion may help to express aspiration, exaltation, freedom from matter and weight. In treating a religious scene, for instance, we may learn something from the lofty, vertical, ascending lines of the Gothic cathedrals. From the view of a kneeling devotee we may pan up to a sacred image, we may show views of candle flames and upward movement of the incense smoke, and also we may include an effervescent fountain in the monastery garden.

A cheerful mood may be enhanced by the revolving, circular motion. Most of the devices in the amusement places are using this motion to make life merry for the customers. Many folk dances are performed in circles. The same motion is also expressive of another form of exuberance, that of mechanical energy, as in revolving wheels of machinery.

The diagonal, dynamic, motion suggests power, overcoming of obstacles by force. A battle sequence may be made very effective by using short sharp diagonal clashes of arms; flags, guns, bayonets, lances and swords cutting the screen diagonally, soldiers running uphill, flashes of battle shot with slanting camera.

There are many such fundamental expressive motions and the possibilities of their combinations are unlimited. To mention briefly only a few more:

Descending motion: heaviness, danger, crushing power (avalanche, waterfall, etc.)

Pendulum motion: monotony, relentlessness (monotonous walk, prison scenes, caged animals, etc.)

Cascading motion, as of a bouncing ball: sprightliness, lightness, elasticity, etc. (Douglas Fairbanks.)

Spreading, centrifugal motion, as the ripple on the surface of a pool after a stone has been thrown in: growth, scattering (mob panic scenes), explosion, broadcasting, etc.

Indeed a whole grammar of motions could be written, analyzing the elements of the cinema language. And by means of that language many new and wonderful things are yet to be told.

I firmly believe that there is no scene in any picture which could not be made more effective, emotionally—more intense and artistically more lasting by imparting to it the proper rhythm and devising some significant motion which would best express the given mood.

A perfect motion picture would be comparable to a symphony. It would have a definite rhythmical pattern, each of its movements would correspond to the mood of the sequence and each individual phrase (scene) would be an organic part of the whole. And like a symphony it would be interesting at every moment of its development regardless of the meaning or story it has to convey. In other words: *a motion picture should be visually interesting even if we entered the theatre in the middle of the performance; we should be visually entertained even if we did not know the beginning of the story.*

In the present article the subject of cinematography has been treated only from the visual point of view, which will always remain the most important one. The invention of sound devices has opened new and almost unlimited possibilities. To discuss these in relation to the theory here expressed would require much more space than is permitted. But we can mention the obvious fact that the sound can be made to harmonize audibly with whatever is given on the screen visually, and that it could enhance the cinema's original power of expression to an immense degree.

There is no cause for alarm if the present pictures seem to have lost some of the tempo they formerly had, no matter how primitive it was. This is a period of experiments and adjustments. Eventually the sound apparatus will—like the camera—evolve from a merely reproductive into a creative instrument.

ERNEST B. SCHOEDSACK (1893-)

The team of Ernest B. Schoedsack and Merian C. Cooper produced some of the most physically impressive documentaries of the silent screen. In films like *Grass* and *Chang* they gave audiences mass tribal migrations and raging elephant stampedes, while Flaherty focused on the day-to-day existence of Eskimos and South Sea Islanders. Their great flair was for dramatic showmanship, and eventually the pair drifted into the use of documentary material for background alone, as in *The Four Feathers,* and finally ended up as makers of pure Hollywood fiction. But they never forgot their roots, and the lessons learned from their years as documentarists ("keep it distant, difficult and dangerous") served as the credo for their Hollywood studio films as well, including *The Most Dangerous Game, Dr. Cyclops, Mighty Joe Young,* and the most famous of all, *King Kong.* The fact that this film deals with a documentary filmmaker who leads an expedition to the uncharted regions of the Pacific is only one of the self-referential asides that abound in this curiously personal work (that Schoedsack and Cooper are the pilot and gunner who pick Kong off the Empire State Building is another). While Cooper had by this time settled comfortably into the role of a major Hollywood producer, Schoedsack was still happiest roaming the world with his cameras, and in the winter of 1932-33 was in Syria shooting material for a project called *A Fugitive from Glory,* which he describes here. Unfortunately the film was never completed: production of large-scale documentaries was deemed no longer practical, and Schoedsack returned to Hollywood to direct *Son of Kong.*

WARRIORS OF THE DESERT
ERNEST B. SCHOEDSACK

Fuaz, sheik of the Rualas, has sent one hundred and twenty-one brave men to green pastures not known on their desert. So the story goes. I cannot disprove it. Fuaz by his deeds and the wish of Nuri, his grandfather, became a sheik before he reached thirty.

Intrigue brings about many strange happenings, especially on the desert. When only eight Fuaz hid in a camel pack to accompany his tribesmen on a raid. With a dirty rifle, he killed the opposing chief. Within two decades six-score others fell before his weapons. Rapidly he attained power over the Syrian desert. Once in a desert pass he met two of his own brothers, reputedly plotting his downfall, and removed them from further temptation.

So the stories go!

I can testify to certain points. I do know Fuaz today rules the Rualas with an iron will. Is he not sheik? As such, no command, no action, of which he disapproves, is permitted among his followers. He must never lose face, for to do so would result eventually in losing position.

His swift *deluhls*—single-humped freighters and fighters of the burning Syrian sands—carry him rapidly from camp to camp. Burning sands? Strange contradiction. When I slept on them they nearly froze my bones. The desert achieves many strange contradictions. The sands of the desert can grow cold, very cold, as I learned during a month on the lava-strewn bed of the ancient lake near Damascus.

But the *deluhls* and the Bedouins, with Fuaz ever present to demonstrate their great prowess, provide a colorful picture as they race in fighting column across the sands. The scene extends far back into antiquity. This color the camera can never record.

From *Travel*, August 1933.

Ernest B. Schoedsack (left) with his partner Merian C. Cooper during the shooting of *The Four Feathers* (1929). More than a passing resemblance here to *King Kong*'s Driscoll and Denham?

A changing civilization has left little of its imprint on the Bedouins—*Ahl el beit* or people of the tent, as they term themselves. *Ahl Bedu*, "dwellers of the open land," really fits them better, even though they nominally make their homes in black flimsies made of goat hair. I could never call these smelly tents home. The open land calls incessantly to the visitor who perforce enters into discussions and occasionally partakes of food within a sheik's consultation chamber.

Fuaz had promised many things before we began to turn cameras on the local scene. But the promises of a Bedouin may mean much or little. The more formality attending the giving of a solemn undertaking, the less it probably means to the one guaranteeing its fulfillment. His word may be as of the wind or as of granite. It gives way before a whim (or without reason) or stands firm as an earthly rock for equally little reason.

No one can explain this strange contradiction, least of all the Bedouin himself.

As I sat with Fuaz, a magnificent specimen of young manhood, and his chiefs within his dingy tent, breathing the aroma of goats and dogs and hot, musty hair-canvas, I could vision in my mind the romance of the desert. But not with my nostrils.

Hurriedly I spoke to the sheik through an interpreter and received at last formal words of friendship and promise.

But the morrow! What would it bring!

Picture the scene. Here we were sixty-five miles southeast of Damascus, our little party of four with hundreds of Bedouins gathered from many parts of the desert. Scattered across the Syrian sands as far distant as twelve miles our so-called camp was collected, ready for the more serious business of acting for the picture we had come here to take, *A Fugitive from Glory*.

Bir Kassab was the place. Fuaz calls it a water hole, and so be it known. Bir Kassab means the "well of the liar." How well named! The deep hole contains little water, a sunken monument to the man who found it and passed along the misinformation to other weary travelers many centuries ago. Or do I commit an injustice? Possibly it ran freely in those days and he had no notion that he would establish his memory for posterity.

"Sheik Fuaz," I said, "we have come a long distance to see you and your people. We have come by steamer and by the great airplane now tethered with your herd. We are ready to photograph you and your men and your herds."

I could not repress a smile as I looked on the solemn faces of the sheik and his head men, squatting on the cold ground. Gravely they discussed my remarks in their tongue of the desert as I awaited the reply.

What a far cry from Hollywood! No ornate conference room here, with secretaries available to run for fresh data in case our deliberations reached an *impasse*. Just we eight—seven to one—mapping the month's plans, already arranged in advance.

The tent consisted of a woven covering of goat hair, spread

rather tightly over several poles. It must have measured nearly forty feet from front to rear; though this is exceptionally long even for a sheik's place of abode. Tall as I am, I could stand easily without being forced to bend my head.

Ordinarily one finds rough mats on the floor of Bedouin tents, yet we sat on the rough earth. Camel-saddles, halters, ropes and other gear of the march, together with a few platters, drinking vessels, a goat skin and several cooking vessels seemed to complete Fuaz's list of household belongings. They represented his badge of mobility. In less time than an American circus requires to strike its tents and move on, the Bedouin tribe can clean up its camp and vanish across the sands.

The interpreter brought me up sharply from my reverie.

"We, too, are ready," he spoke. "Tomorrow morning when the sun is high."

Now the Bedouin enjoys work, but only when he considers that work to be play. How well I was to learn the truth of this observation during following weeks. After all, we only wanted the Bedouins to perform certain simple acts: to pitch and break camp, to advance in column as though to attack, to run to their tents as we dove on them from the air, to water their stock and go about some of the routine business of camp life.

So on succeeding days Fuaz would lead his fellow Rualas, together with a scattering from other nearby tribes, out onto the lava field marking the dry lake bed. There we would discuss the day's plans, always through the interpreter.

"Today," I would say, "I want you first to trot the camels in column past the cameras. We must photograph this scene several times."

Fuaz considered. Nearby stood his assistants, lesser chiefs.

"I think it better," the interpreter finally interpreted, "to bring the camels by slowly at first. Later they will run."

"Ah," murmured his aides. "Fuaz is sheik. Fuaz takes no orders."

And so the camels walked! Fuaz lost no face. The fact that I was paying the bills had not the slightest bearing on his decisions.

Meantime Menake, a giant Nubian servant, stood at my elbow. Menake proved to be a quite remarkable fellow. As chief servant to Fuaz, it was his function to minister over the other lackeys. Once a slave, now Menake and his kind serve much as did American Negroes immediately following the Civil War— receiving their bed and keep in return for labor. Yet they can hardly turn elsewhere, for there is no place to which they can go.

Menake served me well. When I waved my hand, he waved his hand. When I signalled stop, he signalled stop. Rapidly he learned many English words, until, before we departed, I was able to learn from him much of tribal custom not available from the Bedouins themselves. Too, I learned that when we distributed coins among the servants, Menake took his toll. The servant concession was his; and the first man who failed to give him a "cut" was struck from the list when again wealth invaded the camp. As chief grafter, none could surpass Menake; though I suspect we got as much information from him as he received from us in cash.

The Bedouin has a queer sense of humor. I suppose, however, we should excuse one of the rascals for they certainly were not accustomed to the presence of an airplane. Possibly we really provoked the incident.

I had had a commercial plane meet me at Paris. From there we flew by way of Nice and Malta to Syria, a hard journey in anybody's language. When first we reached Damascus, I spent several days flying over the desert, sometimes as distant as two hundred miles from habitation, seeking an ideal location for our activities. At last we settled on Bir Kassab, for here is a combination of low hills, desert and hard ground that would permit speedy action.

At last, having filmed many scenes among the encampment, I decided to take to the air in the hope that the Bedouins would prove themselves capable of registering a little excitement as we dove on the camp, to simulate fright at an air raid. The tents were arranged in a large group, each separated from its neighbors by distances sufficient to indicate preparedness against these fights from the air.

We mounted one camera in the front cockpit, looking out

through a window. A second camera was located in the passengers' cabin that other shots might be taken as the pilot pulled up and away.

To the interpreter I said: "Please ask Fuaz to have his men standing around the camp at ease until we start down in the dive. Then they must look up in excitement, wave their arms and dash for the safety of their tents."

Fuaz agreed and his followers nodded understanding.

Samuel Wheeler, the British pilot who had been assigned to the expedition, took the plane off from the lake bed. We roared off into the distance as the plane circled to gain altitude. Near the outskirts of the camp, Wheeler nosed the ship down and the Bedouins began their unusual act with the abandon of veterans.

But hold! One fellow halted in his flight, stooped, then flung an object into the air. To my amazement, he struck the swooping bird. The plane made off as though mortally wounded and in a minute we came down to a bumpy landing. As the ship drew up to a halt I saw my brother, Felix, jump from the cabin.

"Get Raswan," he shouted. (Carl A. Raswan was the interpreter.)

"Tell Fuaz to find that fellow and I'll give him a good old-fashioned American licking."

Felix was excited, and justifiably, because the chunk of lava had crashed through the window, showering Wheeler with glass. Wheeler dared not open his eyes after the crash, fearing he would be blinded by razor-edged splinters, and had brought the big ship down with his eyes almost closed. Of course I did not permit Raswan to communicate our anger to the sheik, for I knew the complaint would result in promises of an investigation and no punishment would follow. Later, when viewing the scene on the screen, I saw the fellow deliberately heave the rock, though I could not possibly have identified him.

It is difficult to understand some of the fierce hatreds that prevail among the desert tribes. Yet over a period of centuries many changes have come about. A stranger, I learned, entering the desert without first having obtained permission at a moderate fee from the local sheik may suffer death at the hand of some minor band. Yet the same stranger, provided he has complied with the formality, will find himself handed along from tribe to tribe with the same unctuous care he would expect in more civilized countries.

The Bedouins have intense pride. They consider themselves the "best people in the world." In comparatively recent times they moved on to the lowlands of Syria and Egypt. They are today a poor people, those in Syria tending their flocks under French eyes and endeavoring to increase their herds that they might profit thereby. During the days of our own prosperity, a good *deluhl* would fetch as high as $250. Today the camel is worth only $25. Such is the cost, even on the desert, of a world depression!

No doubt their present poor circumstances explain some of their marauding tendencies, though they have their roots in antiquity. We found it necessary to recruit other tribesmen since Fuaz could not gather enough of his Rualas in a short time, and on the day we completed our shooting schedule and the visitors were ready to depart Fuaz sent a flying squadron among the outlying camps to check up on the "foreigners." I don't suppose they were surprised to find several Ruala camels, though they did receive a rude shock when the riders of one camp opened fire and killed two of the party.

Fuaz immediately organized several of his best riflemen. The camp made no effort to hide its excitement. Then, just as the warriors were about to set out across the desert—"to teach the dogs a lesson"—a six-man camel troop of Frenchmen rode into camp and broke up the raiders.

"Hold," cried the leader, "we will punish the guilty."

The French maintain several posts over the desert, old-timers in desert warfare who shift constantly. They know an outbreak of this kind might plunge two tribes into new warfare any day. They have remarkable success in quelling incipient fighting.

Since the days of Roman occupation—evidenced by the forgotten city whose remains may be found near Bir Kassab—these hatreds boil perilously near the surface. Yet two thousand years ago water disappeared from the district and the white race departed for greener lands. Today the Bedouins have sole possession, a privilege whose value I question.

Without Fuaz's sanction I do not know how we would have fared when we left the plane at Damascus for a series of reconnaissance trips on the ground. He sent with us two stalwart guides, who proudly carried shining pistols and rifles and bore a general demeanor of bravery they may or may not have felt. Around the campfire one evening Ateba, the fiercer of the two, sat quietly polishing his rifle. After an hour of this he removed his pistol and worked industriously on its barrel. At last he drew out his cartridges and, one by one, polished the already gleaming bullets to a higher degree of brilliance.

Without speaking, I reached out my hand for his rifle. Proudly he passed it to me. With the excellence of his work I could not take issue. Then I slid back the bolt and, turning the stock toward the flames, looked down the bore. Now I understood why the Bedouin is such a poor marksman. I doubt if a cleaning rag had touched the inner surfaces since the piece first had come into Ateba's possession. Show! All show!

The Bedouin does not think in terms of annual change. He reckons as new that custom or law that dates back to Mahomet. Since the wise prophet formulated his laws bloody feuds are rare exceptions, though they take on the complexion of fierce warfare. Today the Bedouin can be bought. Menake told me that in the days of old when a Bedouin visited a rival family bent on killing an enemy, he shouted his name as he pulled the trigger so that the relatives might know with whom they should settle.

Though such private feuds exist today, they usually are confined among a few individuals. And the murderer must pay, with his life or in kind. They call blood money the *diya*. Instead of life for life, the *diya* may be expressed in terms of camels, from a dozen to a half-hundred, depending upon the position occupied by the deceased. Mahomet decreed that a reasonable *diya*, when offered, must be accepted. Only in this way, the prophet must have reasoned, could widespread bloodshed be averted and his numbers increased.

Nearly all the Bedouins consider themselves good Mohammedans. Yet again they present a strange contradiction, since few visit Mecca and only a small number follow the ceremonies prescribed by the Koran. The Rualas, I found to my joy, do observe the annual fast of the Ramadan. During this period they declined to eat during the day, breaking their fast only after darkness had settled over the desert. Only during the Ramadan were they willing to work throughout the day without stopping abruptly before noon for their version of lunch.

Fierce though they look to the Occidental, the Bedouins really are small in stature. The men are quite active when following their manly pursuits, but perform none of the chores of the camp. Their women churn the butter, gather wood and prepare all the meals. The men sit quietly before their tents, reading and smoking, while their several wives—of whom constancy is seldom demanded—perform back-breaking menial tasks.

Though the Ruala stands ready at any time to exhibit his riding prowess, there comes a time, as I learned, when he demands a price for such exhibition. Believe it or not, even these faraway people have heard that Hollywood pays fabulous sums indiscriminately for personal services, and I spent many weary hours convincing Fuaz that the report has little basis in truth and that recent economic changes make the assertion even more untrue.

Fuaz indicated, not alone by actions, but also by vigorous language, that he considered himself as important to the production as any actor Hollywood might produce. Were not the Rualas to be featured? Was he not to lead them? I did not dare ask if he had ever seen Valentino on the screen. He might have understood.

Fierce though he looks, like the proverbial mountaineer the Bedouin likes to spend most of his waking hours sitting and thinking. Excepting for the surroundings and his appearance, the Ruala could easily be visioned squatting in front of a small cabin in the American foothills. But tomorrow he will have moved on, leaving behind him in the empty desert only the darkened stones that served for a few days as a cooking hearth.

ERNST LUBITSCH
(1892-1947)

Lubitsch was perhaps the most successful of all the European talent imported by Hollywood. He had quickly developed the recognizable style of romantic comedy which came to be named after him, the pointed and patented "Lubitsch Touch," and was widely recognized by audiences and adored by critics. His career blossomed even more successfully after the arrival of talkies, when in such films as *The Love Parade* and *Monte Carlo* he demonstrated that sound was a particular asset to the graceful style he had developed in the silent period. One major reason for the ease of Lubitsch's transition from Germany to America, and from silents to sound, was the carefully programmed way in which he approached the production of his films. "How vital it is, then, for every scene, every action, to be detailed down to the very last raising of an eyelid," he writes, and this describes rather well his entire approach to filmmaking. He would closet himself with writers like Hans Kraly, Ernest Vajda, or Samson Raphaelson, work over the text of some obscure central European play, and emerge with a blueprint for a film that was followed on the set with the precision of a great master craftsman. Perhaps only Hitchcock approached the degree of pre-planning practised by Lubitsch, an approach responsible for a good many of the similarities in their style. While creating an air of spontaneity was never Lubitsch's strong suit, so long as he kept producing clockwork masterpieces like *Trouble in Paradise* or *Design for Living*, nobody seemed to mind.

FILM DIRECTING
ERNST LUBITSCH

I am constantly asked: "How do you decide on those touches that stamp a film? Do you think of them as you go along? Do the players sometimes insert them? Or are they all decided before the production is started?"

When I have answered and settled those little problems I shall have given you a very good idea of my side of this wonderful business of making pictures.

For it is a wonderful business; a fascinating, romantic profession that becomes more and more intriguing with each film.

Always one must be thinking of fresh ideas; new ways to keep an audience interested; different methods of conveying a meaning to them. In the Maurice Chevalier picture *One Hour with You*, I allowed Maurice to take the audience into his confidence, by facing them and, in a typical Chevalier manner, blandly ask what he shall do next! At the beginning of the film, too, he tells the audience that, contrary to their belief, he really is married. There you get a different touch that all directors strive to insert into their films.

How is that "different" touch found?

I am given a story. Let us say, for example, as I have already mentioned Chevalier, that it is to have Maurice and Jeanette MacDonald as the stars. With this fact before me and being in possession of the main theme of the story, I practically lock myself away from the rest of the world, with my script writer and technical staff. For two or three months we will pore over the work. Every detail is worked out. Perhaps for days I think round a particular scene. Nothing is decided hastily. After a good deal of anxiety and thought, someone perhaps hits on a happy solution. We believe we are ready for further development.

From *The World Film Encyclopedia*, edited by Clarence Winchester, London, 1933.

Ernst Lubitsch investigates the possibilities of the sound camera.

The very next week I may visualize quite differently the way that scene should be done. Back we go, retracing our steps, scrapping ideas and whole scenes, if necessary, just to fit in with this new angle. Gradually the whole production is built up. In my mind's eye I can see exactly how that film will appear on the screen. I may revolve an idea round my mind for days, thinking it out first this way and then that. Would a song be better inserted in such and such a place? Is it likely to hold up the action if it is put in?

Here is why it is essential to view the film as a whole before starting on production. The story is divided into many little scenes—each photographed separately. It is possible that scene 40 may be the first to be "shot." The 39 earlier scenes may even be kept until the very end before the camera records them. Thus, one's mind's eye must have a very clear view of the whole production if one is to tackle the problems connected with it.

Why are scenes "shot" out of order? There can be a variety of reasons. The players needed for these scenes may be engaged on another picture, they may be ill. There may be scenes that are needed away from the studio altogether; there may have been a hitch in the construction of the set through some unavoidable mishap. All sorts of accidents or delays may arise to throw the best laid plans temporarily out of gear. And all the time there is a schedule laid down which strictly limits the time allowed for the whole of the shooting. So it is that the scenes are made in what looks like the most haphazard order.

How vital it is, then, for every scene, every action, to be detailed down to the very last raising of an eyelid. If I were to go into the studio with only a hazy idea of how I was going to treat the subject, muddle and chaos would result. At least it would in my case, although different directors have different ways of working.

Sometimes, of course, even after months of labour and careful preparation, a sudden flash of inspiration when the story has started may alter things a little. It would be foolish, in these circumstances, to adhere rigidly to the fixed schedule of the story. One must have a rather "elastic" mind; be able to see how this new idea is going to affect the rest of the production. Few producers would be thanked by their companies, for instance, if, after the film was half-way through, a completely different complexion were put on the story through a flash of inspiration, and all the film was scrapped, for work to start again on the new way.

That is why I stress the importance of thoroughness. That is why I do insist on my players knowing their scenes several days before they are "shot." It is useless to expect an artiste to come on the set, give him his scene, push him in a corner to "run it over," and then imagine that he will act it as it should be acted. An artiste must be given time to know every word perfectly; to understand exactly what he has to do, and to have a chance to "get into the skin of the part." In some films you may have noticed a disjointed effect. They fail to reproduce the harmonious whole that all of us strive to obtain.

A film should appear, when it is completed, to have been "shot" from beginning to end in one complete piece. That, as you will understand, can seldom be achieved in fact; but careful preparation can give the impression of a complete whole. It would be useless for me to begin shooting on scene 35, for instance, following scene 67, if I had not a complete idea in my mind of what I wanted. Preparation, then, is everything. That is why I spend so long on the preparation of a story and, once I have begun "shooting," am able to get that completed in eight weeks or less.

What so many people forget when they criticize the work of a film director is that he has to cater for varying tastes, all over the world. When a play is produced on the New York stage, for instance, the producer can stress certain points, introduce definite "business" which he knows will appeal to the New York audience. If he were to produce the same play in London, he might change his method drastically, because he knows that London would appreciate certain situations that a New York audience would miss; and vice versa. Imagine, then, the enormous difficulties that face a film maker. He has to produce a screen play that will appeal, not only to New York and London, but also to the Middle West towns of America, the Irish and Scottish peasants, the Australian sheep farmer and the South African business man. This will give you some slight idea of the difficulties with which a film director has to contend and why so much time and thought are necessary if a worldwide reputation is to be secured.

Sometimes, of course, scenes are made twice for different countries. I can give you an example of this. In *The Smiling Lieutenant*, I had all those scenes where the word "lieutenant" was pronounced "lootenant" done again for Britain, with the players saying "leftenant." That was a definite case where it was impossible to cater for both countries with the one picture. American people would have been shocked to have heard "leftenant." Britons would have laughed at "lootenant."

IV

THE DREAM
FACTORY
(1934-1940)

KING VIDOR
(1894-   )

One of the most independent minded directors who ever worked in Hollywood, King Vidor tried on more than one occasion to finance and produce his films outside the regular channels of production. At one point he even had his own small studio (dubbed "Vidor Village"), but economics have always been against such operations, and he was inevitably forced to return to the arms of companies like M-G-M. His privately produced *Our Daily Bread* remains a museum classic, but Vidor's studio films often display in even more striking fashion his main preoccupation, the role of the individual in the group. *The Crowd* is still the finest of these, but such later films as *Northwest Passage*, *An American Romance*, and *The Fountainhead* demonstrate that Vidor was well able to take advantage of studio financing and facilities to create works of equally personal expressiveness. Indeed, while film historians have generally tended to demean Vidor's work after *Our Daily Bread*, it could easily be argued that only in the 40's or 50's do his heroes and heroines develop the richness of personality that characterizes any director's mature style. Certainly no one else created such florid and fascinating roles for actresses as the parts Vidor gave Bette Davis in *Beyond the Forest*, Mercedes McCambridge in *Lightning Strikes Twice*, and Jennifer Jones in *Duel in the Sun* and *Ruby Gentry*. Unappreciated in their own time, these bravura performances have only increased in interest with the passing years, and seem especially rare in an era which creates no film roles for its actresses at all.

RUBBER STAMP MOVIES
KING VIDOR

A producer was planning to make a picture against a background of German submarine activities during the World War. I was to direct the picture. The story was insignificant and I was not enthusiastic. I had used every manner of argument to talk the producer out of his plan, to no avail. Over a week-end holiday, I learned from several friends that five other studios were preparing the same type of picture. This fact, I thought, would be my defense against having to make the submarine picture, so Monday morning I eagerly awaited the producer to report my findings.

When I told the producer that if our submarine picture were made it would be the sixth, as five others were already in work, his reply, to my utter astonishment, was: "That proves I'm right."

Walt Disney makes fantasy popular with his delightful *Silly Symphonies* and Paramount produces *Alice in Wonderland* and makes a bust of it. Before *Alice* was rated a failure, Goldwyn planned to do Frank Baum's *Wizard of Oz*. Now he will be in a complete quandary because of the continued success of Disney fantasy and the failure of Paramount's venture.

A producer told me that the success of *Little Women* was due to the fact that the public was beginning to demand costume plays. Ridiculous! As if the public all got together and passed a resolution demanding costume plays. As a result of the success of *Little Women* there will be a flood of similar films and a consequent raid on the "classics" until the public is nauseated and yells for mercy. One exhibitor when asked what picture he liked best last year replied *Three Little Women*.

Five years ago when sound pictures were first inaugurated, musicals were extremely popular until the producers made so many of them, and all exactly alike, that the public simply

From *New Theatre*, September 1934.

King Vidor on the set of *Street Scene* (1931).

went out on strike against over-teethed sopranos. The same thing happened again because Warner Brothers sneaked out with a grand little picture, *42nd Street*, and the flood was on.

After many months of dickering, the Greater Garbo was persuaded to return to Santa Monica and a new contract. Then followed months and months of story conferences and many, many changes of writers to get the proper vehicle to carry the "I-tank" girl to her poor clamoring public.

Actually one year was spent on the story but when the picture reached the theatres it was the same old story that has been produced dozens of times before. John Gilbert should know by now that that pretty blonde he meets in the crowded tavern in the snow country is a woman and not a pansy. Think of the time he loses. Anyway, the story is so familiar I think even Marion Davies would have rejected it.

What causes all this, you may be thinking. Well, the first offender is high-cost. For example, an author may write any book he cares to, and the production cost against the completed article could be as little as: Food and lodging for three months, $86.10; paper and pencils, $3.16; clothes and barber shop, $0.00.

But if a motion picture director gets a big idea he has to dig up a hundred thousand some place even if he does go without shaves and haircuts. A man will gamble two bucks on an old horse at a race-track but if he bets a thousand he's going to pick out the horse that's won the most times before. Consequently, in the movie business the final decisions are made by business men, not artists. If a writer or director could finance himself, and if his work of art could fail completely without the artist going to the poorhouse for the rest of his life, more interesting pictures would be made more frequently.

But the purse-strings are held as I said, by business men and not by artists and when they weigh those hundred thousands on one side and the director's talents on the other the decisions are generally made in favor of the pot of gold.

Many original ideas are accepted for production in Hollywood studios but by the time they reach the screen they appear to have been poured from the same mould as all the others. With a few exceptions all pictures that make a definite step forward come from outside studios and individual producers.

On account of the high cost of production Hollywood producers are afraid to take a chance. They will spend all kinds of money on a picture but they will not gamble with subject material. The hopeful public continue to frequent the picture theatres but in most cases comes away unmoved. The physical aspects of the picture are beyond reproach—direction, casting, acting, photography, settings, dialogue, are the best money can buy. But what of it? The inspirational basic idea has been distilled out of it and what does the public get for its money that it hasn't gotten hundreds of times before?

Intelligent people try to forget the picture as quickly as possible. The result is usually a bad taste in the subconscious. How long they'll continue to abuse themselves in this manner no one knows, but the gross attendance has been falling steadily off and the people will stay away in mobs as soon as they find something better to do.

A few years back they used to say, "Let's go to the movies tonight," now they say, "Let's see if we can find a picture tonight." And usually they are unsuccessful. Sometimes they go anyway and the evening ends with the ultimate resolve to be more careful next time.

One of the different obstacles in production is the fact that a script or scenario is only the foundation on which something else is to be built. That is, the scenario that the director submits to the supervisor is the skeleton upon which his finished picture is going to depend. If the scenario expressed all the emotion that the finished picture will contain it would have to be written in literary or book form. The supervisor with his lack of visual imagination, is unable to fill in the gap between the scenario and the finished article. Consequently he orders that each detail of the script be so obvious and over-written that when the ingredients of good-direction, good-acting, and good photography are added the ultimate whole is all too obvious and dull. The audience cannot use its imagination, and it is the use of the imagination that is the psychological meaning of most entertainment. That was the great value of the silent picture. In the silent picture the audience was compelled to use its imagination at every moment. That is why Charlie Chaplin will do a lot of thinking before he makes a talking picture. We, in America, have never thought of Charlie as an Englishman while watching one of his pictures and neither have the natives of Afghanistan. But let him speak, and English he will be, and all your imagination will not be able to make him anything else.

A scene in a silent picture could be more intense than a similar scene in a talking picture. A talking picture is literal, you take what you are given. In a silent picture we could mix in our sound and dialogue to taste. As soon as some of our stars of the silent days spoke they were finished. Their voices couldn't live up to the imaginative aura with which we had surrounded them. This, however, is not true of Chaplin. Charlie is just as amusing audibly as he is pictorially.

The second drawback to better pictures is "catering to the

mob." Pictures, being expensive, are made for what the producers call the "mob taste," synonymous in their minds with "infantile." Every other project has the element of discrimination in its appeal. Imagine trying to make a pair of shoes that would satisfy every human animal from nine to ninety, male or female. Anyone who can solve that riddle is not only a Houdini but a phenomenon. Even with as universal an article as a newspaper you can read what you like and ignore the rest. But with a picture you must swallow it all. Silent pictures did have the element of flexibility: they could be seasoned to individual tastes by adding imagination.

But this is not supposed to be a discussion of silent pictures or talking pictures but a bark at the producers with a hope that it will have a widespread effect and an ultimate beneficial result.

Pictures would be better if they were not controlled by big business. Big business could make better pictures at much less money by dividing its studios up into individual units and encouraging individual expression instead of throwing all creative endeavors into the same stew-pot.

HAL ROACH
(1892 -   )

When Mack Sennett loosened his grip on the title "king of comedy" in the mid-20's, Hal Roach was there to grab it. This he accomplished critically (his comedians were better reviewed) and commercially (his films were bigger box office), but somehow he never replaced the image of Sennett in the public mind, and Roach's reputation is even today eclipsed by that of his better-known predecessor. The differences between them were considerable, and important to an understanding of why Sennett ultimately failed at a time when Roach's silent comedies were still flourishing. Roach worked with his comics to develop stable characters whose reactions to given situations could be predicted by the audience. We can anticipate how Laurel and Hardy will react to a given situation, and our amused imaginings are only reinforced when they do indeed react that way. This comedy of ritual was a considerable development over Sennett's "wild man" theory of comic construction, which spun off gags like an eccentric pinwheel. Roach was interested in making his characters believably human, and his firm grasp of dramatic structure enabled comedians like Harold Lloyd, Charlie Chase, and the Our Gang kids to appear as identifiable individuals, rather than as stylized comic types—Sennett's approach with Turpin, Sterling, and the bathing beauties. In the final analysis, their own comedians made the crucial decisions on the effectiveness of the competing styles. Chaplin, Arbuckle, and Langdon fought with Sennett and abandoned him, but Roach's troupe remained remarkably intact until the mid-30's when economics put an end to the short comedy.

THE GAG'S THE THING
HAL ROACH

In the motion-picture industry the situations that produce laughs are called gags. Gags are the life and breath of comedy. They cover every type of humorous situation from the pie-throwing incident of pure slapstick to the man who finds his prized watch in the pocket of the person he has just ducked in the pool.

A comedian can be just as funny as the situation will allow, and no funnier. True, some comedians can make a funnier situation of a certain incident than others, but that is merely a measure of ability. It is the gags, the incidents in a comedy, that are remembered, and not the story itself. This is as true in dramatic productions as in comedies. In drama the high spots of the play bring emotional reaction from the audience, tears, smiles, or even hisses. In comedy they bring laughter—and are called gags.

A gag is a situation that is turned from the expected into something humorous and unexpected. An automobile going down the street is just an incident, but if it comes to an abrupt stop there is a shock to the senses of the observer, and the incident may have become dramatic, depending on the story involved. But if this car, traveling along in a very ordinary way, suddenly stops and does a complete back somersault, that is a gag. An extreme example but it illustrates the point.

In movie comedies there are several kinds of gags. There is the funny situation that is building up to the climax of the story, and is a necessary part of the story itself—that is called comedy business. There is a bit of business, injected for an incidental laugh, that will stand by itself—an incident that would be funny whether the story existed or not—and that is an incidental gag. Then there is the running gag, so called because it is represented at intervals through the picture. A gag is capped

From *Popular Mechanics*, May 1935. Reprinted by permission.

or topped, in movie parlance, when it reaches its climax. The comedy business gags throughout the picture are capped individually, and then are double-capped by the sub-climaxes of the story, the high moments of a series of connected incidents. The incidental gags are capped also. Almost every gag is good for at least three laughs, one at the gag itself, another at the incident that caps it, and a third at the reaction of the players. A flash from the reaction of one player to that of another will often double the laughs there.

The test of a gag is, of course, whether or not it is funny. Until we show a picture, we have no standard by which to judge it other than the old standby, "Is it funny to me?" There is no such thing as an average intelligence or a certain level at which to aim our humor. Comedy situations appeal to old and young alike, and the roughnecks will laugh at the same thing that amuses the college professor. We have to judge entirely by our own reactions. Sometimes we are fooled, and the thing that seems funniest to us will fall flat, while some bit of "must" business, put in because it had to be there to advance the story, will get the laughs instead.

Since the old pie-throwing slapstick days, the gag has changed but little in substance. It is still a situation that is given a humorous turn. But in execution it has changed a lot. The gag started as pure physical humor—a man slipping on a banana peel and falling or a car running into a telephone pole. Those incidents were exciting and funny in a day when little happened in people's everyday lives. Now the gags must be more subtle. The broad humor of that day will produce only laughs of derision today. Along the same line, the gag must now have a reason for its existence. It must advance the climax of the story, bring out some phase of a player's character, or, in the case of the incidental gag where more license is allowable, it must at least fit in with the action of the previous gags. No more is a comedy a series of funny situations thrown together with no regard to their relation to each other.

The talkies have done much to change comedies. Formerly, we photographed our action at the rate of twelve frames per second and projected it at twenty-four per second. That made our action appear on the screen twice as fast as it had actually been acted.[1] Now, we must record both sound and sight at the projection speed, twenty-four, and the action must be carried out at the speed at which it is to appear. The talkies also cut out a lot of action that formerly was necessary to explain the story. Now, to make it clear that a woman's husband is a policeman, she mentions it in the dialogue. Before, she would be shown kissing him goodbye as he left for work. The dialogue now possible also is responsible for some of the laughs in spoken lines, which the titles in the silent picture days could not get across.

These are mechanical changes. Broadly speaking, the comedy has not changed much with the years. Even the same old bits of business are sometimes given a new presentation, a new setting, or are worked out from a different angle. Of course there are many variations of the old laugh-getting situations. Some of the methods, such as the combining of animation and sound in the animated cartoons, are new—and there is even a new gag occasionally. But with new methods or old, the gag's still the thing that makes or breaks comedies.

1. While such under-cranking was *occasionally* used for specific effects, the idea that silent comedies were projected at double speed is simply not the case. Imagine one of Roach's Charlie Chase or Laurel and Hardy comedies projected in this manner!

ROUBEN MAMOULIAN
(1898-   )

"Psychological truth" has always been at the heart of Rouben Mamoulian's work, and stylization of image and sound the chosen means of achieving it. Born of Armenian parents in Russian Georgia, Mamoulian studied at the Moscow Art Theatre, and by the late 20's he had directed many important productions in London, Rochester, and New York. At the start of the talkie period he signed with Paramount, and in his very first film (*Applause*, 1929) pioneered imaginative sound-recording techniques which helped free the moving picture from the would-be tyranny of the microphone. By the time of *Love Me Tonight* (1932) he was displaying a mastery of contrapuntal audio-visual editing unrivaled even in Europe. It might seem ironic that such technical innovations came to the cinema from a theater director, but Mamoulian even on stage had experimented with expressionistic staging in such productions as *Porgy* (1927), always seeking a way in which the formal elements of the medium might be marshaled to express the emotional values of the text. Thus when he came to direct *Becky Sharp* (1935), the first feature film made in the perfected three-color Technicolor, he had not only some clearly defined ideas on the expressive potential of color in film, but a reasonable sense of how it would ultimately change the cinema. His late career was marked by greater stage than screen success (he directed the original stage productions of *Porgy and Bess*, *Oklahoma*, and *Carousel*), but he did leave the cinema at least one more masterwork, the brilliantly Technicolored *Blood and Sand* (1941).

SOME PROBLEMS IN THE DIRECTION OF COLOR PICTURES

ROUBEN MAMOULIAN

Ladies and gentlemen: As I sit here, I am amazed at the quality and nature of this meeting. I have attended meetings concerning the arts of the theatre, music and literature, but never have I witnessed the overwhelming scientific atmosphere that prevails here. I must say that this unusual atmosphere of the present meeting is characteristic of the whole industry and art of motion pictures.

No art has ever depended so much on science as the art of motion pictures. In that sense it is truly the most modern of arts. It begins where science ends and it has a hard time, and not always a successful time, in artistically keeping up with the progress of the scientific and technical achievements that are taking place constantly in motion pictures.

Seven years ago motion pictures were revolutionized by the advent of sound. Theretofore silent, the screen acquired the gift of speech. Today, as another result of scientific achievement, color comes to the screen and to my mind, it is just as much of a miracle as sound was. I would like to pay my most respectful tribute to those people whose names one doesn't hear who work in the silence and solitude of their laboratories. I refer to the scientists that compose the body of Technicolor, whose destinies are guided by Dr. Kalmus.

Now the main question today is: "Will color last or will it not?"

I have no doubt that color on the screen is here to stay. I have also no doubt that there will be as much skepticism for the first few months in regard to color as there was in regard to sound.

From *The International Photographer*, July 1935. Originally presented at a meeting of the Technicians' Branch of the Academy of Motion Picture Arts and Sciences.

Rouben Mamoulian with Miriam Hopkins and Cedric Hardwicke on the set of *Becky Sharp* (1935). Director of photography Ray Rennahan sits beside the giant Technicolor camera at left.

Some say that what we haven't got, we don't miss. No one ever missed electricity until it came to replace oil and gas. No one missed dialogue on the screen while the screen was silent. However, let a dumb man, after thirty years of life acquire the gift of speech, would he want to give it up and go back to his silence? Speech came to the screen and stayed—victorious. Now, let a man with ailing eyesight wearing black glasses through which the world looks grey, suddenly recover his sight, throw away his glasses and see the luxury of the color of the sky, the earth and the flowers; would he ever want to go back to his black glasses?

We never missed color on the screen because the very art of the cinema was born black and white. It was a convention which had to be accepted, but once real color comes on the screen, we shall feel its absence as forcefully as we feel the absence of sound when looking at a silent film made some years ago.

I do not mean to say that necessarily all the films will have to be in color, but certainly the great majority of them will be. As in the art of painting, while we admire and love black and white drawings and etchings, could we ever do without paintings? So far the screen has been using a pencil; now it is given a palette with paints.

I don't want to be misunderstood. I don't want to imply that the black and white film is not beautiful nor that the color film completely displaces the black and white. As a matter of fact, the black and white has a beauty of its own that could never fade away. The very unreality of those pale shadows moving on the screen and that remote quality of a dream, constitute the attraction and the spell of the black and white film that could not be destroyed. There will always be room for certain subjects to be treated in terms of these fascinating grey shadows. But color comes to the screen now as a new spring to the earth. It comes as an inspiring and exciting gift, which opens new horizons of creation for the artist and enjoyment for the onlooker.

I am stating this now not merely as a theoretical point, but as a result of an actual experience I went through recently. This experience was directing *Becky Sharp*, the first full-length feature in color. That was a new and wondrous adventure. It had all the thrill and excitement of pioneering in a new field and discovering a theretofore unexplored fairyland.

Color is one of the most powerful and fascinating attributes of nature. Just imagine what the world would look like if you took color out of it. What would life be if we were forced to spend it among sky, trees, flowers and all things black, grey and white! Having known the living joys of color, we would probably die of melancholia.

Love of color and susceptibility to color is one of the strongest instincts in human beings. If you want to discover the most organic, basic elements of the sophisticated human being of today, go to children and go to savages. You will find that next to food, they love things of vivid color and sparkle. That instinct is alive and strong in every one of us.

In relation to motion pictures, our need for color has so far been ungratified. We accepted the situation just as we had accepted the fact of moving on solid ground until we learned to fly. But once color comes to the screen, we will be unhappy without it. It brings a new terrific power to the screen. Our strongest impressions come through vision. So far visually, we are dealing with light and shade and compositions on the screen. Now we have an additional element of color. This, not merely to superficially adorn the images in motion, but to increase the dramatic and emotional effectiveness of the story which is being unfolded to the spectator.

Color, like all power, can be harmful and destructive when used badly, life-giving and creative when used well. Animals and human beings have always been and are unconsciously subject to a hypnotic influence of color. How many times have you walked into a strange house and felt depressed because of the color of the wall paper? How many times have you found consolation in the rich riot of shades of a gorgeous sunset?

Apart from pure pictorial beauty and the entertainment value of color, there is also a definite emotional content and meaning in most colors and shades. We have lost sight of that because like all important and inevitable phenomena, it has become subconscious with us. It is not an accident that the traffic lights of a city street today are green for safety and red for danger. Colors convey to us subtly different moods, feelings and impulses. It is not an accident that we use the expressions "To see red," "to feel blue," "to be green with envy" and "to wear a black frown." Is it for nothing that we believe that white is expressive of purity, black of sorrow, red of passion, green of hope, yellow of madness, and so on.

The artist should take advantage of the mental and emotional implications of color and use them on the screen to increase the power and effectiveness of a scene, situation or character. I have tried to do as much of this in *Becky Sharp* as the story allowed. To quote an example of this, I would refer to the sequence of the panic which occurs at the Duchess of Richmond's ball when the first shots of Napoleon's cannons are heard. You will see how inconspicuously, but with telling effect, this sequence builds to a climax through a series of inter-cut shots which progress from the coolness and sobriety of colors like grey, blue, green and pale yellow, to the exciting danger and threat of deep orange and flaming red.

The effect is achieved by the selection of dresses and uniforms worn by the characters and the color of backgrounds and lights. There is a little of homecoming feeling in this for me as the use of color and colored lights was one of my main joys and excitements in the theatre. Surely, the effectiveness of productions like *Porgy*, *Marco Millions* and *Congai* which I have done in the theatre world would have been sadly decreased if I were forced not to use color in sets, costumes and lights on the stage.

Of course, in each art, different subjects are expressed best through different forms. Undoubtedly, there are some stories which beg for color on the screen more than others do. Off-hand, a story of historical period of the past, when life and clothing were much more colorful, or stories with the backgrounds of countries like Spain and Italy, even of today, would ask for color more than some stories of our modern age and civilization.

The black and white films will still have their place on the screen, but most assuredly as time goes by, there will be less of them and more of the color pictures. For even though our life today is grey (and because of that) we have a great love and longing for color. Is it not to be more attractive that women dress their bodies in beautifully shaded gowns and touch their faces with the subtle magic of a discriminate make-up? Is it not the same impulse that drives the grey and tired families of working-men out to Sunday picnics somewhere where there is a touch of blue sky, a green blade of grass, a tree or a flower?

Everything that is beautiful to the eye is a great gift to humanity. Color on the screen is such a gift. The only danger of it that I can see during the first stages of the color picture, would be the danger of excess. Talking pictures did not avoid it during the first months of their existence. There was too much talk and too much noise on the screen. The cinema must not fall into another trap and must not go about color as a newly-rich. Color should not mean gaudiness. Restraint and selectivity are the essence of art.

WILLIAM DE MILLE
(1878 - 1955)

This sly little article tells us nothing about the films of William de Mille, but plenty about the tongue-in-cheek humor of the man whose film career was always overshadowed by the success of his younger brother, C.B. William had more modest pretensions all around, not only in retaining the family's non-capitalized "de," but in the scope of his film work as well. Eschewing the spectacle, he felt that the interplay of human emotions was more than enough to fill any screen and he achieved considerable acclaim in the late 'teens and early 20's with such thoughtful, literate films as *Conrad in Quest of His Youth* and *Miss Lulu Bett*. He had originally been brought west by his brother to help establish Lasky's script department, and turned inevitably to directing soon after. Few of his films survive today, but those that remain tend to bear out his reputation as the more intellectual of the brothers, the one given to introspective dramatics leavened with bursts of wry humor. This humor is in ample evidence throughout the following article, which stops to analyze the recent victory of Popeye the Sailor over Mickey Mouse in a national popularity poll. He discusses this poll with a mock seriousness that parodies that of the *Literary Digest*, claiming to see, among other things, a general swing toward fascism on the part of cartoon watchers. The deadpan seriousness with which the rest of Hollywood reacted to both the poll and de Mille's analysis of it can only be imagined!

MICKEY vs. POPEYE
WILLIAM de MILLE

Whenever the motion-picture industry creates an outstanding piece of work like *David Copperfield,* it points with pride to the wonderful effect this picture will have upon the youth of the country.

When the same industry puts forth a gangster story, it takes great pains to explain that the youth of the country is in no way affected by what it sees on the screen; that the portrayal of vice and crime can act only as a warning to little would-be murderers and racketeers; and that by producing these pictures in sufficient volume the cumulative effect upon the younger generation will be to disgust it with all criminal activities, through sheer boredom.

Thus, to the studious observer, the general effect of feature pictures upon our young remains in a state of academic obscurity.

But the animated cartoons give a surer indication of how our future citizens react to life's values once they are divorced from tedious reality. In the cartoons we find super-nature in the raw, and it is even less mild than nature under the same conditions.

A vote was taken recently among schoolchildren of the United States, to decide which of the well-known cartoon characters was the most popular. The ordinary adult would say at once that Mickey Mouse, the "little friend of all the world," would win in a walk. But the election went otherwise.

Popeye, the Sailor Man, carried many States by safe majorities, and, while the balloting as a whole was close, it is probable that Popeye has carried the country by a small number of votes.

This is amazing and revolutionary.

Do the kids want a new deal in their two-dimensional he-

From *The Forum,* November 1935.

roes? Must the gentle altruism of Mickey bow to the rugged individualism of Popeye?

There have always been two schools of juvenile thought in the land—the party of the Right, based upon the firm rectitude and irreproachable philosophy of Sanford and Merton and the various examples of youthful perfection as drawn by Horatio Alger, and the party of the Left, whose ideals are founded upon the more violent careers of Nick Carter and Jesse James. Under the drive of modern progress and world mechanization, each of these schools has evolved its screen symbol: Mickey, a veritable Sir Galahad, polished, courteous, unselfish, and full of a great desire to help the world; Popeye, sinister, self-assertive, worshiping strength rather than justice, determined to dominate rather than to help.

Should Popeye commit an uncouth act, which he does frequently, he excuses it by the nearest approach to an apology he can find in his nature—"I yam what I yam, and that's all I yam."

It is saddening to see Popeye, like a Hun from the north, threatening the more cultured supremacy of Mickey, Minnie, and the intelligent and devoted Pluto.

That Popeye and his ever-present companion, Olive Oyle, should be accepted as Mickey's and Minnie's equals indicates a definite degeneration of domestic ideals.

Mickey, the devoted husband, the generous provider, Minnie's infallible refuge in times of storm and strife, and Minnie, the faithful helpmate, presumably the fond mother of those hundreds of little mice who from time to time form part of this joyous household—these two stand for the integrity of the American home.

Nothing less than violent abduction causes Minnie to notice any male but her own; no blandishment or seductive female charm ever lures Mickey to forget for one instant the sanctity of his hymeneal vows. Their relationship forms an inspiring picture of perfect matrimonial union which cannot help encouraging those children who attend the theater after witnessing an unpleasant tiff at the breakfast table between dear Papa and darling Mamma.

What are we to think, then, when we find young America accepting with equal gusto the vague and somewhat equivocal relationship between Popeye and his not-so-charming Olive Oyle? There is certainly no indication that they are legally wedded. On the other hand there is no suggestion that they are living in sin. They remain perpetually *in statu quo*, a sort of permanent engagement without the object of matrimony. Popeye's treatment of his girl friend is not only extremely boisterous but at times positively rude. Such gestures of affection as they indulge in are distinctly anatomical rather than spiritual. It may be that their remarkable powers of recuperation from physical shock would make a less strenuous gesture inadequate to express their true feelings.

In physical type Popeye and Mickey and their respective companions represent two distinct schools of aesthetics: Mickey's voice gentle, childlike, charming; Popeye's rough, raw, and raucous, with a suggestion of salt air blown through adenoids. Mickey's graceful movements and his long and expressive tail are poetry, whereas Popeye's movements are uncouth, jerky, expressive of power without beauty.

Mickey's whole life suggests the beloved Don Quixote, with Minnie as the fair Dulcinea and good old Pluto fulfilling the duties of Sancho Panza. Popeye, on the contrary, is more like Captain William Kidd, taking his own or anyone else's where he finds it and being not so much interested in righting the wrongs of the world as in seeing to it that the world takes no advantage of him.

Strange that two such contrasting figures should divide the affections of our children. The idealized mouse and the human figure which falls so far short of Grecian standards of beauty; the lovely, fascinating tail of Mickey against the hideous but terribly powerful forearms of Popeye. When Mickey smiles we feel that the sun is shining and all the little birds are singing. Popeye's infrequent grin is that of the absolute sensualist.

One quality they have in common, and it may be that in this lies the secret of their influence over the youngsters. That quality is courage. No two heroes since the world began have so frequently dared the impossible as these two. By all the laws of nature and man the two have died a thousand deaths; but Mickey's ingenuity and Popeye's remarkable anatomical construction have always brought them through unscathed. In this respect Popeye has one great advantage over Mickey. That advantage is spinach.

It is the one practical lesson in living that Popeye has to offer his admirers. When the youthful but prehensile mind comprehends the amazing effects that a few mouthfuls of spinach can achieve in deciding the outcome of a major battle, it undoubtedly eases the lot of millions of American mothers who find difficulty in persuading recalcitrant offspring that the homely vegetable is a desirable food.

To be fair to Popeye, it must not be thought that he is not always willing to fight for his Olive. He is fond of his own and ready to protect the weak; but he fights for her because she *is* his own; he is protecting his property, not rescuing a loved one; and when he comes to the aid of strangers in distress we cannot help thinking that he is reveling in his own prowess rather than feeling the glow of civic virtue which comes from doing justice.

These two strange figures, Mickey and Popeye, products of a humorous but desperate age, have won the hearts of those to whom we will, tomorrow, turn over the country. What is their secret? Probably power.

They both achieve. Each in his own way strives to solve the world's problems. It will be interesting to see which will dominate the future thought.

As Mr. Gilbert once remarked:

> Every boy and every gal
> Who's born into this world alive
> Is either a little Liberal
> Or else a little Conservative.

So the Mickey Mousians of today will be the New Dealers of tomorrow, whereas the Popeyesians will breed a race of Fascists.

JOHN CROMWELL
(1888-   )

Long a successful actor and producer on the stage, John Cromwell was associated with William Brady for twelve years before contracting with Paramount to direct talkies in 1928. He brought over a theater director's respect for the actor and the writer, a quality which gave his work a uniformly high performance standard. Yet even his earliest films display a grasp of cinematography and editing that eliminated any unwanted qualities of staginess. His recently discovered *The Dance of Life*, for example, has been acclaimed as one of the most fluid and sophisticated of the early talkies. These skills made him the perfect team director for a producer like David O. Selznick, for whom he directed such films as *The Prisoner of Zenda* and *Since You Went Away*, peaks of Hollywood craftsmanship. To Cromwell the work of the director was not to throw off individual sparks of creativity, but to fuse the efforts of the entire creative team for the best interests of the finished work. Such selflessness has always been rare in film-making, and Cromwell has long been overlooked by critics and historians alike. But recent reassessments of his work, notably such bitter late films as *Caged* and *The Goddess*, have established him as a director of substance as well as style, not merely the hired *litterateur* of Paramount, RKO, or Selznick.

THE VOICE BEHIND THE MEGAPHONE

JOHN CROMWELL

When I first came to Hollywood from the theater, I was told upon my arrival, as a preliminary to my first assignment as a director, to look for a story. This was some eight or ten years ago when the talking picture was in its infancy and before so many fine minds had been attracted by the new medium. I set about looking for a story in the files of the studio story department (naturally I was asked to make my selection from the material on hand). For several weeks I read lengthily, if not too well. Finally I came across a story which appealed to me, and, anxious to get started, I hurried to the author to discuss with him certain changes which in my capacity as a director I felt were necessary. He agreed with me on all of them. But when I asked him how soon he could make these changes, he looked at me in great surprise and said, "You don't want *me* to make them, do you?" "Why, who else but you?" I answered. "Well," he said, "we write a story out here and hand it in. If it's accepted, we're delighted. But we don't expect to hear any more about it until the preview and then if we have the good fortune to find one scene of our own that we recognize, we feel very flattered." I explained that in the theater it was considered a very poor breach of etiquette to consult another writer about changes on a script, unless the original author had given up completely. This screen writer looked at me in some astonishment and I have been told his encounter with me was his topic of conversation for some time following.

At that time, it was believed impossible to obtain a successful screen story without employing a great many writers. In fact, their number measured its success. This belief probably grew out of the demand for competent screen writers which far exceeded their supply. All this, as I have said, was some

From *We Make the Movies,* edited by Nancy Naumburg, New York, 1937.

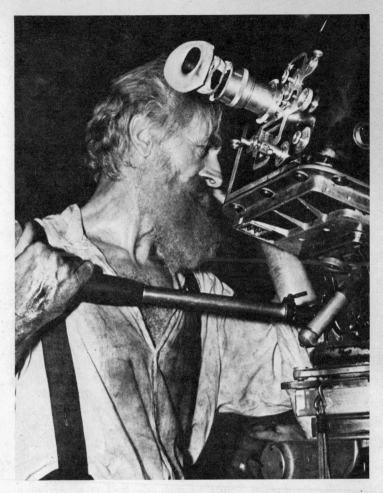

John Cromwell, in make-up for the part of John Brown, checks a camera set-up on his *Abe Lincoln in Illinois* (1939).

eight years ago, and since that time pictures and the making of pictures have come a long way. I have come also to certain very definite theories about the motion picture and the varied processes it must undergo before it is given to me to translate into living situations and personalities for the screen. I have come to believe that if studios would look at what the author has created as the thing worth producing, and would take the trouble to develop writers—especially young writers—to a point where their efforts are worthy of production, pictures would be much better for it. Not until a determined effort is made to develop writers who have something to say, and have learned to say it in the medium of the motion picture, will the motion picture as an industry really have some claim as a creative art.

Once the story has been agreed upon, the producer, writer and myself enter into a general discussion as to its treatment. This will vary, of course, if the story is in the form of a novel, short story, an original story or a play. I believe there are very few plays in their original form which lend themselves to the motion picture, because the medium is so totally different. In most plays the story is static, and it needs a great deal of ingenuity to transfer it to the visual medium. A screen story must flow, it must tell its story through the eye and the emotions: a play, on the other hand, tells its story through the mind and the emotions.

Having conferred thoroughly on the treatment, dramatic construction and character of the story with the director and producer, if the latter has anything to offer, the writer goes away to make a first draft. This is then submitted to the producer and myself and adjustments are made on this basis. In working out the treatment the author may have found flaws which were not apparent at first, such as in the logical development of the story. It has sometimes been necessary to change a dramatic story into a comedy so that the writer could take more liberties with the plot line.

In *The Prisoner of Zenda*, for example, we were confronted with an antiquated, nostalgic story. Our problem was either to tell it realistically as well as possible, to tell it with our tongue in our cheeks, or to endeavor to create a period in which our story would seem credible. The first two methods would obviously not stand up today. But, in the third, we were able to realize enough of our original intentions to make the result both interesting and exciting.

When a director gets a story, he has a pattern which includes the original idea of the writer and his comment on the story. These are uniquely his; they should not be supplemented by any other writer who might blur the final conception of the story. The director adds only enough interpolations of his own to give the story the fluidity a screen story must have. It must then be conceived and formulated by the writer and director as a complete entity. How the director will interpret this is the next step in its proper place. His own individuality is apparent in the way he shoots and edits the picture, and the manner in which he builds up the story expresses his point of view.

While the writer prepares the final shooting script, the director confers with the producer, art director and cameraman as a matter of course. The completed script contains a full description of the locale and atmosphere of the scenes, explicit camera angles and effects, detailed descriptions of the characters as well as the dialogue and sound effects. This is then sent to all departments so that each will be as familiar as possible with the director's requirements. These departments of the motion picture, in the main, are in safe hands. Most art directors and most cameramen have real understanding and feeling. The art director should be able to understand from reading the script just what is needed in his interpretation of the story in terms of the sets. He must be sure to cover it from every conceivable camera angle. For example, in designing a large ballroom set, he must have enough variety of angles to cover the length of the scene when the cameras are placed in various positions.

The interpretation of the cameraman is also brought to bear on the script. Usually we discuss our viewpoints in a fairly exhaustive conference. The cameraman often makes valuable suggestions which may necessitate changes in the script. I have already laid out the general pattern of the camera angles or shots in my mind. But the greatest danger to avoid is any set or predetermined ideas about camera angles which are not amenable to suggestions from the author, the art director or the cameraman, or, later, to circumstances on the set. Camera angles should never be completely fixed in the script. Very often they are changed to facilitate a more dramatic emphasis in a scene or a more interesting way of telling the story.

On the premise that a director to be a director should be able to determine what it would cost to shoot successfully the story agreed upon, he should be allowed, and invariably is, to determine how the money should be spent. Of course the production manager supervises the various details of the budget, which include the estimates of all departments involved in the production. But this budget must always have enough latitude so that the director can completely effect his visualization in terms of the finished film.

As the pre-shooting preparation proceeds further, the director is confronted with innumerable problems which must be solved before the production gets under way. In this he is given invaluable aid by the assistant director who has charge of all routine matters connected with the production and who has mapped out the script into the various shooting days, so that it may be finished with the maximum efficiency. Now every department clamors for his attention with a hundred and one details.

First there is the casting problem to settle. His star or stars have already been chosen by the producer. He must accept or reject the casting director's final choice of players. He must look at the tests made under his supervision of these players or at their work in previous films. With the casting settled, he must confer with the wardrobe department on costumes for the principal players and later make tests of them in their wardrobe and make-up to see that they are in character. He must make a final inspection tour with the art director to see that the sets are properly built and dressed or decorated. He must pass on all properties to be used. He must confer with the musical director as to how much and what type of background music is required. He must confer with the location manager on a suitable site, if the picture is to be shot on location. He must confer with the art department together with the special effects department on any miniature sets which must be built, and with the special effects and camera department on process or transparency shots, which generally form a part of every feature production. And he must confer at frequent intervals with the producer on the progress in the preparatory stages of the production.

I like to rehearse the entire script with the players at least two weeks before I start shooting. The value of rehearsals is twofold: they enable the director to get a view of the whole story and they permit the actor a complete conception of his part, so that if we shoot according to schedule, starting with the middle of the story, jump back to the beginning, ahead to the climax and then back to the second third, the actor will have the complete conception of his part so thoroughly in mind that his acting out of continuity will not greatly disturb him.

The greatest factor against proper rehearsals is the fact that very few stories permit them because of economic reasons. Of course, I cannot blame a producer who has paid a large sum of money to an actor in an important part for concentrating on that part. If it is spread out over the script, the producer naturally will try to concentrate it into one week's work instead of three or four, by adjusting the shooting schedule. But it has always been my contention that I could find economies in the usual picture which would make up for the expense of carrying important actors from the date of their first rehearsal to the first day of shooting, and this certainly curtails the actual shooting time.

There are two schools of directing. In the first, the director is and insists on being all-powerful, so that any creative thought on the part of the actor is apt to infringe on his ideas. What he most desires is to manipulate facile and clever automatons which are nevertheless possessed of great screen personality. In the second school, the director wants actors who are really creative, so that he can mold these various creations into a whole which fits in with his idea of the story. I liken a director of a picture or a play to the director of a symphony orchestra in which his job is merely his interpretation of the author's idea through which he makes his personal comment on the story. This presupposes that each actor with whom he works is a creative artist in his own right and that the director's job is merely to guide and fuse these individual creative interpretations into a harmonious and expressive whole.

The old theory about acting in pictures seemed to be based

on the common belief that the screen required no acting in the proper sense of the word. Actors were little more than puppets with a talent for mimicry or an abundant supply of facile tricks, so that when they came on the set, bolstered up by personality, their stock question would always be: "What do I do in this scene?" As director, I deplore the lack of initiative and imagination in the great majority of screen actors. I would go so far as to say that I could count on two hands the actors in Hollywood who are truly creative. The majority have not the slightest conception of what the word creative means. This lack, and the inability of the actors to realize it, may be due to the essential difficulty of screen acting. Few actors are conscious of the fact that their whole conception of a part must be completed before they start on a picture. In the theater, that conception is a matter of growth through from three to eight weeks of rehearsals and trial. In pictures, all this must be accomplished before shooting begins. Nor have screen actors learned to consult their directors exhaustively in this process. To conceive one's role completely beforehand requires great personal integrity of an actor, because he must accomplish this in spite of the many and persistent obstacles of studio routine. I am frequently amazed at actors of great integrity and purpose coming from the theater to do pictures and supinely yielding to that routine.

When the director starts shooting, he has the story so completely in mind that he knows exactly what he wants. The old style of shooting a scene was to take an establishing *long shot*, play the scene through with a *medium shot*, and then use a *close shot* for the characters. This was called "being thoroughly protected." I think that a director should save all that time and energy by learning the art of film-story-telling, and cut his picture as he shoots. Fundamentally he has a choice of two kinds of technique: starting on a fairly close shot of some action that is either revelation of the characters or story, then proceeding back to a revelation of time and place, or establishing the locale first and then progressing up to the characters. Using the first method, the picture might open on a close shot of a newspaper lying on the pavement with the camera *tilting up* to the little boy who is standing over the newspaper reading it, and from there moving horizontally or *panning* over to a man standing on the street and watching the little boy, when the story begins. Using the second method, you might open on a long shot of the street, then move the camera towards the little boy in what is known as a *trucking shot,* and finally pan over to a shot of the man as the story begins.

The most effective way of telling a story on the screen is to use the camera as the story-teller, selecting and concentrating upon objects which are the center of dramatic interest. The camera may be used objectively or subjectively: as an onlooker or as the eye of one or more of the characters in the story. It is enabled to do this because of its mobility: it can see objects from a distance or it can magnify them; it can move freely or remain fixed; it can turn or tilt, swing, peer through keyholes, swoop or crawl.

Sometimes the camera uses objects as a means of creating suspense. In *The Prisoner of Zenda* we had a scene in the king's hunting lodge on the morning after a hard night of drinking. Ronald Colman as Rudolf Rassendyll is still asleep, and extraordinary means are necessary to awaken him. Here we used a silver water pitcher to create suspense and to introduce the characters in the scene. We began with an extreme close shot of the pitcher filled with ice-water and carried on a tray by Joseph, the servant. As he enters the main room, the camera travels ten or fifteen feet seeing only the water pitcher. Then the camera stops and we see a hand grasp the handle of the pitcher, draw it back and throw its contents. The camera now draws back to show that the water hits Ronald Colman full in the face, as he is sleeping in a chair. This shot is held until he reacts to the sudden shock of the water, then cuts to the man who threw it.

Each shot here was a separate *set-up* or camera position and each had to be made individually. Here no additional protection shots were necessary; we used our judgment in the amount of footage. Before we started shooting, I rehearsed part of the scene for the action, then once for the cameras and lighting and once for the sound department, which checks the level and position of the actors' voices. Generally not over three *takes* or separate film records are made of each set-up. We may do a scene of half a minute or of four minutes, but we always rehearse it thoroughly first before taking it. The number of set-ups which can be made each day depends on the amount of change of the position and lighting. A good cameraman should be able to make one set-up in about forty minutes, or at least eight set-ups a day.

During production, the script girl is of indispensable help in taking detailed notes of everything connected with the shooting: all business, all placements of the actors, use of props, the footage, angle and lens used for each scene. Without these notes the director's task would be infinitely more involved.

The shooting schedule varies from forty days to sixty or seventy. Every evening the director looks at the rushes of the previous day's work, selecting the best takes and discussing with the editor the feeling and tempo he wants for the entire film. When the picture is finally cut, and scored by the musical director, it is then ready for preview. The reactions of an audience are his best guide for the necessary changes; these are made until he feels the film is right. When the negative is cut to correspond with this positive, the picture is ready for the screens of the nation.

The advantages of the screen director are obvious: he has more money at his disposal than the stage director; he has unlimited technical facilities at his command. But he does not have the human emotional reactions of direct contact with his audience; instead, he must be his own audience. Perhaps his greatest handicap is the lack of understanding of his supervisors. In most cases, he should be allowed the final say on the production he is directing. Nor should he be forced to do stories in which he does not believe. He should be allowed to do stories in which he *does* believe, even if they involve censorship. Next to supervision, censorship is the most difficult handicap to overcome and he is always obliged to compromise. The story must either be abandoned or the director must change the story to such an extent that its entire meaning is lost.

It is desirable for a director to have a limit to the number of pictures he directs each year. This should not exceed three. There is not sufficient time to make more because one production alone takes from twelve to twenty weeks, of which eight weeks are spent in the pre-shooting preparation. And he must have time to see the production through to its completion.

As the problem of color is entering more and more into the making of pictures, I would like to include mention of it here. When the mechanics of color will have been perfected, there will be no more difficulties in the production of color pictures than there are now in black and white. I believe that color should be the perfect stage setting for the story, as are some of the stage designs of Robert Edmond Jones, which so caught the mood of the play that they completely satisfied the eye and the author's conception of the setting without even slightly intruding themselves on the audience. When color reaches the point where audiences take it for granted and are not startled into a lack of attention of the story itself, then it will be an added means of telling the story as dramatically as possible.

All through the production the director must co-ordinate the work of the technical departments, which check the numerous processes, and the hundreds of indispensable workers engaged in the making of a motion picture—to the end that a story may be translated from paper into film. If, in spite of the many minds contributing to its shaping, the visualization of the director is achieved, then the coordination has been successful and the dominance of one mind is apparent. And if the technical and mechanical factors involved are subservient to the director's conception, there results an individual expression in terms of a motion picture.

W. S. VAN DYKE
(1887 - 1944)

Woodbridge Strong Van Dyke was one of the most interesting of the house directors at M-G-M in the 30's, someone
who was often able to breathe life into the most stultifying
of that studio's processed entertainments. Originally an
actor, he had been one of Griffith's assistants on *Intolerance*,
then began moving from company to company until winding up at M-G-M in the late 20's. Here he became a specialist on "outdoor stuff," everything from Tim McCoy
westerns to an abortive collaboration with Flaherty on
White Shadows in the South Seas. His excellent work on
this film has consistently been downgraded by those who
prefer to see it as a "butchered" version of Flaherty's original concept, but they would do well to take another look
at this strangely affecting work. M-G-M sent him on other
expeditions, notably a disastrous one to Africa to shoot
Trader Horn, and he left his vigorous stamp on *Eskimo*
and *Tarzan, the Ape Man* as well. Such action stuff was a
bit out of the ordinary at M-G-M, and the studio soon
brought Van Dyke indoors to handle more typical projects
like a series of Jeanette MacDonald musicals, and *The Thin
Man*, of which he writes here. But he still seemed best
suited to the outdoor epic, and if a large, action-filled property like *San Francisco* was being developed, Van Dyke
was the no-nonsense director M-G-M invariably assigned.
A man with a keen eye for movement and action, his best
films often achieved a certain rough grace, but Van Dyke
seldom wasted a minute on fancy effects: he wasn't called
"One Shot Woody" for nothing.

R FOR A THIN MAN
W. S. VAN DYKE

Looking back into the infinite past, I seem to recall that a certain motion picture was made and that I had something to do with it. It stirs restlessly in my memory, for it was immediately seized by the theatre public as a picture that started a new cycle in screen entertainment. In Hollywood, things are often done by cycles—gangster cycles, G-man cycles, historical romances, sea stuff, even Shakespeare. Somebody starts it and others fall in line to catch the shekels that bounce to the floor after the first jack pot.

Many pictures have been filmed requiring from one to two years to complete and costing in the neighborhood of one or two million dollars. Yet quite a few of these super-colossals failed to arouse the exhibitors' hosannas that *The Thin Man* did.

From the first scene, when Myrna Loy made a perfect three-point, one-take landing on a dance floor, to the final shot of Miss Loy, Bill Powell, and Asta in a train drawing-room, *The Thin Man* was filmed in just sixteen days.

Then why has this picture been accepted as a paragon of perfection for other pictures of a certain type to follow? Even today, three years later, we now and then read of pictures in the critics' reviews . . . "Almost equals *The Thin Man*" . . . "As funny as *The Thin Man*" . . . "Another film in *The Thin Man* mood."

Perhaps there are several answers to that question. It did start a new cycle in screen entertainment. It proved that murder mysteries on the screen necessarily did not have to be morbid nightmares; that, with sparkling wisecrackery and a chain of kaleidoscopic situations that keep an audience guessing to the last frame of the film, a murder mystery can be turned into

From *Stage*, January 1937.

Director W. S. Van Dyke (in hat) and cameraman Clyde De Vinna check out the short wave equipment they intend to use during the shooting of African locations for *Trader Horn* (1930). They hope to stay in direct radio communication with Hollywood throughout production.

pleasing, laughable entertainment and still retain every element of first-class baffling mystery.

The picture shattered Hollywood traditions in several other ways. It awakened the theatre public to the truth that romance actually can exist happily among more matured married persons. There had been so many stories, novels, and screen plays of puppy love that audiences sickened of the overdose. Romances among mature people are as old as the universe itself, but apparently they had been obscured by the petting parties of flaming youth on the screen. Mature romances contain more understanding. In them the instabilities of youthful love affairs and quarrels have been overcome, all of the obstacles have been conquered and marriage progresses under full sail. *The Thin Man* was the first example of the possibilities of happy, mature romance.

Also, the picture had other advantages. It already possessed the title and the story of the best-seller mystery novel in many years, which that admirable and sage critic, Alexander Woollcott, praised as "the best detective story yet written in America," and which was authored by Dashiell Hammett, the unquestioned master of detective-story fiction. It was adapted to the screen by the ablest scenarists, Albert Hackett and Frances Goodrich, who faithfully transferred the humor and the mystery of the book to their script without losing one whiff of the original flavor. It was produced by Hunt Stromberg, who possesses a rare insight into mass psychology and the wants of the theatre patrons, who has the touch of Midas in turning daring production ventures into box-office gold and who, as far as I can recall, has never turned out a flop. Then, lastly the picture had as its stars the ideal Mr. and Mrs. of the screen, Myrna Loy and Bill Powell—not to forget Asta.

The Thin Man already was marching across the theatre screens, kicking the dollars into the cash tills, when rumor arose that a sequel to the picture was to be made. In the Hollywood vernacular, the word "sequel" is a bugaboo that frightens most directors, and I am no exception, for if the sequel fails to approach its parent picture in public favor or financial returns, it is the director who is left holding the bag. Sequels have made money in the earlier days, in such breath-takers as *The Perils of Pauline* and *The Demon Eye*, and, in later years, the *Tarzan* pictures, but sequels of Class-A pictures with Class-A stars offer a different problem.

The Thin Man had the additional advantage of not only being adapted from a best-seller novel that had rung up a sale that reached into the hundred thousands, but also of serialization in a nation-wide chain of newspapers that were read by an additional three million people. Seldom has any film production had the benefits of such advance exploitation. But exploitation alone cannot make a good picture. The picture first must be good upon its own merits and then the exploitation serves as a means to tell the world that it is good.

Hence the apprehension of every one concerned, myself included, with bringing the clever Nick Charles and his amusing wife, Nora, back to the screen in a *Thin Man* sequel to solve another perplexing murder case. The return of Nick and Nora in a second mystery would not have such helpful allies as adaptation from a best-selling novel and universal ballyhoo through newspaper serialization. This time it must be an original story written solely for the screen, yet it must retain an interest equal to, if not greater than, that of the first story. Too, it must be as good, if not better, than the first.

Here was the first problem. To lift a character out of the pages of a popular book, such as Nick Charles, and build it into an idol in the public's imagination is one thing. To transplant this idol to an original screen treatment and keep it at its highest level comparable to the book idol is something else. Hunt Stromberg had the courage to do it and I dared to back him up.

Dashiell Hammett had his problems. In *The Thin Man*, Bill Powell and Miss Loy had brought the story to a happy ending in a drawing-room aboard a train that was speeding them back to San Francisco. And Asta, the frisky, wire-haired fox terrier, had his final close-up in Myrna's hat box.

Obviously, *After the Thin Man* could not be filmed without Powell and Myrna—and Asta. As they were last seen returning by train to San Francisco, the new murder mystery must have its locale in San Francisco. They had trained out of New York about the day after Christmas. Allowing for time to cross the continent, the new story must be picked up on New Year's Eve to permit Nick and Nora to continue their madcap marital adventures without leaving too wide a breach between the two chapters of their hectic honeymoon.

Here, at least, was to be something new in film fare—two distinctly separate motion picture mysteries, linked together with the same major characters and with less than a week's time elapsing between the finale of the first and the beginning of the other. Yet, three years had swept away between the shooting of the last scene for *The Thin Man* and the first scene for *After the Thin Man*. How well we could accomplish that job was the thought that gave us many sleepless nights.

I have felt very fortunate in having the same personal staff on the pictures I have directed for many years, particularly the same script clerk with her photographic mind, the same prop man, the same sound engineer, and others. A trifling thing such as the dog leash that led Asta onto the train in the last scenes of *The Thin Man* could have become an irritating problem had not my prop man not only remembered the style and color of the leash but had kept it stored in his prop box, for Powell leads Asta from the train in *After the Thin Man* by the same leash.

The same scenarists, Goodrich and Hackett, fell heirs to adapting the new original story, but it was no easy task for them to grope back through three years of time to catch the same characteristic idioms voiced by Bill and Myrna in the first story. Too, Bill and Myrna had grown three years older than the original Nick and Nora, and had alienated themselves from those characterizations by many successive screen roles of varied interpretation, so it was necessary for them also to step back three years into the amusing, delightful characters of Nick and Nora. Picking up these threads was no simple job for Bill and Myrna.

The tempo of the second Hammett story had to parallel the first if it were to be as successful and entertaining as its predecessor. New actors had to be carefully selected to adapt themselves to the unusual new characters, as intriguing as *The Thin Man* characters if not more so, created in *After the Thin Man* to muddle the element of mystery, for in such detective fabrics as Hammett weaves, unusual characterization is one of the more important structures of fictional enigma.

Since *After the Thin Man* has San Francisco as its theatre, I chose to capture the true atmosphere of the city so the picture might breathe its true life. Although confronted by many handicaps, such as over-enthusiastic crowds who interfered with the shooting, and low-hanging stubborn fogs, we did succeed in filming most of our exteriors up and down San Francisco's throbbing streets and around its historic landmarks, with the mighty Golden Gate and San Francisco-Oakland Bay bridges, symbols of the new and greater San Francisco, constantly in the background.

Once the foundation for *After the Thin Man* was firmly laid, no major obstacle presented itself in our path toward completing the picture. We had an excellent story from the author of the parent production. We had a flawless script from the same capable team who had adapted *The Thin Man*. We had the same two stars, Powell and Miss Loy—and we still had Asta, who, though he, too, had aged three years, had been going through three years of special training for his repeat performance.

After the cameras started rolling, the picture progressed with precision and with the finest cooperation from every person who had a hand in it, and I feel that we have turned out a worthy successor to *The Thin Man*.

Such is the prescription for success for any good motion picture: A perfect story written by an expert in his field, a finished script that needs no alteration after the picture is under way, and a wisely chosen cast who can be depended upon to do what the director wants them to do . . . who know how to do it . . . and who do it.

If he has all these, no capable director should fear the bugaboo of a sequel.

LEWIS MILESTONE
(1895 -   )

There is a miniature history of Hollywood and its directors contained in this nostalgic survey by Lewis Milestone, one of the 30's more independent spirits. But the picture he paints is a sad one, painfully aware of the severe erosion in the director's freedom that paralleled the rise to ultimate power of the studio producer system. The only possible solution is compromise, he states flatly, bending like a twig before the huffing and puffing of studio potentates like Irving Thalberg (a much revered figure today, but one whom Milestone cuts down to size). He leaves his own fate open, but like many of the pioneer directors he cites (note the obeisance to Neilan and Cruze) his relation to the studio system at the height of its power was not a productive one. Milestone was a Russian émigré who arrived in Hollywood in the late 'teens and worked up to a director's position by 1925. His silent films were hailed for their freshness and vigor, but the best of them (*The Cave Man, Two Arabian Nights, The Racket*) have not been seen for many years and are difficult to assess today. His most important films were from the early talkie period, *All Quiet on the Western Front* and *The Front Page*, but by the late 30's the innovative flair that had marked his earlier work had dampened, and the latter part of his career was marked by only sporadic flashes of creativity, a veritable forest of saplings graced by only one or two solitary oaks.

THE REIGN OF THE DIRECTOR
LEWIS MILESTONE

A sapling stood in the shadow of a mighty oak, so mighty that the appearance of the little sapling filled the oak with both pity and disgust.

A storm hit the forest. The oak proudly faced it, refusing to bend or even sway before it, but the little weak sapling bent to the ground with each blow of the wind. Such humility filled the mighty oak with disgust, and proudly, and more stubbornly than ever, he faced the fierce storm.

But when the storm had spent itself the sapling stood as before. The mighty oak that had refused to sway and bend lay prone to the ground, torn out by the roots—dead.

I first arrived in Hollywood at the end of 1919. That and the subsequent three or four years can be called "the reign of the director"—a power supreme and absolute. D. W. Griffith! *Way Down East! Dream Street!* James Cruze! *Covered Wagon! Merton of the Movies!* Eric von Stroheim! *The Devil's Pass Key! Foolish Wives!* Rex Ingram! *Four Horsemen of the Apocalypse! Scaramouche!* Mickey Neilan! Another Neilan picture! What difference does it make who's in it or what the title is—it's a Neilan picture! Who can afford to miss it? The latest and the best in comedy, sophistication, speed. Another lesson in what the best motion pictures can be like. Learn about inference, power of suggestion, subtlety; the most told in the shortest possible footage. *Why Get Married! Go And Get It! Fools First!* Raymond Griffith is born—again Neilan!

And then came the storm. It started with a tiny gust of wind.

Irving Thalberg, the baby producer, the important general manager of the very unimportant Universal Manufacturing Company. And the first oak hit was von Stroheim, then directing *Merry-Go-Round.*

From *New Theatre and Film*, March 1937.

Lewis Milestone points out an angle to cameraman Arthur Edeson during the shooting of *All Quiet on the Western Front* (1929-30). Dialogue director George Cukor waits in the rear of the trench.

The saplings (all unemployed at the time), Richard Wallace, W. K. Howard, Bill Wellman, and the writer of this piece, were sharing a borrowed dollar at Levy's Cafe. We sat through the lunch hour and long past it. The subject of conversation was (Hollywood forgive me!)—pictures.

"Let's start a rumor," said Wallace, "let's start a rumor that Irving Thalberg—you know, the little fellow at Universal— well let's start a rumor that Irving Thalberg fired von Stroheim —took him off the picture."

When the laughter subsided we agreed that a more startling tale couldn't have been invented by Munchausen himself, and we promptly scattered to circulate the rumor. But Wallace must have been psychic. That evening Hollywood was shaken like no earthquake ever shook it. Newspaper headlines carried the startling news that Irving Thalberg fired von Stroheim— took him off the picture. At first we, the members of the con-spiracy, thought it was the result of our own work, for no place in the world can you spread a rumor more quickly than in Hollywood (with the exception of an Army latrine). Im-agine our surprise when we found out that we started the ru-mor simultaneously with the actual happening.

Well, that was the beginning of the storm and the end of the reign of the director, the mighty oak. The storm grew fiercer. Following the birth of the first producer, Irving Thalberg, came others, each adding to the ferocity of the storm, each out-doing the others in establishing his absolute power, and when the storm subsided there was no D. W. Griffith, no Cruze, no von Stroheim, no Ingram, no Neilan. These men knew only one way of working—the way of a director; select the story, have a hand in the writing of the story, cast it, cut it, etc. De-prived of that method they couldn't function. They were forced to go and they went.

A comeback for a top-notch director is practically impos-sible. The reason is simple. To make a good picture the director needs the producer's absolute trust and confidence and a great deal of money, money to buy material, cast, etc. Once fallen into disfavor he gets none of these things, yet, because he had a great name once, the producer expects him to deliver a pic-ture up to his old standard.

And, since I started this piece with a fable I suppose I should finish it with a moral, but I'm afraid I can't, for I have been both a sapling and an oak. What am I now? You have to wait until the next storm to get the answer.

GEORGE CUKOR
(1899-)

Cukor, who had spent the 20's on Broadway as an actor and director, was called to Hollywood with the arrival of talkies, and his initial film assignments were as "dialogue director" on such films as *All Quiet on the Western Front* (see the illustration on page 319. While the old Hollywood hands learned dialogue delivery from him, he learned film technique from them (that was the general idea, anyhow), and, after the other dialogue "experts" had been sent on their way, Cukor remained to direct films on his own. His work has always been strongest on performance, a fact he readily admits here, and *Dinner at Eight, Holiday, The Women, A Star Is Born,* and *Travels with My Aunt* all project that impeccable sense of timing and style that is Cukor's own. A superb director of actresses, Cukor finds it particularly relevant to speak here of his work with Garbo, Shearer, and Hepburn, who under his direction delivered perhaps their finest performances. In this essay he very modestly describes his main contributions as pre-production consultation and "on the floor" direction of the performers, giving the rest of the creative team full credit for their efforts and regarding warily those directors whose films are a "brilliant exercise in cinema technique." The reference to the producer as the director's "superior officer" may be taken as a reference to David O. Selznick, with whom he was closely associated in the late 30's, and for whom he was at this time involved in laborious preparatory work for *Gone with the Wind.*

THE DIRECTOR
GEORGE CUKOR

It is no more possible to dogmatise about the methods of work of a film director than it would be to lay down laws about how an author should write his books. In both cases generalisation can go no further than the primary and superficial details of routine. An author about to write may be safely assumed to sit down somewhere with a block of paper and a pen or typewriter. A film director stands (or more often sits) by the camera while the players go through each scene in the script. But beyond that, no two directors work in the same way.

The popular idea of a film director is, I think, of this figure beside the camera, usually sitting in a canvas chair with his name painted on it in large letters, bawling raucously at intervals through a megaphone. I have no wish to dismiss this traditional conception, for directors often do sit in chairs, these chairs often have their names painted on them, and there may even be times when a director uses a megaphone. But I would like to make it clear at the start that the work "on the floor," the actual supervision of dialogue and action, is only a comparatively small part of the director's work. Indeed, the shooting of the picture is the more or less routine part of the work for everybody concerned. When the time comes for a scene to be shot, the director and the players have already tackled and solved their various problems, and have—or ought to have—a very clear idea of what they want to achieve.

In most cases the director makes his appearance very early in the life story of a motion picture. There are times when the whole idea for a film may come from him, but in a more usual case he makes his entry when he is summoned by a producer and it is suggested that he should be the director of a proposed story. If a director has a reputation and is free from the pressure of simply finding work to do, he will probably be told

From *Behind the Screen*, edited by Stephen Watts, New York, 1938.

George Cukor discussing the script of *The Philadelphia Story* (1940) with Katharine Hepburn. She is holding a "hand test," a short length of film taken to check the lighting and composition in advance of the actual shot.

the story proposed and asked if he would like to do it. There usually is some good reason why he, of all the available directors, has been approached. It may be a type of story he is known to handle well. It may be destined for a star with whom he has had previous experience and success. He accepts the assignment, and then begins a series of collaborations which go on from that moment until the film is ready for showing. He collaborates with his superior officer, the producer, and with the author or authors. Let us say the film is to be made from a successful novel, and two writers have been assigned to do the screen play. The director may not write a word—for myself, I never do because writing is not one of my accomplishments—but he will sit in conference with the producer and writers and talk over the story scene by scene and line by line. He may be a writer himself and thus able to contribute more than ideas. Some directors are very good writers. But the presence of even a non-writing director like myself at these script conferences is essential, because it is he who will finally have to convey the writer's work to the screen through the media of players and camera, and his first necessity is to equip himself with the best possible screen play that will treat the subject as he plans to treat it, and extract from it every ounce of dramatic value. A scene brilliantly conceived in a writer's mind may be impossible of execution in practical terms of production. The director, who probably knows by this time who is going to play in the picture, will always use his influence to guide the growing script along lines most suited to the style and personality of those players.

This collaboration of director and writers is typical of what must be the director's attitude to everybody connected with him in the making of the picture. I would set down as the essence of the directorial approach to a film the art of knowing exactly how much to take from each of his collaborators. They are all experts in one department or another of film production. They know all about their own departments. The director knows a certain amount about all the departments. On the one hand, he must not approach his task with rigidly preconceived ideas of what he wants. If he does so he will lose the value of his expert collaborators and whatever spontaneous, original ideas they may have. On the other hand, he must not be bullied by his experts. If each of them is allowed to pour in ideas of treatment unrestricted, the result will be a chaotic film, lacking that central line and integrity of purpose without which no work of art, nor even of efficient story-telling and entertainment-making, is possible. He must exist throughout the making of the picture in a curious elastic, yet firm, state of mind. From each individual concerned with him in the creation of the picture, he must constantly select and reject, extract, modify, repulse and refine a continuous output of suggestion. He must be prepared to let beloved ideas of his own go when a better idea appears, from whatever source it may come. But he must also be prepared to stand staunchly by a conception of his own if he believes in it, no matter how it may be assailed or made difficult to bring about. It will be seen already that the artistic side of the director's work flows over into the technical and the personal. His collaboration with the art department is an example of the merging of all three. A good art director, having read the script, has a clear idea of the settings required. Much of a film's atmosphere comes from its settings. The director has his own ideas about the physical background against which his screen story is going to be told. Together, director and art director, in conferences with their producer, must thrash out their problems. The ideas of one or the other may be inclined towards a lavishness so costly as to throw the picture's budget out of balance. The director may want things which the art director knows would not be practical.

I hope I am not making these preliminary consultations sound like a lengthy wrangle between the director and various departmental experts. Co-operation—the tradition of pride-of-craft and mutual help—is astonishingly strong in the studio. Everybody concerned with a new film, from the producer to the property boys, knows all about it and genuinely and unselfishly works for the common end of making the best possible picture.

So the date scheduled for the beginning of shooting approaches; the conferences with dress designers, with the stars themselves, with the cameraman, go steadily on. In the modern studio there is no room for inefficiency, for anything but clean-cut, fool-proof preparations. If your cameraman has not been given a chance to see the designs for the settings, you may find that a beautifully built scene simply cannot be lit to advantage, nor action in it photographed properly. If a discovery like that is not made until the picture is actually in production, the waste of time and money is enormous.

There are personal problems enough to be dealt with in these preliminary stages, but they are trivial compared with the problems during the actual shooting. As I have explained, the work of direction "on the floor" is almost entirely routine from the *technical* point of view. But from the *personal* standpoint, the director's troubles have often only begun when the picture goes into production. The first cause of this is the physical strain of studio work. Everybody on a picture works long hours, and all those who are creatively concerned are keyed up all the time. It is not too much to say that the mood prevailing in a studio, even when the camera is not turning, somehow projects itself into the finished film. And it seems to me from experience that the mood, the psychological pitch, if you like, comes from the director. In Hollywood I have found one has a great advantage in the basic good humour and natural high spirits of the people with whom one has to work. If a director is friendly with the people around him, is enthusiastic, energetic, considerate, and can engender a spirit of co-operative good-will, extending from the man operating a spot-light to the feminine star playing the principal rôle, he is on the way to making a successful picture. This is not always easy. A democratic manner, a happy disposition, and confidence in his fellow-workers' ability to give him the result he has dreamed of, are not enough. So the director, however amiable and sympathetic he is by nature, must be capable of being a despot and a bully when the occasion demands. His relationship with his principal players is the most delicate of all. I find with every new film that there are always a few days in which a kind of settling-in process goes on. A woman star arrives to work with a director she has never met before. She may have seen his last film and disliked it intensely. She feels that this man is completely incapable of understanding her and that, with her reputation to think of, she must constantly be on guard against his bullying her down to what she believes to be his level. Or, without any prejudices for or against the director, she may be going to play a part about which she has very definite ideas. Preliminary meetings with the director may merely have served to show her that his ideas and hers do not tally. She is determined to play the character the way she sees it. The director may be equally determined that it shall be done his way. If he bullies her into subjection he will almost certainly get a lifeless and unconvincing performance. If he lets her have her own way he may get an unbalanced result, with the star rôle played in a style completely at variance with the rest of the picture. The director, if he is wise, will not only be diplomatic and do all he can to inspire the star with friendship for and confidence in him, but will also examine carefully the points of difference between the two conceptions. If, as I have said before, he has started with a clear, but not hide-bound idea of what he wants, he may find that a blending of some of the star's ideas with his own will result in an all-round improvement. But if all the star's ideas are completely wrong to his way of thinking, then he has to tackle the difficult task of winning her round to his ideas, without losing her confidence or any of the initial enthusiasm she brought to the picture.

I have gone into this question of the personal relationship between star and director fairly fully, because I achieve practically all my film effects through the actors and actresses. Other directors are less dependent on their stars. They are, perhaps, more strictly *film* directors, with vast knowledge of camera work, lighting effects, and other purely cinematographic devices in which I, with my stage background, may not be so well versed. I find that, because the human beings in my pictures are the instruments through which I must tell my story, my relationship with them, while we are working, is of the highest importance.

The great difference between the stage director and the film director is the extent of control which is necessary in the film studio. In the theatre the director may rehearse assiduously, and the actors and actresses may model their performances scrupulously on his instructions, but when the first night comes along—and on every succeeding night too—they step out of his control, go on the stage, and the responsibility for what happens from the moment the curtain rises until it falls, perhaps three hours later, is entirely theirs. In the film studio the player never steps outside the control of the director. That does not mean he, or she, never makes a movement other than that prescribed by the director—that would make the actor a robot, which is the last thing the screen, with its intimate personal contact between player and audience, wants. But it is true that every scene which reaches the screen has passed the censorship of the director; he cannot plead to be absolved from responsibility for the merest flicker of an eyelash, because it was at one time within his power to remake that scene and remake it again until he had the effect he desired. The fact that the scene is in the final film is proof that he decided it was good enough to be there.

I said at the beginning that no two directors have the same working methods. I can go further and say that no director has exactly the same working methods in any two pictures he makes. Certainly no director who, like me, gets his effects mainly through the players. In my case, directorial style must be largely the absence of style. It is all very well for a director whose reputation is based on a certain hall-mark which he imprints on all his work to subject every new story and scene to his own style and artistic personality. He may achieve wonderful results. He may take a poor story and poor performances, and by making them merely the groundwork of a brilliant exercise in cinema technique, evolve a distinguished picture. But such directors are very rare, so I shall stick to my own case of the director whose end is to extract the best that all his fellow-workers have to give, and who is best pleased when the finished picture shows to the layman in the audience no visible sign of "direction," but merely seems to be a smooth and convincing presentation by the players of the subject in hand. Such a director must alter his methods with every film.

The good director brings to each job of work, not only his technical equipment and clear-cut idea of what he is trying to achieve, but also an instinct trained by experience for the solution of the human equation, which is certain to present itself. I can best demonstrate this by examples from my own experience. When I met Greta Garbo to discuss *Camille*, in which I was to direct her, I sensed that she was a little distrustful of me. Having her own very clear idea of how she thought *La Dame aux Camelias* ought to be played on the screen, she was not unnaturally afraid that I, too, would have ideas on the subject, and that a clash would develop when we faced each other as director and star on the studio stage. I sympathised mentally with her attitude and set about to persuade her, very gradually and gently, that I was genuinely anxious to hear her ideas about the character. When we went into production I took the line of letting her play a scene in rehearsal without any instructions from me, instead of telling her how I wanted it played. This was not merely tact or strategy in order to get my own way, because the ideas of an artist like Garbo are well worth serious consideration. After I saw how she wanted to play a scene, I talked it over with her, and made suggestions from *my* mental picture of the scene. But at the same time I made it clear that I respected her conception, and that she had given me fresh ideas which I was more than willing to blend with my own. Nor was this merely a kind of artistic compromise. She, as a woman and a sensitive artist, was, I found, always prolific of ideas, and when she had admitted me to her confidence and friendship—which she did quickly when the initial barrier of distrust was broken down—we had formed an ideal collaboration for our mutual benefit as actress and director.

With other stars—other methods. Norma Shearer, for instance, I found when I made *Romeo and Juliet,* is a nervous, highly self-critical woman who has schooled herself to give an impression of self-confidence. If one had accepted that impression one would have gone far astray in working with her. She needed sympathy and reassurance. Another way in which Miss Shearer might mislead a director—as I am sure she continually misleads herself—is in the matter of physical resources and sheer stamina. She becomes so engrossed in her work, so keyed up with a kind of taut, nervous energy, that she is apt to overtax her strength. She will play a long, exhausting scene over and over again without appearing to lose an atom of her freshness and verve. When it is over, she will tell you she feels fine—and believe it. Then she will go to her dressing-room and collapse. If one worked her as hard as she seems to want to work, she would be worn out before the picture was half finished. With her, a director has to reverse the normal process of inspiring his star to greater efforts. He has to persuade her to spare herself. The greatest joy of working with Miss Shearer comes from her complete lack of vanity. Far from bridling at minor criticisms as many actresses do, she will criticise herself with a penetrating, almost unfeminine, impersonal judgment. When she sees the "rushes" (the unedited versions of the previous day's work which are screened in the studio every day), she seems to cease to be an actress and to look at her own work on the screen with the shrewd and critical mind of a producer.

I wonder what a director with a fixed style of approach to the problem of handling his stars would do if he went straight from directing Norma Shearer or Garbo, to making a picture with Katharine Hepburn. This fine actress is more than a personality. She is a human dynamo. Without meaning to be, and simply because of the vigour of her own mind and the intensity of her attitude to her work, she can be, if given the chance, what I would call an artistic bully. When I directed *Little Women* I had to develop a new technique to ensure the best results from the collaboration of Miss Hepburn and myself. I do not say that if I had decided to "lie down" to her from the start, a less good picture would have resulted. But a director with a conscience will fight tooth and nail to get the picture as he wants it. Let me hasten to say that Miss Hepburn and I did not fight at all. I confess freely that I used many weapons in dealing with her—simulated rage, ridicule, and good-humoured cajolery. She has a great sense of humour, and is quite capable of directing it against herself.

There is in every star something strictly individual which he or she has to give to the public, and the director must be careful not to stand in the way of that direct, personal and subtle communication. The case of the late, beloved Marie Dressler comes to my mind. When I directed her in *Dinner at Eight* I found myself at first making alterations in her treatment of a scene which the old lady, with the greatest desire in the world to please me, seemed to have a certain difficulty in carrying out. She did not complain, and tried very hard to do things the way I wanted them. Then suddenly it dawned on me that all I was doing was subtracting from the very essence of Marie Dressler and tampering with the bond which she had fixed so firmly between herself and the public. At once I went back on my tracks and let her do everything she had to do exactly as she felt it, without interference from me. The result, of course, was magnificent.

You will detect through all I have written one theme running continuously—that the art of the director is to hold the delicate balance between giving something to, and taking something from, the people with whom he works. That is, to my mind, the root of the matter; that is why a director must never think of his work as a one-man job; that is why I, as a director, always want to have the best possible help in all departments. I want to make not only the stars but the assistant electricians feel that they are there to supply something to the composite whole of the finished picture that nobody else can supply. I want them to know that I, frankly and freely, confess my need of them, my need of every scrap of assistance they can give me.

If, throughout the making of a long and difficult picture, everybody concerned comes to the studio each morning with undiminished eagerness and enthusiasm for the new day's work, for its adventures, for its achievements—yes, and for its fun—I think I have laid one of the surest foundations of a good picture.

TAY GARNETT
(1898 -   )

While many critics (and even some directors) were decrying the stultifying effects of the late 30's studio system, Tay Garnett was proposing a radical revision in the most basic aspect of Hollywood production. This operation focused on a stable of contract talent both before and behind the camera, and resulted in a given studio producing films in conventional cycles designed to take advantage of expensive talent already at hand. Garnett suggested putting everyone on a percentage of profits basis, something which would break up the stagnant and unimaginative production cycles then dominating American films. His innovative plan was disregarded with the sudden prosperity of the war years, when tampering with success was hardly likely to attract much of a following. But with the box office decline of the late 40's the old system did indeed break down, the large stables of contract talent dissolved, and percentage deals turned stars like James Stewart into formidable powers quite capable of dictating terms to the now shaky studio heads. Garnett never achieved this kind of power himself, but moved around comfortably throughout his career, now producing a few films for one studio, now working independently, always finding some outlet for his seemingly boundless energy. His best films are an oddly mixed bag, ranging from *Her Man* (a sparkling early talkie) to *Seven Sinners* and *The Postman Always Rings Twice*, films which reflect the rugged quality of his own life. He has been remarkably active into the 70's, working in television and low budget features, and finding time to publish a noteworthy autobiography on the side. His most recent film, *Challenge to Be Free*, continues Garnett's contributions to innovative methods of production and distribution.

THERE'S PROFIT IN SHARING PROFITS

TAY GARNETT

While it may be premature in some critical quarters to speak of the art of the motion pictures, there can be no violent denial that under the guise of "prestige" pictures, Hollywood is earnestly trying to achieve classical greatness. But the sturdy esthetes of Los Angeles are under handicaps ("gigantic" and "colossal") peculiar to no other art.

An insolvent poet, for instance, may write a sonnet equal to Shakespeare's; a dispossessed sculptor may hew a masterpiece worthy of the Metropolitan Museum of Art; and a painter with only a relief check in his pocket may smear a Mona Lisa on a bar-room floor. Even in the theatre—without scenery, costumes or overhead—it is possible to produce a play that is great Theatre. All that is needed is the inexpensive magic of dialogue and direction.

But just try to produce a motion picture on a shoestring. While there are instances where it could not be done for even $2,000,000, it positively cannot be produced on what the industry fondly terms a "herring." It is financially impossible for a director with an ideal to go out and shoot a classic on a private bankroll. And, at the same time, it is just as difficult to accomplish with all of the money from Wall Street.

To begin with, a tremendous amount of capital was required to launch this industry (it is among the ten leading industries of the country). There is, to point at only a phase of the picture business, the tremendous investments throughout the country in motion picture theatres. Every city with a population of 25,000 or over has its quota of "palaces." Comfortable theatres are essential for the proper enjoyment of pictures. And so, it is not at all remarkable that with the millions of dollars involved in the picture business it is difficult to find a dreamer in the industry.

On the set of Walter Wanger's *Stand-In* (1937) director Tay Garnett takes time out to speak with a visiting Portland society girl.

However, Hollywood citizens have not been entirely unaware of the higher implications of the camera. Good pictures are still the aim of all. And the solution of the curse of too much money, I believe, will be found in the percentage-salary plan.

The plan, simply, is for the artists to get so much of the total profits from the pictures produced. We earnestly believe that is a profound improvement in making pictures, and will benefit all concerned. The industry as a whole will benefit by better pictures. A star, for instance, gets a flat salary for, say, five pictures in five years. The tendency is to get the pictures out of the way and then for "that much needed vacation." It is only human that if you are paid for doing something in advance, your work is not so likely to be as good. This, I believe, is one of the fundamental (for want of a nicer word) evils of Hollywood. Putting a star on a percentage basis actually makes him part owner of the film—even though the amount of money he receives under both set-ups is the same. He is going to do his darndest to cooperate in making it a great picture.

Many stars have professional pride and try to do their best under any circumstances, but they are only human, and the terrific pace of Hollywood makes them slipshod in their work. Not necessarily their work before the cameras, but the work in which the public seldom sees them. Such little details as cooperating with the publicity departments or attending story conferences are often overlooked.

And the same thing holds true of directors, camera men and producers. If their salary depends on the merit and quality of their inspiration, they will naturally try to eliminate some of the slipshod movie boners found in pictures. And, of course, if they make great pictures, they are justly entitled to all the rewards. Speaking as a director, there are some directors—Mervyn Leroy, Frank Capra, Gregory LaCava—whose names on a marquee mean as much as any star—Shirley Temple excepted. I believe that with a producer directly responsible for the success of a picture, better cinemas [sic] will be produced.

WILLIAM K. HOWARD
(1899 - 1954)

Howard was one of the mere handful of directors with any experience in the distributing end of the business, breaking in as a salesman and exchange manager for some of Vitagraph's midwestern offices. After service in World War I he turned to production, quickly working his way up to the direction of small-scale action pictures. He first achieved a reputation with the sensitive late silent *White Gold*, a pictorially imaginative film noticeably influenced by European models. Howard's early talkies were similarly visual, especially *Transatlantic*, *Surrender*, and *The Power and the Glory* (all photographed by James Wong Howe), but his handling of actors was less assured. By the late 30's his films had clearly turned away from the usual run of Hollywood product (*Mary Burns—Fugitive* is one of the strangest American films of the period) and his move to the east coast was no doubt an attempt to get out from under the usual Hollywood studio pressures. His Astoria picture, *Back Door to Heaven* (which he refers to by its working title, *Frankie*), was an extremely personal project, and its failure marked the end of the creative phase of his career. The Astoria studio suffered a similar fate: *Back Door to Heaven* and *One Third of a Nation* were the last films produced in that facility, which was later used by the Signal Corps for the production of training films. But in late 1975 the studio was reopened with much fanfare for the production of Herb Gardner's *Thieves*, and it is to be hoped this time its future will be brighter.

FILMING IN ASTORIA
WILLIAM K. HOWARD

Frankie is my first venture in Eastern production, after almost 20 years of directing pictures in Hollywood and recently in England. And, accordingly, not a day passes but that I am asked whether I prefer working here to California or Denham. My invariable reply is that I prefer working in any studio where I have the equipment, time and opportunity to express my ideas on the screen.

Given a good story and these essential factors, a director is well on the way to turning out a worthwhile motion picture. East or West is a minor consideration, for art—and by that I mean the art of motion pictures as well—knows no geographic barriers. Good pictures can be produced in Hollywood, Paris, London or New York as long as production conditions are favorable.

I have found such conditions in the East and am perfectly satisfied to remain at the Astoria studios. The technical equipment here is entirely satisfactory and up-to-date, while the available talent surpasses Hollywood's. The Broadway theatre yields new faces for picture production that are a welcome contrast to the familiar types of Central Casting. New York, the world's greatest talent center, is only a nickel subway ride from the studios.

Equally as important is the fact that the studio overhead in Astoria is negligible. Before a picture even goes into production in Hollywood, forty percent of its final cost is already marked against it on the budget because of the immense studio overhead. Here, unburdened by this additional cost, a class A motion picture, enhanced by the best production values, can be turned out for as little as $200,000.

It is sometimes forgotten, I think, that pictures originated in the East, that Edison and the other pioneers of the screen pro-

From *TAC*, December 1938.

William K. Howard gives direction to Aline MacMahon during production of *Back Door to Heaven* at the Astoria studio (1938-39). Director of photography Hal Mohr consults with script girl at left.

jected the first films here. The Biograph studios, where D. W. Griffith, Mack Sennett, Mary Pickford and many others developed the newborn art of the cinema, flourished in New York City at the turn of the century. Picture production migrated to California to take advantage of the more favorable climatic conditions, but these factors have long since been eliminated by modern studio conditions. Perfected process and trick work have removed almost all necessity for outdoor work and brought the outside world within the four walls of the studio.

But most important is the artistic freedom a director enjoys here. Since the financial investment is smaller, there is proportionately less adherence to the true and tried clichés of picture production that Hollywood relies upon to appeal to the largest common denominator of moviegoers. There is more room for new story material and for new methods of story telling. I myself undertook to produce *Frankie* with the agreement that I was to have complete and sole say over the script, casting, and direction, without any interference from the front office. This is a condition rarely existing in Hollywood.

Frankie is something that I have been planning for a long time, for the story, which I wrote myself, is based on an event of my childhood. I was born in St. Mary's, Ohio, together with Jim Tully and Charles Makeley. Tully later became an author, while Makeley fell in with the Dillinger gang, killed a sheriff and was condemned to death. In attempting to escape from the death house with an ink-stained soap revolver, Makeley and another convict were shot to death by the guards.

I distinctly recall, and Jim Tully corroborates this, that Makeley was a swell kid. It might have been either Jim or I who would have gone wrong instead of Makeley, for "there, but for the grace of God, go I." Around this, I have written the story of a boy, Frankie, essentially a good fellow, whom environment, heredity and adverse circumstances forced into a life of crime.

The story of *Frankie*, a simple one, takes place in an ordinary mid-western town. The characters are first seen as children, and the picture follows their careers until fifteen years after their graduation from school. A large number of characters and a widespread background have been given unity by a tightly-knit script, which was written by my friends, John Bright and Robert Tasker, both ace Hollywood scenarists.

My intent in *Frankie* is to point out that our destinies are irrevocably molded by outside factors, and that we all do the best we can under the circumstances. Frankie, who had all the makings of an admirable human being, was unfortunately born on the wrong side of the railroad tracks and never given a chance to develop himself in the right direction.

The juvenile actors in the cast have largely been recruited from Broadway productions, and even bit parts are taken by well known actors, something which is financially prohibitive on the coast. Stage performers are able to double in theatrical productions and motion pictures here, without trouble.

The present films at the Eastern Service studios are no fly-by-night ventures, but ambitious productions enlisting the services of well known stars, writers and technicians. My colleague, Dudley Murphy, has already completed . . . *one-third of a nation* . . . , starring Sylvia Sidney, Leif Erickson, Hiram Sherman and Myron McCormick for Triple-A. *Frankie,* an Odessco production, numbers in its cast Wallace Ford, Stuart Erwin, Aline MacMahon, Patricia Ellis and Bert Frohman, while both Hal Mohr, the cameraman, and Gordon Wiles, the art director, are former Academy Award winners. Both pictures will be distributed by Paramount as major releases. The units will not disband after their present production, but continue to function.

All this will not be enough, I realize, if coupled with the necessary artistic freedom for the director, and the relatively low costs for the producer, the final result in both material and treatment is not of the highest level. It is with the production of significant and popular films that we in the East must here concern ourselves. That, after all, is the true test of our success.

WILLIAM DIETERLE
(1893-1972)

Of all the members of Hollywood's German colony, Dieterle is perhaps the most under-appreciated today. His career began as an actor on the German stage, then moved over to films for directors like Dupont and Leni. He was directing his own films by 1926, and in 1930 was in Hollywood to work on "German versions" of talkies. He made a fairly smooth transition to the Warner's production mill with such lean and stylish works as *The Last Flight* and *Fog Over Frisco*, then in 1935 co-directed *A Midsummer Night's Dream* with Max Reinhardt. This established him as a top "prestige" director, and he followed up with the cycle of biographical dramas for which he is mainly remembered today. Highly regarded in their day, these films have since come under attack for allegedly puffing up the crisp Warner style beyond recognition in an attempt to emulate the "class" look of an M-G-M picture. But while they do tend to be over-reverent and perhaps over-simplified, the best of them—like *Juarez*—have a distinct visual grace and a sophistication of performance, especially from the supporting players, that could not have been expected from one of the studio's less stylish directors. Compare *Pasteur* and *Zola* with Mervyn LeRoy's *Anthony Adverse*, for example. At any rate, Dieterle survived his biographical period and went on to such films as *Love Letters* and *Portrait of Jennie* (two other sadly under-rated works). Not so flashy as Curtiz, or so dramatic as Lang, Dieterle's films are reflective, graceful, and thoughtfully low-key, a sensibility that often makes him seem more French than Germanic.

THOUGHTS ABOUT DIRECTING
WILLIAM DIETERLE

It is always difficult for a man to speak about his own work. Goethe once said: Bilde Kuenstler—rede nicht! Which means: Create artist—don't talk! I believe he was right.

What I have to say as a motion picture director—you can best read from the screen. There you find all that the subconscious force—(the only *real* creator in my opinion) wants to tell.

It is all right for bystanders to enjoy a blooming flower without knowing anything about it, theoretically; but as an expert gardener one should understand the flowering—and to understand one has to know something about the inter-relations of soil and air, water and sunlight, which conditions the growth of plants. To understand is a matter of experience. So I shall try to tell you about my experience as a director, with incidents from the *Pasteur* and *Zola* pictures.

Taking for granted that you all have seen the picture of *Zola*, I will give you a few highlights, from the first conception of the idea, to the final showing of the picture. To make *The Life of Emile Zola* was suggested, not by the studio, but by a European friend, Mr. Heinz Herald, now a writer with Warner Brothers. The studio, quickly convinced of the great screen possibilities of the story, bought it for Paul Muni. As the writing progressed, research on the subject began to embrace, directly and indirectly, French, German, Austrian and English literature.

I well remember a few years ago, when at my repeated insistence upon historical correctness, I got the customary answer: "Who knows the difference?" Strange as it may seem, studios did not have a very high opinion of people's knowledge of history. I said *did* not—because they now do have. Much criticism has been received which proved that the audi-

From *Cinema Progress*, December-January 1938-39.

Dieterle claimed that his habit of wearing gloves while directing was a carryover from his early days in the theater—where he was often called upon to stop acting or directing and help move the scenery around.

ence *did know*. So, today, there is a thorough check-up, down to the most minute detail.

But a director should do more than check-up; he should know more than just the principal characters; he should become acquainted with the spirit of the entire period—its social and political set-up—its relation to other countries, to the world. This work may appear to be a detour, but it is not. It is the perspective of your main characters. Just think of primitive paintings and you know what the lack of perspective does. That is exactly how a dramatic character would look, without the perspective of its period. No such figure can live, or will be capable of exciting human interest.

In this research work your characters already begin to live; from that moment on they will never let you alone—they demand to be brought to life; they become so insistent, that they actually hold you up. At this moment, please be careful. Don't let them corner you—keep out in the open. Too much detailed knowledge, as well as too little, would hinder you. Don't over-rate the value of anecdotes and sayings. They are generally as untrue as the last words of famous men.

There is not a picture of historical character ever announced but what I am flooded with information about all the known and unknown anecdotes and episodes relating to the given character. To follow these well-meant suggestions would mean almost certain destruction to any story. Anecdotes, wonderful as they may be, often destroy the artistic continuity of the composition.

The real fascination of a picture lies in the suspense with which the audience follows the hero, eager to find out whether or not he will justify its opinion of him. This relation between our characters and our audience we must try to understand, if we are interested in the development of motion picture stories. You will see best what I mean, when I tell you a little about the opening scenes of the *Pasteur* picture.

In the first script, Pasteur was introduced *right in the first scene*, taking for granted that everybody knew who he was. But when I spoke in the studio or in public about him, I always heard the remark: "Pasteur? Pasteur? Oh yes—the milk-man!" and that caused me considerable worry.

For days I pondered, until I came to the conclusion that, when so many people of a good average education didn't know about Pasteur, then I could not expect it from the general motion picture audience, either. So I set out to find a way to combat this ignorance. Then suddenly one night it came to me, right out of the very atmosphere of Pasteur's time.

I opened the picture in this way: A doctor is murdered by a man who considers that his wife was killed through the un-cleanliness of the doctor. As proof, he shows a leaflet, appealing to all doctors to clean their hands before going from one patient to another, written by a certain Pasteur. And this leaflet becomes the highlight of the investigation. Nobody knows Pasteur, neither officials nor doctors, and when the matter finally comes to the attention of the emperor, he, himself, doesn't know but calls for the unknown scientist, *Louis Pasteur*. So the audience was led from ignorance to knowledge in a highly dramatic way, without cheating on historical facts.

Let us take another instance: the finish of the Zola picture. As you may well know, Zola died several years before Dreyfus was rehabilitated. Fearing that the early death of Zola, occurring before the rehabilitation of Dreyfus, would check further interest for the audience, the authors changed historical facts for a dramatic climax in this way: after Dreyfus leaves Devil's Isle, he is immediately rehabilitated. Then Zola is shown at home, working, and after going to bed he is suffocated, and then the funeral.

Such a finish would take a great deal from the success, because, as I saw it, it was not dramatic. It was a finish in a matter of fact way, besides being historically incorrect. So, I suggested with the very same facts, the finish you saw: after Dreyfus' release, Zola is working on his last book, in which he intends to tell the world of his recent experiences, and is overcome by poisonous carbon-monoxide gas. Then follows the Dreyfus rehabilitation and thereafter Zola's funeral at the Pantheon. In this way, we have an ending full of suspense, still building up, holding the audience to the very end, without changing history. Zola dies before Dreyfus is reinstated. Minutes or years before, that doesn't matter—the screen has no real time. The spiritual truth, that and that alone matters. So much about the work with the writer.

Now let's visit the art director. Of him the public knows very little, and yet he is of the greatest importance in the process of making motion pictures. Naturally, he has to be correct in the style of the period, yet to the director, it is just as important that he builds his sets correctly for the dramatic continuity of the picture.

The law of *directional continuity* is one of the most neglected laws of all. Many motion picture people are not even aware of its existence. They have to be bothered about directions. And yet it is in this way, that a screen story is properly told.

Take, for instance, a thief running away from the police.

Let's say our thief runs from right to left and the police follow him. No matter how many cuts the thief runs away from the police, where, or in which direction has the thief to run? From right to left, as he has started. That is the correct answer. Otherwise, the thief runs right into the hands of his pursuers. But please watch your next picture and you will see.

Now, before we come to the actual making of the picture, one word about casting. The work of finding the necessary actors, conforming to the requirements of the script, is one of the most difficult tasks of the director. In *Zola,* for instance, the actors had not only to look like the original characters, they had to be militaristic, too—which means they had to have good figures, and above all, had to know how to walk, something very few actors know; and to make it worse, they all had to look European. Yet with patience we succeeded.

Now that the picture is an accomplished task, it all seems very simple, but it was not so at the time. Take, for example, the part of Dreyfus. After innumerable tests with different actors, we tried Mr. Schildkraut, who, coming from Broadway where he was a stage star of first magnitude, had his own ideas of how the part should be played. Just as most actors playing an important part, he had the conception that he must show this importance and played more the monument in honor of Dreyfus, than the humble officer, himself, who, through tragic circumstances, became a worldknown figure.

Yet, after a little revision, Mr. Schildkraut created something marvelous, as you most likely have seen. It is important to know that, in pictures, one cannot "play a part"; one must possess a sum of real qualities, clearly expressed in the external, in order to obtain the desired effect. This leads to the question: has the screen need of actors, or of personalities?

All I can say now is: the personality who is not an actor is to me impossible—I prefer the actor with personality. It should never be necessary for the director to compel an actor to create something that is not in him; therefore, casting is important. The greatest difficulty for the motion picture actor is to overcome the surrounding conditions under which he has to work and, above all, to overcome the presence of the camera.

So the director must achieve a proper creative state, which will help the actor to the birth of inspiration. The rest will come about subconsciously—by nature. Not the actor alone, but all cooperators, whom I consider as important as the director, himself, give of their best only in a favorable atmosphere, which is the supreme task of the director to create. How can anyone, not to mention an actor, work if he is embarrassed, or if he feels a sense of inefficiency, of failure? To create success one has first to create the spirit of enthusiasm; that is, the spirit of success. This works miracles.

The job of the director is, in my opinion, like that of a gardener, who puts a stick here, to help a plant to grow straight, and cuts a branch there, that the whole tree may thrive better and a good harvest result. Of course, this way of directing requires intelligent actors. At this point I would like to mention Mr. Paul Muni, whom I consider one of the most intelligent actors of our day. Imagine, Zola's tremendous scene in the courtroom was the first and only take! Contrary to the common opinion, I believe in first takes. When a scene is taken over and over again, the actor is tired and bound to become self-conscious. Then his acting is not at its best. So, since intelligence is rare among actors, too, proper casting is one of the main factors of success.

Now, I take it you all know the significance of the camera. It is through this medium that the story is told. Since the camera is handled by a specialist, the director has to work closely with that man, which is the cameraman. This relationship cannot be too intimate. He is really to the director, what the brush is to the painter. It is through the technical possibilities of the cameraman that the ideas of the director can be transformed from abstract to concrete form. Therefore, director and cameraman should have almost the same philosophy of life, but by all means the same artistic viewpoints. Only then, the beautiful unity of conception and form will enchant the audience.

In order to get this completeness, the camera should always be in the right position and should never move at the wrong time. Camera technique is what diction is to the writer—the director's style of expression. Yet two men never see alike, never react alike, and the tragedy of relativity is frequently discovered too late, in the projection room, and not all studios allow retakes, especially not for "technical reasons." That is exactly what the studio calls it when you are artistically not satisfied. That is of minor importance to them. But, if a kiss or a leg is not shown long enough, then you can be sure of retakes.

Only sometimes there are retakes asked for other reasons. For instance: the scene when Dreyfus leaves the prison on Devil's Island was at first not so well liked. I was asked to shoot it once more, showing Dreyfus closer and having him leave the prison directly, without going back and forth. I did as I was asked, to prove that the first form of the scene was right, and, in the end, my original scene was chosen.

This proves to you the importance of a definite setup of the camera. The quality of your film depends not only on *what* you shoot—but *how* you shoot it. This must be planned by the director and carried out by the cameraman. How you can *make* or *break* a scene through a set up, I will show you with another example:

The scene between Zola and his wife—so superbly performed by Miss Gloria Holden—after Cezanne leaves Zola and he tells his wife what Cezanne had said to him and all his reflections on the break of this friendship. This scene was written to be played while walking from one room into another. That would have spoiled a beautiful scene, because not only had Zola walked with Cezanne through the rooms a few moments before, but after the tragic break the scene must come to a rest.

Therefore, I decided to play it as you have seen it: Zola with his wife sitting at the fireplace. Only in this way, the value the writer wanted was brought out. Very often, as in the case just mentioned, a scene may in itself read all right, but the picture as a whole, and not the scene, has to be considered. This leads us to another vital point in motion pictures—the rhythm. And with rhythm is connected film cutting.

Cutting is not merely a method of joining separate scenes or pieces, but is actually a method of deliberate and compulsory guidance for the spectators. It is quite obvious that such an important task should not be done without the director. Visualize, if you can, a major operation being performed by a first-aid man. He could not help cutting into the life-giving arteries and sinews, which only the surgeon knows how to avoid. The same goes for motion pictures. Only the director can avoid hurting the life of the story, so cutting should be done in consultation with him.

But film art is yet in its childhood. As time goes on, the motion picture artists, not the directors alone, will continue and eventually win their fight for creative freedom, for the benefit of better pictures, to enlighten intelligent audiences.

FRANK TUTTLE
(1892-1963)

Tuttle was a director of some skill who showed occasional flashes of talent, but for the greater part of his career he buried himself in irredeemable studio assignments. His earliest silent films (produced independently for organizations like The Film Guild and Hodkinson) seem to have been fairly innovative and exciting, yet little is known about them today. Instead, a long string of routine films, mainly for Paramount, leaves the impression that Tuttle was a hack with no personal style and no particular skill at grabbing the more interesting assignments. The few occasional exceptions are mainly lightweight thrillers like *The Glass Key* (1935) and *This Gun for Hire*, films of a certain interest that somehow never achieve complete success. Ironically, his best film might be the silent *Kid Boots*, a wonderful Eddie Cantor vehicle that is not at all typical of Tuttle's usual work. What are we to make, then, of the burning idealism and naïve expectations for world betterment that we see in this article? Hardly the words of a worn-out studio drudge. Tuttle, in fact, had never lost his youthful zeal, and even after years of racing through projects like *Waikiki Wedding* and *College Holiday* still maintained hopes of creating something not merely artistic, but "meaningful," rather like the fictional director in Preston Sturges' *Sullivan's Travels* (there are other points of resemblance here as well). But Tuttle had neither the talent nor the clout to achieve his aims. The well-intentioned schemes he describes here never amounted to anything, and he soon returned to the practically anonymous production of studio potboilers.

HOLLYWOOD BITES DOG
FRANK TUTTLE

It's not news when fascism takes a crack at Hollywood. Handsome Adolf himself resented Charlie Chaplin, even if Charlie was there first with his little mustache. Hitler and Mussolini censored Hollywood so much that people wondered if the film capitol was supposed to be a suburb of Berlin.

Hollywood took plenty from the Blood-Bunds of Germany and Italy, Kaiser Adolf's propaganda machine described the Hollywood workers in very uncomplimentary terms. The Black-shirt Magpie bellowed about Hollywood's treatment of the Italian home and fireside.

Hollywood bent over backwards, and then things happened. The Dashing Duce sent over one of his brood to learn the picture business. Hollywood read what Vittorio had said about the beauty of bombing Ethiopians, and the film colony rose in wrath and kicked Papa's movie-struck eagle in the seat of his fascist film ambitions.

Then Hitler sent his girl-friend, the glamorous Leni. Hollywood gave her the cold-shoulder. A leading night-club refused to allow her to enter. None of the major studios would give her a studio pass.[1]

Berlin and Rome crackled with indignation. It wasn't news when the axis took a crack at Hollywood, but it *was* news when Hollywood hit back.

Mussolini thought of a clever answer to Hollywood: take the American movies and pay the American companies in wooden nickels. Hollywood's reply was to withdraw all American films from Italy. Today the Italians have thrown rocks and eggs at Mussolini's film screens. Mussolini wishes he had Holly-

1. In 1938 the German director Leni Riefenstahl had visited Hollywood in an effort to promote her film *Olympia* and meet with Hollywood filmmakers. The only studio which she was able to visit was Disney.

From *TAC*, June 1939.

Frank Tuttle directs Jack Benny in *College Holiday* (1936).

wood's pictures back, because the masses are beginning to wonder what has happened to the circuses that disappeared with the bread supply.

Berlin and Rome crackled with indignation, and Hollywood chuckled. Warner Bros. went to work on *Confessions of a Nazi Spy*. MGM rather cautiously dragged out *Idiot's Delight*. Charlie Chaplin decided to make something out of Hitler's stealing of his mustache, and announced *The Dictator*.

So Hollywood got excited about it. The next thing to happen was the organization of Motion Picture Guild, Inc., to make films in the interests of democracy.

Writers, producers, directors, actors and craftsmen formed the Motion Picture Guild. Every studio in Hollywood and every branch of the industry was represented in its membership.

Everybody wanted to make an anti-Nazi picture first of all. The problems of America were definitely on the schedule, but that crack at Hitler was going to come first. There would be a picture on the 1940 elections, a history of the New Deal, the story of American youth, something about the sharecroppers—but first on the list was the anti-Nazi picture.

Everybody in Hollywood has read Erika Mann's book about education in Hitler Germany: *School for Barbarians*. The members of the Motion Picture Guild were enthusiastic about it, but some of them wondered how it could be made into a picture.

A production board was organized and the writers went to work on Erika Mann's book. There was a wealth of material that suggested situations. The writers developed a story that came right out of *School for Barbarians* as though it had been intended by Erika Mann.

The story line was discussed with Miss Mann and she approved it. At the party in her honor, given by the Guild at the home of Helen Gahagan, she spoke in high praise of the enterprise.

In three months of exciting activity, Hollywood has created a vital new organization. *School for Barbarians* will go into production this summer. Already plans are being laid for a second feature picture to follow it.

These Hollywood artists and craftsmen are among the finest in the industry. Producer Frank Davis and writer Tess Slesinger, Ace Cameraman Floyd Crosby (*Tabu*), Director Herbert Biberman, Writer John Wesley and two-score others of Hollywood's best are out to see that the cinema industry bites fascism here and abroad before fascism gets a chance to bite first.

Documentaries and short subjects also are in the plans of Motion Picture Guild. A film on sharecroppers in the South is now being edited for immediate release. A program of 16 mm documentaries is under way.

A group of young cartoonists from Hollywood's animated cartoon studios are preparing plans for cartoons to knife the dictators right in their Mickey Mice. Motion Picture Guild is sponsoring them in their production.

Handsome Adolf and Bouncing Benny started it. They snapped and crackled for six years, and the Motion Picture

Guild is the answer. It isn't news that the boys from Berlin don't like it, but it is news that Hollywood likes it.

Hollywood has suffered many a foul gust from Kaiser Adolf and his gang of cut-throats, but the wind has changed . . . it blows from Hollywood now, and the first hurricane to strike Berlin and Rome and even Tokyo is going to be *School for Barbarians*. That old wind might even blow down a few of those Little Brown Houses that are messing up our American landscape just now.

INDEX

(Numbers in italic refer to photographs.)

INDEX